Praise for
Spoken For

"*Spoken For* is the kind of book every Christian teenage girl wants to read: a perfect mixture of truth and love story and Jesus and humor. Robin and Alyssa have practically written the handbook for every young woman looking to understand how God feels about them."

—ANNIE DOWNS, author of *Speak Love*

"*Spoken For* is filled with life-changing truths that will help you discover, strengthen, or reclaim your true identity. This book will teach you how to embrace the person God has created you to be...a must-read for every young woman who longs to know her true value, beauty, and purpose."

—ALLIE MARIE SMITH, founder of Wonderfully Made

"I highly recommend this relevant and essential book to any young woman trying to understand romantic relationships, navigating her way through the dating world, or even considering marriage. Robin and Alyssa are candid, thoughtful, and wise as they share personal stories and universal truths. A great tool for mothers and daughters, book clubs, and youth groups."

—MELODY CARLSON, author of the TrueColors series

"Robin and Alyssa have delivered such a timely and beautiful truth in this book! As daughters of the King, we are loved to the core by the One who will never leave or fail us. We are never forgotten, pushed aside, or up for anyone's taking, but we are covered and pursued by Jesus."

—REBEKAH LYONS, author of *Freefall to Fly*

"Alyssa and Robin have written a book that is so tender and true, full of encouragement for all of us as we try to understand the love of the Savior. You will walk away from this book changed for the better and celebrating the fact that you are truly loved by the One who knows you best, the One who created you with a plan and a purpose."

—MELANIE SHANKLE, *New York Times* best-selling author of *Sparkly Green Earrings*

"What makes *Spoken For* unique is the authors' ability to internalize and understand that we are in the midst of a divine love story! Alyssa and Robin casually and eloquently remind us not only of who we are but whose we are and that we are wanted, loved, and spoken for."

—BIANCA OLTHOFF, speaker, teacher, and chief storyteller for the anti–human trafficking organization The A21 Campaign

"In *Spoken For,* Robin's and Alyssa's gentle honesty and personal stories made me feel as if we were out having coffee together and talking about our love for the Lord. This book is a perfect reminder of how great his love is for us and how sweetly he cares for us."

—ERYNN MANGUM, author of *Paige Torn*

"Anytime two unique voices come together with a unified message, there is power in it. Robin and Alyssa have different perspectives and life stages, but both have experienced God's relentless love and now want to give it away. *Spoken For* will help you remember your infinite worth because of Jesus Christ and what potential abounds if you will only embrace it."

—JENNIE ALLEN, founder of the IF:Gathering and author of *Restless*

Spoken For

embracing who you are and whose you are

Robin Jones Gunn
and
Alyssa Joy Bethke

MULTNOMAH
BOOKS

SPOKEN FOR
PUBLISHED BY MULTNOMAH BOOKS
12265 Oracle Boulevard, Suite 200
Colorado Springs, Colorado 80921

Trade Paperback ISBN 978-1-60142-597-3
eBook ISBN 978-1-60142-598-0

Published in the United States by WaterBrook Multnomah, an imprint of the Crown Publishing Group, a division of Random House LLC, New York, a Penguin Random House Company.

MULTNOMAH and its mountain colophon are registered trademarks of Random House LLC.

Library of Congress Cataloging-in-Publication Data
Gunn, Robin Jones, 1955-
    Spoken for : embracing who you are and whose you are / Robin Jones Gunn and Alyssa Joy Bethke. — First Edition.
        pages cm
    Includes bibliographical references.
    ISBN 978-1-60142-597-3 — ISBN 978-1-60142-598-0 (electronic) 1. Identity (Psychology)—Religious aspects—Christianity. 2. God (Christianity)—Love. 3. Gunn, Robin Jones, 1955- 4. Bethke, Alyssa Joy. I. Bethke, Alyssa Joy. II. Title.
    BV4509.5.G83 2014
    248.4—dc23
                                                              2013045130

Printed in the United States of America
2014

10 9 8 7 6 5 4 3

SPECIAL SALES
Most WaterBrook Multnomah books are available at special quantity discounts when purchased in bulk by corporations, organizations, and special-interest groups. Custom imprinting or excerpting can also be done to fit special needs. For information, please e-mail SpecialMarkets@WaterBrookMultnomah.com or call 1-800-603-7051.

From Robin:
To all my nieces: Amanda, Ashley, Alyssa, Katherine,
Hannah, Karen, Susi, Gabi, and Sami.
May you always remember who you are
and whose you are.
You are deeply loved by the One who created you,
more than you will ever know.

From Alyssa:
To Jeff: Thank you for showing me
how God is the Relentless Lover
through your unending and gracious love.

To my mentors: Mom, Amy, Dani, Robin, Jill, and Jeri.
Thank you for teaching and showing me that we are spoken for
and that his love is truly the greatest of all.

Contents

One

An Epic Love Story—
Yours

One bright April morning Alyssa and I (Robin) were busy in my kitchen preparing food for a youth event at church. All the windows were open. A gentle breeze cooled us. The television was on in the background, but we weren't paying much attention. I reached for the remote to turn it off but accidentally changed the channel.

"Oh, wait," Alyssa said. "Leave it there. I love this part."

I had happened upon an oldie-but-goodie chick flick at just the right moment. It was one of my favorites too. Alyssa and I stopped what we were doing. We stood together in a sweet silence and watched as the fair maiden ran into the arms of her hero. We sighed and looked at each other. Alyssa had tears in her eyes. So did I. We pointed at each other and laughed. "Why are we crying?" I asked. "I'm sure we've both seen this a dozen times."

"I know," Alyssa said wistfully. "But it's such a great love story. And love stories get me every time."

It's true, isn't it? Love stories draw us in. Honestly, who doesn't love a good love story? The pursuit. The suspense. The drama. The mystery. We cry, we laugh, we cheer—all for love. We are captivated by our favorite movies, television shows, and books when the romantic elements capture our imaginations and enliven our hopes.

Even if you don't see yourself as a girlie girl and didn't have a favorite Disney princess when you were growing up, you know in your core that you want to be loved like the heroines in all the best films and stories. You want to see love conquer all.

The desire to be loved, cherished, and adored never goes away. All of us long to believe someone is out there who wants us. Someone who will come for us. Someone who will take the role of the hero in our lives and love us, deeply love us, not for what we do or how we look but simply for who we are.

What if you could know that you *are* loved that intensely? You *are* sought after. You *are* the bride-to-be in a love story that's unfolding in your life right this minute. You are spoken for.

This love story began once upon a time long ago before you were even born. Almighty God, the Creator of the galaxies, thought of *you*. He carefully fashioned *you*—your voice, your fingers, your mind, even every one of your eyelashes. He carefully and deliberately crafted you. For all time there only has been and only will be one of you.

He saw all your days before you took your first breath. He knows all your thoughts before you speak them. He knows everything about you. From the very beginning you were known, and you were wanted. He is pursuing you like a tenacious bridegroom with a perfect proposal. He has set his affections on you. Why? Because he loves you, and he will never stop loving you. You are his first love, and he wants you back.

How do you respond to such unwavering, unending, unstoppable love?

In this book we will unwrap the ancient truths from God's Word about what it means to be loved, to be sought after, to be spoken for. You will see how the Bible is a love letter written to us.

Through that love letter God makes it clear that he desires to be with us forever. Alyssa and I will share details from forever-love stories and show how our love for God grew as he pursued us.

Our goal is simple. We want you to see what happens when you respond to the invitation of the true Bridegroom and step into the center of an epic love story—yours.

Two

You Are Wanted

Embedded in our souls is a quiet wish, a secret hope we carry with us always.

We want to feel wanted.

Yet we struggle to fit in and to be included. It's more common to experience rejection than acceptance. We're more familiar with the bitter sting of being left out than with the delight of being sought out. All of us know what it's like to be overlooked and unwanted.

When was the last time you felt that way?

Was it last week when a group of friends decided to get together and none of them thought to include you? Or was it last month when you poured your heart out to a guy who expressed interest in you, only to find out that he didn't share any of your romantic feelings?

Perhaps the ache of feeling unwanted hit hardest when you were a child. You overheard your parents fighting and came to the conclusion that your presence on planet Earth was an inconvenience to them.

Or maybe more recently you were caught off guard when you applied for the ideal job. You waited days for the call. After convincing yourself you would be hired, you were told in an impersonal way that the position had been filled. You were not wanted.

Yes, we all know the wrenching pain that comes from experiencing rejection. Our hopes are crushed, our feelings ignored, our hearts broken. What do we do? We pull back. We draw inward and give way to doubt and distrust. We brace ourselves against further hurt, and with a straight face we say that we don't care. It doesn't matter. No one can hurt us.

And yet...

The longing to be wanted continues to be the cry of our hearts. We dream of being sought out, included, welcomed, and warmly embraced. But living as we do in the rubble of a fallen world, rejection, not acceptance, seems most often to accompany us on our life journey.

So why do we keep hoping? Why does the secret wish to be wanted never go away? The hope lingers over us like a lullaby because we were created to experience love and to give love. We were made to belong, to be accepted, to be included. We were created to be in community with God and with others. He has reached out to us so that we might know *who* we are and *whose* we are.

You see, you were bought at a great price. You belong to the One who made you. You are spoken for. Almighty God, your heavenly Father, will never leave you, never reject you, and never say "Go away." He moved heaven and earth to make known to you this steadfast truth: you *are* wanted.

Robin

The worst rejection I ever experienced came when I was twenty-one.

I was engaged to a guy I'd met in college. I thought we had done everything right. We were friends first, dated in group settings at the Christian college we attended, and waited until after he graduated before we became engaged.

Then one February afternoon he looked me in the eye and spoke words that broke my heart: "I can't marry you. I don't love you. I don't want to spend the rest of my life with you."

My wedding dress was hanging in the closet. The invitations had been selected. In a single moment I went from believing I was loved and wanted to being told I was not wanted. I was very much unloved.

He went on to reveal big pieces of his life that he had kept hidden from me. I was not his one and only. I was, in his opinion, absurdly romantic to have written letters to my future husband declaring my loyalty to him and praying for his faithfulness to me. My unrealistic expectations, he said, had caused our relationship to fail.

I will never forget how that rejection felt. I was so confused.

For days I tried to make sense of it. I struggled to separate the truth from the lies. Acidic thoughts kept me awake at night. *The problem is me. It is. That's why he ended our engagement. I'm too idealistic, like he said. I put too much pressure on him when I gave him the letters I'd written to my future husband. If I hadn't romanticized our relationship, we'd still be together.*

A destructive cycle of thinking kicked in. I thought that if I worked hard to make improvements in my personality, my body shape, my looks, and especially my beliefs, then he would want me again. I would be accepted by him, and we could be together.

He would take me back. He would love me again if only I would change. I *had* to change.

Yet it soon became clear that none of my efforts would change his heart. He had made his final decision, and I was out of his life for good.

Not to mention that none of the changes I might attempt would be lasting, because they wouldn't be true to who I was and what I believed. Temporary adjustments to please him wouldn't alter who I was at the core. Eventually my true personality, opinions, and values would come through.

The raw and horrible truth was that I was unwanted. Cast aside. Unloved.

The only thing—and I do mean the only thing—that kept my heart above water in the wake of that life-altering rejection was that I knew, really truly knew, Someone wanted me. Someone who took me in just the way I was. Someone who had already invited me to be his bride. My relationship with him was sealed for eternity. He was my way out of the hurt. He was the One who spoke truth to me. He was the One who showed me true love.

That Bridegroom was Jesus. He loved me. He wanted me. Always.

My journey with Christ began when I was twelve years old and went to summer church camp. My main objective during that week was to be included in the popular group. I wanted to share the inside jokes and be invited to hang out at the camp pool with my new best friends. I dearly wanted to be wanted.

My efforts met with success, and by the last night I was sitting in the front row with the most popular kids at camp. I even knew the clever hand motions the group had made up to go along with the songs. It felt great being on the inside.

Acquiring that favored position had taken a lot of work, but it came with a fleeting reward. In the morning when camp ended, all of us would go our separate ways. I remember feeling sad that our gang was going to be dismantled.

Then the speaker said something that grabbed my attention: "God doesn't have any grandchildren. Just because your parents are Christians, that doesn't automatically make you a Christian."

What got to me was the way the speaker explained that God doesn't show us favor because we're part of an insiders' group. He doesn't give us special consideration because of our families. He invites us to come to him as individuals. And that night I did. I responded with my whole heart to receive Jesus Christ as my Savior and Lord.

If anyone would have asked me prior to that last night at camp if I was a Christian, I would have said yes. I'd grown up going to church, so of course I was a Christian. It seemed to me the same as if someone had asked me if I were an American after having lived in the United States my whole life.

But I had never personally responded to the invitation to enter

God's forever family. My prayer that night was simple. I knew that I could never be good enough through my own efforts to be right and pure before God. I needed to receive the gift of Christ's sacrifice. I needed to ask God to forgive all my sins.

My camp counselor prayed with me that night, and I calmly surrendered my life to Christ. As soon as I looked up at her, big, sloshy tears streamed down my face. I was overwhelmed to realize that God wanted me. He loved me. He wanted me to be in a close relationship with him. He promised he would never leave me. He would never give up on me. He accepted me into his kingdom. I felt so loved. So wanted.

The first thing I did after summer camp was start to read my Bible. I remember one day reading somewhere in the middle of 1 John and feeling as if I was reading a love letter. That's when I made the heart-pounding discovery that the Bible is a love story, an epic love story, in which every page is laced with evidence of God's unending love for us.

See what great love the Father has lavished on us!
1 John 3:1

For years after that night, I read God's Word and memorized his promises and eternal truths. Some days during my time alone with God, I felt as if I were on a treasure hunt, searching for the nuggets of truth that applied to what I was going through at the time.

That's how the Bible touched my heart right after my fiancé ended our engagement. I remember opening my Bible and my heart fully to the Lord. I felt so raw and vulnerable. I was looking for comfort, and I found it. Throughout God's beautiful love letter, I discovered reassuring evidence of his unfailing love. I started a list of verses and titled it "What God Says About You."

Whenever I felt discouraged about what my ex-fiancé or others said about me, I went to the list of what God said about me and found my heart filling up with life-giving hope. I even found a verse, John 3:29, in which John the Baptist referred to Jesus as the "bridegroom" and those who followed him as his "bride." His Word healed me. I knew that no matter what happened with any other relationship, Jesus would always want me.

A few years later I met the man who is now my husband. My heart was anchored, and I was much more prepared for marriage because I understood more fully what it meant for Jesus to be my First Love. My hopes were realistic because they were founded in his truth.

I also discovered that I *was* realistic to hope for faithfulness and to grow in a relationship that was flooded with the light of God's truth and forgiveness. Even though my letters to my future husband had been given away and never returned, the man I did marry was the answer to the prayers I had written from my hopelessly romantic heart when I was a teenager.

I encourage you to take some time alone with God to go through the list of "What God Says About You" at the end of this chapter. Look up the verses, and mark your favorite ones in your Bible. Soak up the truth of how deeply God loves you and how much he wants you. Believe me when I say that the anchor of God's truth will keep you steady through every stormy relationship.

> So I want you to realize that the LORD your God
> is God. He is the faithful God. He keeps his
> covenant for all time to come. He keeps it
> with those who love him and obey his
> commands. He shows them his love.
> —Deuteronomy 7:9, NIrV

Alyssa

Just like Robin, I discovered how much God loves me when I was a teenager. I also discovered how painful it can be when you realize you are not wanted.

My freshman year in high school was a season of big changes. I'd graduated junior high, surrendered my life to Jesus, started high school, formed new friendships, and experienced my first real love. (Big changes, people, big changes!)

Now, I had had crushes in the past. Oh boy, did I have crushes! But *this,* this was the real deal. This boy was different. He and I would talk forever. E-mailed each other. Served with each other in our youth group. He was the first boy I knew who really loved Jesus. He was the first boy who made me want to love Jesus and seek him more. This guy pointed me to God, and I was in love.

Yes, I was in love with Jesus but also in love with this guy. I spent hours thinking about him and our possible future together. My best friend and I would stay up until the wee hours talking about the boys we liked. We would analyze every conversation and every thought and anxiously wait for those guys to pursue us. Oh, how desperately I wanted to be with this guy. How much I wanted him to want me too and to choose me.

However, as the months wore on, instead of my dream coming true, he and I were growing further and further apart. He gave no indication he liked me. He never pursued me and never called to hang out, as I had so hoped. No, he didn't want me. I wasn't his choice. He was a great guy and definitely a friend, but he didn't reciprocate my feelings.

I can't tell you how many nights I cried myself to sleep. How many prayers I prayed. My heart was broken.

Until one night I finally gave up. I gave it all to the Lord—my heart, my dreams, my longings, and this guy. I was done. I couldn't bear the rejection anymore. I asked God to take over and mend my heart. To show me his unfathomable love and how *he* wants me. I didn't heal overnight. The feelings didn't go away immediately, and the loneliness and hurt still stung. But slowly the Lord revealed himself to me. Slowly the Lord showed me how deeply he loved and cherished me, how he was ultimately the Love of my life. And slowly the Lord helped me to move on. Yes, it took years.

But the Lord was faithful to walk through those years with me—years of constant surrender and trusting his best for my life.

The summer before my freshman year I had started my relationship with Jesus. No big moment happened. No altar call occurred. Instead, I was bored one day and decided to read a book my mom had bought me, one in the Christy Miller Series by Robin Jones Gunn. I hadn't met Robin yet, so to me it was just a teen romance, but I later learned it was the first novel Robin had written for teen girls.

On those pages I found a friend, Christy—a fifteen-year-old girl who comes to know Jesus. Not just know about Jesus or all the facts about Jesus, but actually comes to know *him*.

This fictional character's life changed after that decision. She fell in love with God, the One who had wanted her so much that he sent his Son to die on the cross for her sins.

Yes, this beautiful Savior transformed Christy's life. Everything changed for her.

I desperately wanted to know, adore, and live for Jesus like Christy did. Through her example I was ushered into a forever relationship with God.

But it wasn't until my freshman year, when I walked through my season of love, disappointment, loneliness, and hurt, that I truly understood Jesus's love for me. Whether I was wanted by a boy or not, Jesus wanted me. *Jesus.* He loves me. He likes me! He wants to be with me, and no sin, no barrier of time or space, would stop him from winning my heart.

It's the same with you.

He wants you.

No matter if you're single, dating, married, or ninety-nine years old, Jesus wants you. He is after your heart. I don't think I would have understood that beautiful truth as deeply if I hadn't walked through my season of rejection.

Robin and I aren't the only ones who know the sting of rejection. Throughout life we'll all experience many kinds of loss and hurt. The opinions and actions of others do not define us. We are known and wanted by the Lord himself. He never changes, never turns on us, never gives up on us.

All the fiery pain from rejection by other people can be put into perspective when you know that you are wanted by the Bridegroom. He made the stars. He tells the sun when to rise each morning. His hand holds back the ocean. His faithfulness endures for a thousand generations. He made you. He wants you. He loves you.

The lies, the memories of past hurts, the ache of rejections—those things burrow deep in our hearts, and most of us spend a lot of time digging those hurtful experiences back up. Whatever your story, whatever pain and hurt you have experienced, God knows. Not only does he know, but he has entered into your story. He has made a way for you to know your Savior, your Healer, your King. He wants to heal you, to make you like his Beloved Son, and to be with you forever. No, this life won't be pain free. But Jesus promises to walk with us through the pain. He never leaves. Ever. He is our Rock.

We will never fully understand why God allows us to go through pain and trials, but one reason is to draw us to him. When we walk through a trial, if we turn to him as our refuge and comfort, regardless of how messy and doubtful we may be, he draws us close into his embrace. He welcomes us in. He showers us with his love.

This is an epic love story that you are part of. You are wanted. Draw in that eternal truth: You. Wanted. Forever.

Come walk with us as we see how God woos each of us into a beautiful love story that will change our lives.

> But the LORD longs to show you his favor.
> He wants to give you his tender love.
> —Isaiah 30:18, NIrV

What Do You Think?

1. Describe a time when you were wanted and what that felt like.

2. Think about a time you were left out or rejected. How did you handle the hurt?

3. How do you think God feels as he waits for us to come to him?

4. If you have given your life to Christ, recall what that moment was like for you.

5. If you haven't made the decision to enter into a relationship with Christ, the Bridegroom, you can do that by praying a simple prayer to invite him into your heart. Why not do so right now? It will be the beginning of your epic love story.

What God Says About You

✦ You were made in my image (Genesis 1:27).

✦ You are my treasured possession, my peculiar treasure (Exodus 19:5, NIV, KJV).

✦ If you seek me with your whole heart, you will find me (Deuteronomy 4:29).

✦ When you are brokenhearted, I am close to you (Psalm 34:18).

✦ Delight in me, and I will give you the desires of your heart (Psalm 37:4).

✦ I know everything about you (Psalm 139:1).

✦ I know when you sit down and when you stand up (Psalm 139:2).

✦ I am familiar with all your ways (Psalm 139:3).

✦ I knit you together when you were in your mother's womb (Psalm 139:13).

✦ You are fearfully and wonderfully made (Psalm 139:14).

✦ All your days were written in my book before there was one of them (Psalm 139:16).

- ✦ My thoughts toward you are as countless as the grains of sand on the seashore (Psalm 139:17–18).

- ✦ As a shepherd carries a lamb, I have carried you (Isaiah 40:11).

- ✦ I knew you before you were conceived (Jeremiah 1:5).

- ✦ My plans for your future are for good, to give you hope (Jeremiah 29:11).

- ✦ I have loved you with an everlasting love (Jeremiah 31:3).

- ✦ I will never stop being good to you (Jeremiah 32:40).

- ✦ I will take pleasure in doing good things for you and will do those things with all my heart and soul (Jeremiah 32:41).

- ✦ I want to show you great and marvelous things (Jeremiah 33:3).

- ✦ I rejoice over you with singing (Zephaniah 3:17).

- ✦ I am your provider. I will meet all your needs (Matthew 6:31–33).

- ✦ I know how to give good gifts to my children (Matthew 7:11).

- ✦ I gave you the right to become my child when you received my Son, Jesus, and believed in his name (John 1:12).

✦ I am the Bridegroom and you are my bride (John 3:29).

✦ I have prepared a place for you. I will come back for you and take you to myself so that we can be together forever (John 14:3).

✦ I love you even as I have loved my only Son (John 17:23).

✦ I revealed my love for you through Jesus (John 17:26).

✦ I determined the exact time of your birth and where you would live (Acts 17:26).

✦ In me you live and move and have your being (Acts 17:28).

✦ I am for you and not against you (Romans 8:31).

✦ I will never allow anything to separate you from my love for you (Romans 8:35–39).

✦ I gave my Son so that you and I could be reconciled (2 Corinthians 5:19).

✦ I am your peace (Ephesians 2:14).

✦ I am able to do more than you could possibly imagine (Ephesians 3:20).

✦ I am at work in you, giving you the desire and the power to fulfill my good purpose for you (Philippians 2:13).

✦ I did not give you a spirit of fear but of power, love, and self-discipline (2 Timothy 1:7).

✦ Every good gift you receive comes from my hand (James 1:17).

✦ I desire to lavish my love upon you because you are my child and I am your Father (1 John 3:1).

✦ My love for you is not based on your love for me (1 John 4:10).

✦ I gave the ultimate expression of my love for you through Jesus (1 John 4:10).

✦ I am the complete expression of love (1 John 4:16).

✦ I will dwell with you in heaven. You will be mine, and I will be your God (Revelation 21:3).

✦ I will one day wipe away every tear from your eyes, and there will be no more crying or pain or sorrow (Revelation 21:4).

✦ I have written your name in my book (Revelation 21:27).

✦ I invite you to come (Revelation 22:17).

Three

You Are Pursued

Have you ever been pursued? Not in a creepy, stalker sort of way but in a good way, like being selected for a job or to be included in an exclusive group or by someone who wanted to have a close relationship with you.

It's humbling and even thrilling to know someone thinks you're worth snatching up.

God's way of pursuing us is by patiently drawing us to him. His love letter is laced together with beautiful, soul-stirring evidence that we humans are the object of his affection. He wants us to be his.

One of the strongest declarations of how God feels about us is in Jeremiah 31:3: "I have loved you with an everlasting love; therefore I have drawn you with lovingkindness" (NASB).

This verse stirs up a reminder of what happened in the Garden of Eden after Adam and Eve disobeyed. God didn't destroy them on the spot. He didn't turn his back on them and ignore them. He pursued them. He drew them out of hiding and provided for their needs.

Adam and Eve were the first to experience the tender ways of God, the Relentless Lover. Because we were made for him, he never stops pursuing us. We are his, and he wants us back.

Alyssa

I've found it easier to understand God's patient, faithful love for me when I think about the way Jeff set his affections on me and pursued a relationship with me.

Our love story began a few years ago when I was twenty-two. Some close girlfriends and I were gathered in a circle on the floor of the church auditorium, enjoying our fast-food burgers. We were giddy with excitement because one of our friends was getting married the next day.

From the other side of the circle a friend said, "Lyss, I know a boy who is smitten with you."

My heart beat a little faster. My hands felt sweaty. Did I hear right? A boy was smitten with me? How could that be? I had been gone from my hometown in Washington State for three years at college and was just home for two weeks before I left for an internship on Maui. Who lived in the area that would have a crush on me when I hadn't even been around?

Her grin grew wider. I gave a little laugh so no one would know that inwardly I was freaking out. I had to ask, "So, who is it?"

"Jeff Bethke!"

"Jeff Bethke? I hardly know him."

"He knows who you are. We've had your senior photo on our fridge since high school. Over the last few months every time he comes over he looks at your picture longingly and asks when you're coming home."

"Really?" I was shocked. Jeff and I had had a few Facebook interactions, but that was about it.

"Yeah," my friend added, "my brother and I are always telling him how great you are. He's dying to meet you."

All I could do was smile. Deep down I was flattered. But I couldn't put much hope in meeting Jeff, let alone starting some sort of relationship with him. I was leaving in a week, and I'd be gone for two years.

In the past I had liked guys as a result of hearsay, but it never worked out. I had never dated before, and let me tell you, hearing that Jeff Bethke might have a crush on me threw me for a loop! Dating wasn't even on my radar, especially dating a guy I had never met in person before. (A few interactions online don't reveal the full scope of a person, no matter how much Facebook skimming one does!) No, I was better off dreaming that God had a surfer husband waiting for me on Maui.

The next day my friend's wedding was beautiful. Like I do at all weddings, I cried. Tears of joy, sweet joy. I was so excited for my friend. But I was also shaking all over because I had heard that Jeff was at the wedding too. He told my friend he wanted to meet me.

Freak. Out.

Toward the end of the reception, Jeff came over to the table where I sat, pulled up the chair next to me, and began to talk. My stomach did flips.

Right away I knew this guy was different. He didn't start in with small talk. He went directly into what God was doing in his life, how he had been saved, how he loved Jesus. He asked me questions that drew me out and showed he cared.

As we talked, I became convinced this guy was special. He captured my heart.

I wouldn't say it was love at first sight. I mean, the dude was handsome, but I had my guard up because I hardly knew him.

Jeff and I had one week from the wedding to the day we both left—me to Maui and Jeff to Oregon for college. Jeff pursued me all week, conspiring with his buddies to figure out ways he and I could hang out. On the day after the wedding, he asked if I wanted to go to church in Seattle with him and his two best friends. I was intrigued by Jeff, so I gladly went. During the drive we rocked out to Taylor Swift and Disney tunes. Seriously!? This was my dream man. (What I didn't know until a couple of years later was that Jeff blew out his car speaker that night trying to impress me, and he had downloaded those songs because he knew they were my favorites.)

The last night we were together, his best friend had a good-bye party for Jeff, and I was invited. We had a blast, roasting marshmallows and hanging out. What I didn't know then was that the whole group was plotting to put us together.

At one point everyone went inside, leaving Jeff and me by the fire. Jeff went deep, telling me more about his testimony and background. He was roasting three marshmallows over the fire as he was talking but then realized they were on fire. He brought them up close to his mouth to blow out the flames when those gooey suckers splatted right in his lap. Jeff dropped the stick and frantically tried to wipe the gooey, on-fire marshmallows off his lap, only to smear them all over his shorts and hands. He excused himself to change his shorts as I held back my giggles.

Way to impress a girl, right? He came back after a few minutes, having doused himself in cologne. Oh yes, this guy was definitely into me!

I stayed as late as I could, hoping that Jeff would say something about staying in touch. Finally I had to leave, so I said my good-byes. Everyone looked at Jeff. I stood up to walk away, when Jeff stood up quickly and sputtered out, "Alyssa, do you have a phone?" (Nervous much!?)

"Yes, I do."

"Um, can I have your number? I'd love to stay in touch while you're in Maui."

Finally. I gave him my number and walked to my car with a huge smile on my face. Oh yes, I wanted to stay in touch with Jeff Bethke.

Over the next couple of months, he called me a few times, and each phone call lasted several hours. The more we talked, the more my heart melted for him. This guy was a true God lover. He was real, honest, smart, funny, and sensitive. We could talk for hours, and it was like no time passed.

Jeff continued to pursue me and to initiate the relationship. After a few months he asked me to be his girlfriend, and we began dating long-distance. He was my first boyfriend. I was giddy. Over the moon. Glowy.

As much I'd hoped and dreamed that an amazing guy like Jeff would be interested in me one day, I couldn't believe it was actually happening. Jeff's deliberate pursuit of me led me to understand what it feels like when God pursues us. Jesus truly has his eye on us. He tenderly, patiently shepherds us and draws us to himself.

> Bless those who belong to you.
> Be their shepherd. Take care of them forever.
> —Psalm 28:9, NIrV

Robin

Alyssa and I met by God's divine happenstance. She was serving a two-year internship at a church on Maui when my husband and I moved to the island. Alyssa and I became instant forever friends. She told me how God had used the Christy Miller books I had written years earlier to play a significant role in her relationship with the Lord. From there we discovered that we both loved communicating with young women and shared a romantic heart when it came to our relationships with Christ.

One afternoon we met to plan an event for the high school girls at church. The day was so glorious that we decided to conduct our business on the beach. We took a refreshing dip in the deep blue before planning the high school gathering.

Somewhere in the conversation I used the term *Relentless Lover* to describe the way I viewed God's pursuit of us.

"How did you come up with that description?" Alyssa asked.

I told her about a radio interview I had more than fifteen years ago. In most interviews I'm asked questions such as "Where do you get the ideas for your stories?" or "What prompted you to write for teens?" This interview, however, kicked off with a startling question.

I had walked into the studio and put on the headset. Then the interviewer looked at me and said, "So, how can you call yourself a Christian and write romance novels?"

We were on the air! Live! People were listening! And everyone, including me, was waiting for how I was going to answer.

"Well…"

The words tumbled out before I had time to consider them. "I think the reason is because when I was a teenager, I read a love story that changed my life."

"A love story?"

"Yes. The relationship starts off well. Actually, very well. And then in the first few chapters everything falls apart. You think they are never going to get back together, but you hope they will, so you keep reading. About three-fourths of the way through the book, he does everything he can to prove his love to her. But still she won't come back to him. Then in the last chapter, he rides in on a white horse and takes her to be with him forever."

The host looked at me skeptically. "How could a book like that change your life? It sounds like a formula romance novel to me."

"Really, a formula romance?"

"Yes. Isn't that what you were talking about?"

"Actually I was talking about the Bible."

"The Bible?"

"Yes. The love story I read as a teenager was the Bible. There's a white horse and everything."

The radio host pulled back and stared at me. For a moment the radio station experienced what no on-air host ever wants—dead air.

"We're going to cut to a station break, and then we'll be right back." The host pushed a few buttons and looked at me, stunned, before saying off the air, "You are absolutely right. I never saw that before. The Bible is the ultimate love story."

"God even calls us his bride," I added.

"You're right. He does."

We went back on the air, and I said, "I think God is the Relentless Lover, and we are his first love. That's why he never stops pursuing us. He's not a vengeful God who wants to 'get back at us'; he's a patient, loving God who wants to 'get *us* back.'"

> Then I saw heaven opened, and behold, a white horse! The one sitting on it is called Faithful and True, and in righteousness he judges and makes war.
> —Revelation 19:11, ESV

The rest of the hourlong interview zipped along with more lively conversation about what it looks like when God, the Relentless Lover, pursues us, his first love.

Evidence of that relentless pursuit is found in the beginning of the Bible. Genesis 3:8 says that Adam and Eve "heard the sound of the LORD God as he was walking in the garden in the cool of the day." Adam and Eve had just sinned by eating the forbidden fruit. Everything that was beautiful in their lives was now broken, including their relationship with God. Yet notice how, even in that painful moment of God's confronting them about their poor choice, the description of that encounter has a romantic sound to it. They heard the sound of the Lord God. He was walking toward them in the cool of the day. He wasn't stomping or charging at them. He was walking toward them to initiate reconciliation.

This isn't the image of a fierce, omniscient power wrathfully flinging lightning bolts, prepared to release his fury on the two rebellious souls. No, this is the sound and image of a broken-hearted Creator pursuing the man he had handcrafted so meticulously from the earth's dust. This is the Giver of Life pursuing the woman he had sculpted so precisely from Adam, for Adam.

This is the Relentless Lover tenderly coming to redeem that which was lost.

He was the One doing the pursuing from the beginning. And he still is today. Right now.

Learn to listen until you recognize the sound of the Lord God walking in the garden of your heart. He's coming for you, drawing you to him because he loves you and wants to be with you.

Let's recognize him as the LORD.
Let's keep trying to really know him.
You can be sure the sun will rise.
And you can be just as sure the LORD will appear.
He will come to renew us like the winter rains.
He will be like the spring rains that water the earth.
—Hosea 6:3, NIrV

The amazing thing about God's unfailing kindness is that he hasn't given up on his creation, us, for thousands of years. Some people delayed nearly a lifetime before responding to the Relentless Lover. They ignored all the nudges, all the whispers, all the times God made it clear that he wanted to be their God. Instead, those stubborn souls kept thinking they could do life on their own without God, even though he is the One who created them. They decided they could handle all their problems without calling on him for wisdom and direction, which he promises to give freely and generously to all who ask.

That concept touched me deeply a few months ago when I came across Genesis 6:6. As a matter of fact, when I read it, I unexpectedly burst into tears.

I'd read that verse many times over the years, but I'd not paid any special attention to it before. This time the verse went deep inside me.

It appears at the beginning of the account of Noah and the ark. Little more than fifteen hundred years had passed since God created Adam and Eve and placed them in the Garden of Eden. During that time most everyone on earth had moved further and further away from God. Very few sought him. Even fewer honored him. Wickedness and violence dominated the planet. None of the good things God had designed for Adam and Eve was being enjoyed.

Genesis 6:5 says that every intent of humanity's heart was "only evil continually" (NASB).

How tragic! God had created a perfect world and given Adam and Eve the freedom to choose to obey or disobey him. When they chose disobedience, that mind-set toward God continued generation after generation. Every intent of their hearts was only evil continually.

The next verse is the one that made me cry. It simply says, "The LORD was sorry that He had made man on the earth, and He was grieved in His heart" (Genesis 6:6, NASB).

My heart ached for God. More than a thousand years of continual rejection. More than a thousand years of patiently pursuing a relationship with the people he had created. But virtually no one wanted him. That loss of relationship grieved his heart, and he was sorry he had made us.

I cried that day because I don't ever want God to be sorry that he made me. I don't ever want him to be grieved in his heart because of me.

Even though God never stops pursuing us and it's never too late to turn to him, none of us knows how many minutes we have left on earth. Jesus even said that, as it was in the days of Noah, so it will be when he returns. No one knows the hour or the day (Matthew 24:36–39).

Let's not be among those who presume on God's goodness and think we have all the time in the world to run off in our own direction and then call out to God to save us at the last minute. He has been pursuing you since before you were born. Stop and turn to him. Let him catch you.

Today is a very good day to start fresh as a woman who knows who she is and whose she is. You are a princess in God's kingdom. One day the Prince of Peace will come riding in on a white horse because he wants to take you to be with him forever. All the fairy tales that were ever dreamed up come from this one true tale. God's story. A story he wants to write throughout your life.

> "Sing and rejoice, O daughter of Zion!
> For behold, I am coming and I will dwell
> in your midst," says the LORD.
> —Zechariah 2:10, NKJV

What Do You Think?

1. How do you view the Bible? How does that view shift if you think of it as a love letter written to you?

2. In what ways can you relate to Alyssa's hesitation to believe that someone was smitten with her?

3. Describe a time when you felt God was pursuing you or drawing you closer to him.

4. How did you feel when you read Genesis 6:6 about God being sad that he had made humankind?

5. What sort of expression do you imagine on the face of Jesus, the Prince of Peace, when he comes for you on a white horse?

Four

You Are Loved

*J*esus loves me, this I know, for the Bible tells me so.

Did you sing that familiar song as a child? How easy it was to believe those simple words when you were young. How comforting to sing it over and over when you were filled with all kinds of hope and a sense of wonder at life.

And then you grew up.

Right?

The simple, innocent faith you had in God and the trust you had in his love for you were rocked when you were exposed to the reality about human nature. Someone hurt you. Something you were counting on fell from your grasp. Terrible thoughts leaked into your imagination. Life became complicated. You became more complex. You tried to sort out the good from the bad, the truth from the lies. Your personal hunt for true love began, and the search was much more elaborate than the elemental foundation "Jesus loves me, this I know."

How is it possible to believe again with simple, childlike faith that Jesus really loves you?

Robin

I'd be the first to say that the answer to that question lies in the second line of the song: the Bible still tells us so. God's one Book is filled with declarations of his love. His Word is true. He keeps all his promises. Nothing has changed about God or his Word.

We are the ones who have changed.

As you look back over your life and all the experiences you've had, I'm guessing you could point to a collection of cuts, bruises, and scars that came from hurts, betrayals, disappointments, and loss. Those wounds are keeping you from believing that God really loves you.

Someone might tell you with confidence and passion that God is your heavenly Father and that he will never leave you because he loves you, but if your earthly father left you, it's difficult to believe your heavenly Father would be any different.

If you read in God's Word that Jesus called his disciples "friends" and that he promised to be with them until the end of the earth, you might think it sounds too good to be true. Why? Because you had a best friend who promised to always be there for you, but now the two of you no longer speak to each other.

You may have memorized a verse that filled your heart with peace because it gave you assurance that Almighty God was faithful and true and wanted only the best for you. But then someone you relied on turned out to be unfaithful and not true to his or her word. In the end that person only wanted what was best for him or her, not what was best for you.

As the list of life experiences grows, it's easy to doubt that love of any kind is real. Parental love, friendship love, romantic love—if someone has let you down in each of those relationships, your battered spirit has no place to put the simple truth that "Jesus loves me, this I know, for the Bible tells me so."

In the second chapter of this book, I shared how my confidence was crushed when I became disengaged and how I went to

God's Word to learn all over again how much Jesus loves me. Part of the reason I needed God's perspective on how he saw me was because of the second wave of rejection that came during the months after the broken engagement.

Some couples joke, "So, who gets to keep our friends after we break up?" In our case my ex-fiancé kept pretty much all our mutual friends. I was quickly cut out of the loop and left off the guest lists for birthday parties and weddings. Every day on my social calendar was suddenly vacant. No plans. No invitations. Nothing but rejection on all sides.

In an effort not to become a hermit, I tried to connect with some of my old friends from high school. Finally I was included in a get-together at the home of a friend from my teen years. One of the guys at the gathering told me he attended the same church college group I went to. It was a large group, and even though we had noticed each other before, we had never met.

By the end of the party, he asked me out to coffee. It had been four months since the breakup, and I was ready for a date. I knew it was super casual and not even a real date, but someone was including me, and that felt good.

However, the next day he called to cancel. He said he would phone to reschedule, but he never did. Later I found out that rumors about me were making the rounds in my old circle of friends. I hadn't told any of my old friends the details of why the engagement ended. I guess that left a few of the creative ones in the group to come up with their own assumptions. It didn't matter that none of the gossip was true; it still destroyed my opportunity to reconnect with friends. What is also true is that gossip spreads like wildfire, destroying everything in its path.

Several girls in that group came to me privately looking for the inside scoop. I chose not to tell them the details. I wasn't sure at the time if that was a good idea because it resulted in a lot of alone time. But somehow it felt right not to share confidential details, even though the relationship was irreparably shattered. I sensed the girls were more interested in the dirt and the drama than they were in my feelings or my friendship.

During that time I learned something powerful about God's love. His love is not like human love. Not at all.

I realized that if I was going to understand the uniqueness and depth of God's love for me, I had to mentally separate my relationships with people from my relationship with the Lord. God's love should never be distorted or diminished by comparing it with the friendship or love of any human who has let me down, rejected me, betrayed me, or lied about me.

During that time my relationship with the Lord matured and grew deeper because I was learning to love him for who he was and not for what he did for me.

At just the right time, some girlfriends from church gathered around me, and those friendships deepened. Four of us took off that summer for a backpacking trip around Europe. We had the adventure of our lives. Every day we sensed God's closeness.

We had long talks on the trains and read the Bible to one

another in the morning while dining on our continental breakfast of hard rolls and coffee at the youth hostels. At the same time I was discovering what a great big world this is, I was also learning that God was greater and more powerful than I'd ever imagined. He was not like anything else or anyone else. He alone was God.

It became clear that when I focused on the flawed love shown to me by humans and used that measurement to think about God's love, I was unwittingly making God human, but of course he isn't.

He is holy. He is almighty, all powerful, and all knowing, and he is love. We can't measure God by any love, friendship, compassion, or loyalty that we have ever known. God is in a category all by himself. His love is true. He never changes. He is always faithful. Always patient. Always good. Always truthful. Always kind.

He loves us. Always.

Understanding God's love meant that I had to wrap my head around God's holiness. He is set apart from all humans.

> But set Christ apart as Lord in your hearts
> and always be ready to give an answer
> to anyone who asks about the hope
> you possess.
> —1 Peter 3:15, NET

If you have found it difficult to believe that God's love is meant for you, start here: Set him apart in your heart. Separate what you know about God from what you know about everyone else who ever said he loved you or wanted to be with you forever or promised to be your friend. Don't compare God to any human. Humans fail. All of us do.

Jesus never fails. He is perfect. Always. In all things. At all times.

So when he says he loves you, that means he loves you.

Forever.

What does God's love for us look like? How does it make us feel? Here's the definition of love that he gave us in 1 Corinthians 13:4–7: "Love is patient and kind. Love is not jealous or boastful or proud or rude. It does not demand its own way. It is not irritable, and it keeps no record of being wronged. It does not rejoice about injustice but rejoices whenever the truth wins out. Love never gives up, never loses faith, is always hopeful, and endures through every circumstance" (NLT).

Now read those verses again and think about how every one of those attributes of love is true of God and his love for you.

Without a doubt you are loved by God. You are eternally, extravagantly, tenderly loved. That truth has never changed, and it never will.

Jesus loves you, this you know. For the Bible tells you so.

Alyssa

Most of the time I dated Jeff, I was on cloud nine. Whenever his name was mentioned, I couldn't help but smile big. My heart melted every time I heard his voice on the phone or received a letter from him. I had fallen for this guy and fallen hard. However, our relationship was all long-distance, which didn't give either of us the full picture of who the other person was.

Even though we dated for a year, we only saw each other when I went home a couple of times and when Jeff flew out twice to see me in Hawaii. The last time he came to visit was for two weeks, which was the longest we had spent time together. In fact, the first week he was on Maui, my parents were visiting as well. The four of us stayed in a small condo—talk about a true act of love...I mean, the poor guy slept on the lumpy pull-out sofa.

The two weeks were wonderful. Hiking. Snorkeling. Cliff jumping. Serving together at church. He had a chance to see my life, parents, friends, church, job, roommates. However, since we hadn't spent much time together, I didn't understand any of his "Jeffisms." You know, what it meant when he was quiet. Or how he felt in group situations. Or how he interacted with my friends and family.

I misunderstood Jeff. I took his sometimes standoffishness as his choosing not to pursue me or cherish me. Instead, he was taking it all in and was a bit nervous. Would my friends like him? What did influential people in my life think of him?

I concluded that Jeff didn't like me, that he didn't cherish me as I so wanted him to. If a guy likes you, shouldn't he bring you flowers and instantly know your favorite Starbucks drink? (Iced soy caramel macchiato, just in case you're wondering.) Shouldn't he want to see you at work or get to know the kids you work with? I thought cherishing a girl was evidenced by those things. I found out much later that those are nice but aren't the foundation of a relationship.

I also felt that this wasn't the right time for us to be together. We were in different seasons of life. He was in college across the ocean. I was done with college and living on a small island twenty-five hundred miles away. I couldn't envision our lives together.

So I broke up with him.

Over the next few months, I was left raw and pretty beat up. Breaking up with Jeff had broken me. I only vaguely understood why I was breaking up with him—I didn't feel cherished, and I couldn't see how our lives were going to come together. But I couldn't wrap my mind fully around why I had walked away from him. My heart was telling me I was over the moon about him, but my mind was saying he didn't totally love me and it wouldn't work out.

Looking back, I know that we needed to go our separate ways. God did amazing things in both of our lives the year we weren't dating.

However, there is no way around it: that summer was one of the hardest seasons of my life. I doubted God's goodness, and I feared his plan for my life. I questioned if God was good enough to ever bring a husband into my life. I was a shattered soul. I didn't want to admit to others that breaking up with Jeff had left me so heartbroken. I mean, *I* was the one to break up. I wanted to appear strong and put together when I was the exact opposite. I was weak, messy, and extremely vulnerable.

In September I started my second year of internship on Maui. I was matched up with a new mentor, and one afternoon as we were sitting in the open courtyard at church, she asked a question that caught me by surprise.

"Alyssa, do you really believe God loves you?"

My world stopped. My heartbeat quickened. Why was she asking me such a question?

Of course I believe God loves me. I mean, I know he loves me. That's what his Word says. But do I believe it? Wow, I don't know.

"I guess I wonder at times," I admitted.

She knew about my relationship with Jeff and my heartache over breaking up with him. Having her ask me that poignant question, though, to say it so bluntly, caused me to search my heart.

What I came to learn during that next year was that God was for me. He is my portion. He is mine, and I am his. I get God. He's all I need. Really.

As crazy as it sounds, sometimes I want to go back to that summer—or entire year, really—because I've never been closer to the Lord. He met me in my pain. He held me. He cared for me. He was intimate. I learned that sometimes our Good Shepherd leads us through valleys to build up our muscles to climb the mountains. And he doesn't let us do it alone but walks with us the whole way, sometimes carrying us until we can walk again.

God proved faithful. He knew my heart's desires but also knew how I needed to let him fill my desires first before he placed anyone else into my life. I needed to see how God was enough—and more than I could ever dream of. Not that being content in God means he will bring a husband into your life; it's not an equation. But see, I had idolized marriage for so long that I needed the Lord to break me from placing it above him. I had thought (although I never would have admitted it) that once I was married, then I would be completely happy, then I could be content and satisfied. That summer the Lord tore down my idol and revealed that he alone was enough. He was my portion, and I was rich to have him.

Knowing and believing this truth didn't come overnight. It took all year for the reality to sink in. I remember one moment in which the Lord showed me his love as I was reading Genesis.

I had decided to study the first book of the Bible, and I remember reading through the story of Abram, Sarai, and Hagar. Sarai was unable to have children, and although God had promised her a child, she didn't wait on his timing but ran ahead and told Abram to sleep with her servant Hagar to have a child. So Abram did as his wife said, and sure enough, Hagar gave birth to a son. Sarai was infuriated and lashed out at Hagar, causing her to run away.

Can you imagine? Being forced to sleep with your lady's husband, getting pregnant, and then having her turn on you? I would be terrified too. But God met Hagar right where she was. He tenderly comforted her and told her to go back. Hagar called God the "One who sees."

The One who sees. This phrase has been woven into my heart ever since I read Hagar's story in Genesis 16. I remember sitting on the couch with a pillow and my Bible on my lap and tears dripping from my face.

God sees me. He sees me right now. I thought God had forgotten about me. I thought he had forsaken me, had crushed my dream, and had forgotten about my heart's desire. No, not at all. God knew my heartache. He knew my desire to be married. He hadn't forgotten or turned his head. Rather, he was facing me, doing what was best for me by crushing my idol and drawing me close to him.

> Thereafter, Hagar used another name to refer
> to the LORD, who had spoken to her. She said,
> "You are the God who sees me."
> —Genesis 16:13, NLT

True love is choosing the highest good for the other person. God loved me so much that he did what was best for me—and for Jeff—and that was our breaking up for a season.

God's love is manifested in many ways. He thoughtfully handcrafted each of us. He gave his Son to die and rise again for us. He sends us the Spirit to dwell in us to comfort, help, teach, and lead us. He gave us his Word. He blesses us with friends and family to walk life together. We are created from community to community. He gives us breath. And he knows our hearts and shows us his love each day. We simply have to open our eyes to see it.

Do you believe that God loves you?

I mean, do you really believe he loves you? It's hard in our culture to know what real love is. I love my parents, and I love berry cobbler served in miniature Mason jars (what girl doesn't!?). But let's hope that the love for my parents is much stronger than my love for those sweet cobbler-filled Mason jars.

We're bombarded daily with messages of what love is that are contrary to what God says. Music, movies, television, and our friends and family show us that love is conditional and that love is all about us. It often can be translated as "You make me happy" because it's all about how other people make us feel. That kind of love is based on what they can do for us, and when they fail, show weakness, or don't "fill us up," we split.

That kind of love is based on emotion, which is scary because there's no security. That's why we hear "Well, I just fell out of love" or "I don't have those feelings anymore, so it's over."

If we accept the meanings of love that our culture feeds us, we question whether God loves us.

But that's not true love. God's love is unending, unconditional, and free. It's not based on what we do or don't do. It's not based on who we are or aren't. It's not promised to us when we're "all good to go," but rather, as God makes clear in Romans 5:8, his love is lavished on us even while we are sinners. This love is based on God's character because he is love itself.

Robin told me once that "love is an unconditional commitment to an imperfect person." That's how God loves us.

> God is love.
> —1 John 4:8

To fully absorb his love for you, you might need to start by choosing to believe that God actually *likes* you. He wants to spend time with you. He wants to hear your heart, your struggles, your joys and pains. He wants all of you. He's crazy about you.

In John 15:9 Jesus said, "Just as the Father has loved Me, I have also loved you; abide in My love" (NASB).

Let yourself fully take in this fixed, eternal truth: God loves you. Believe it. Store this truth deep in your heart. And when you have doubts or go through a storm, remember who God is. What he has done in the past. What his Word says. Ask others to pray with you and for you, that God would show you how deep his love is for you.

> And I pray that Christ will be more and more at
> home in your hearts, living within you as you trust in
> him. May your roots go down deep into the soil of
> God's marvelous love; and may you be able to feel
> and understand, as all God's children should, how

long, how wide, how deep, and how high his love
really is; and to experience this love for yourselves,
though it is so great that you will never see the end
of it or fully know or understand it. And so at last
you will be filled up with God himself.

—Ephesians 3:17–19, TLB

What Do You Think?

1. Do you see yourself as the object of God's affection? Why or why not?

2. Why do you think God would keep loving his children even though they rebel against him?

3. Even if another human has loved you deeply, in what ways do you see God's love for you as deeper still?

4. How can you separate your understanding of God's love from your understanding of and/or hurt over a human's love for you?

5. In what ways would your life be different if you lived each day in the confidence and security of God's love?

Five

You Have Been Called

We have a dilemma. We know God wants a relationship with us, we see how faithfully he pursues us, and we start to believe that he deeply loves us. But we are still bent on going our own direction, and we are unhappy.

Every human since Adam and Eve has had the same problem:

> We want what we want when we want it,
>
> but
>
> when we get it,
>
> we no longer want it.

Why is that?

It has a lot to do with understanding and embracing *who* we are and *whose* we are.

We were created to be in a dependent relationship with God and to rely on him for everything. Yet society tells us to be independent, self-sufficient, liberated individuals. Individuality is strength, the ads tell us. Create your own success. Go after what you want. Be fierce in doing whatever it takes to make your dreams come true.

Magazines show us images of aloof, detached models, and we gaze at them thinking, *Now this is beauty. Such control! Such power!* Our culture praises and rewards the supremacy of self-reliance.

Yet God has called us out of this world and in the opposite

direction of our culture's value system. His Word gives us example after example of people who ran hard after the fleeting prize of fame, wealth, and power, and every one of those independent-minded individuals ended up empty and still wanting.

God's Word is also filled with stories of people who sought him and his standards in the midst of difficult times, perverse societies, and great opposition. History is punctuated by those who put God's kingdom first and lived according to his values. As Psalm 112:6 says, "Surely the righteous will never be shaken; they will be remembered forever." Their lives were blessed for eternity because they chose not to live according to the system of this world.

> Seek the Kingdom of God above all else, and live righteously, and he will give you everything you need.
> —Matthew 6:33, NLT

So, what does it mean to be called?

We have been called *out* of this world and its value system and invited *into* God's eternal kingdom. We belong to the One who made us, loves us, and knows what's best for us. That's why we will be happy only when we fix our hope and affections on his kingdom and all that is eternal.

The big question is, how do we do that?

It begins with a choice. Your choice.

Do you want what you want when you want it? Or do you want what God wants when he wants it?

Alyssa

When I broke up with Jeff, that was my choice but not his. And it was one of the most difficult decisions of my life. The thing was, I really liked him. Like heart-beats-a-little-faster, butterflies-in-the-tummy, smile-from-ear-to-ear, get-a-little-clumsy-when-he's-around, cloud-nine liked him.

This guy had me.

I wanted to marry him.

But, as I mentioned in the last chapter, during the week he was visiting me on Maui, I thought he didn't care for me the way I cared for him. I had to work all that week, and I thought he would visit me every day at work to help out. Instead, he went hiking with the guy interns. At one point when I gently mentioned the big *M* word (*ahem*, marriage), he got uncomfortable and changed the subject. I had so many doubts. Did he really like me? Was he the right one for me? Could our lives blend together? Was he even interested in marriage eventually? Was he ready to lead me?

Looking back, I can see my expectations were too high and my desires weren't expressed. I kept all my hurts and questions inside. I didn't understand how Jeff operated, and I didn't try to see our time together through his eyes. As a result of my not expressing any of this to him, he left Maui thinking our long-distance relationship would continue as it had for the last year.

Of course, that's not what happened.

I kept thinking and praying about our relationship, and I was torn up. The day after he left, I headed out with twenty-five high schoolers on a two-week mission trip. There I was, waiting to board the plane, when I realized I needed to break up with Jeff. I wasn't sure why since I liked him so much. But I knew that's what I was supposed to do.

But I couldn't do it yet.

For the next two weeks I was responsible for focusing on and leading those students, yet I was in deep pain, knowing that I needed to break up with Jeff. I cried buckets of tears. Buckets!

He was my first boyfriend, so not only did I feel as though I was losing a good friend and saying good-bye to a guy I really liked, but I also felt like my dream of ever getting married had died.

I didn't handle the actual breakup conversation well. Actually that's an understatement. It was awful. I was awful. I called him the day after I returned home. Immediately he could tell I wasn't myself.

I kept the call short. No emotion. No tears. No sadness. I just said, "Jeff, I have to break up with you."

He was stunned. He asked why, and I stammered a few sentences, none of which made sense. How could they? I didn't even fully understand myself.

Then the worst thing happened. Jeff cried.

He asked if there was any hope for us getting back together. I said no. It was done. Forever. And that was that. Good-bye. *Click.*

I still can't believe how emotionless I was on that call. I think it must have been because I had wept so much during the two weeks building up to the conversation that I didn't have anything left in me when I finally talked to him.

That call broke him. And it broke me. We've been told that the person who does the breaking up doesn't go through as much pain as the other person. So not true in our case. Jeff didn't know it, but I was left raw for months.

But after that heartbreaking summer ended and I started my second year as an intern, I began to heal. As I explained in the last chapter, I learned from Hagar's story that God sees me. He was shepherding me and showing me how persistently he had been pursuing me.

During that season of healing, another Jeff—"Surfer Jeff"—pursued me. (Just can't get away from those Jeffs.)

Surfer Jeff went to my church. He pursued me for a month before I gave in and agreed to date him. A couple of weeks later Jeff Bethke texted me. He said he wanted to Skype.

I agreed. Let me tell you, the conversation wasn't at all what I expected. He asked me to be his forever. With each sentence he poured out his heart. He had written a list of things to say. Sweet things that every girl longs to hear.

"Lyss, I love you."

"I want to marry you."

"I'll move to Maui to be with you."

"There's no one like you."

I didn't know what to do with such an outpouring of affection and tenderness. I had longed to hear Jeff say those things while we dated. Why was he telling me now?

He wanted me to be set apart from dating other guys so that my heart would be clear and ready for a lifelong relationship with him.

He paused and waited for me to reply. He wanted to hear that everything he felt about me was what I also felt for him.

Instead of affirming words of mutual love, I said, "Jeff, I just started dating someone else."

"Who?"

"Another Jeff."

He ranted and raved about how Surfer Jeff would never love me the way he loved me. He said that Surfer Jeff didn't know what I needed, but he did.

I was infuriated. He was passionately confrontational. But looking back, I love him for it. Jeff was *fighting for me.* He didn't just let me go. He took a stand and fought to win my heart even though I had turned my attention toward this new relationship. It was such a picture of how God doesn't give up on us. How he calls us out of the distractions of our lives into a deeper relationship with him. But I didn't see it that way at the time because I was focused on going a different direction. My dreams for my future were all about Surfer Jeff.

Months went by. Things were going pretty well. I was finishing my internship, figuring out life and relationships and what

God wanted for my future. On Valentine's Day Surfer Jeff told me he loved me as we stood overlooking the ocean, with roses scattered all around us. It had taken me awhile, but I had begun to believe that Surfer Jeff and I could get married. My thoughts were leaning toward what our future would be like together.

Then late one night under a smirking Maui moon, Surfer Jeff broke up with me. Out of the blue. The whole time we had dated I had been the hesitant one. He was the one who had consoled me and confidently led me. Now he was standing before me, spilling out all his doubts along with a list of things he couldn't put up with any longer.

I remember going to Robin's house the next day and being so emotionally and physically exhausted I could hardly tell her what had happened. Robin and her husband told me to go to their guest room, close the door, climb into bed, and not leave until that pillow was soaked with all my tears. I fell into a deep sleep. When I woke up, I still felt pretty awful. Nothing seemed to make sense.

Two weeks later Jeff e-mailed me a short message, asking how I was doing. He had found out that my relationship with Surfer Jeff was over, but he didn't mention that. He just asked how I was doing. At the time I didn't want anything to do with any guy, let alone someone named Jeff.

Finally I decided to reply and told him briefly that Surfer Jeff had broken up with me. He responded immediately, expressing sympathy and care.

As the next month progressed, a bunch of e-mails flew back and forth between us. Jeff was nothing but kind and tender. He pointed me to Jesus. He forgave me for how awfully I had broken up with him and for the way I had treated him after the breakup. He showered me with love.

As we exchanged e-mails, my heart began to heal. I could see how beautifully Jeff loved me. I began to care deeply for him, and I realized I didn't want to be with anyone else.

Jeff had never stopped loving me. He had made his intentions clear when he called me. When I didn't respond with equal devotion, Jeff didn't stop loving me. Instead, he stepped back and waited out my choice to focus my heart not on him but on Surfer Jeff. But he never gave up. He waited. He prayed. He hoped. And then he stepped in when the opportunity came. Jeff never stopped pursuing me.

Our love story is unique and isn't what I would have written for myself, for us. In fact, it's so much better. And one of the things I appreciate most about our story is how it shows off Jesus. It's a perfect example of how Jesus makes his love for us clear and then fights for us even as he waits for us to return to him. How he calls us to be with him, not just once but over and over.

It's easy for us to choose to go in a direction that we think will bring us what we want. Yet that direction will turn into a dead end, like my relationship with Surfer Jeff did. All along God is waiting for us to choose his way and give our hearts to him.

Robin

The longer we walk with the Lord, the more we realize there will always be another Jeff. Someone or something that seems like the fulfillment of our deep longings will pop up at just the right moment. We find it easy to set our affections on that someone or that something while all along our heavenly Father is patiently wooing us, pursuing us, calling us to be his alone.

I remember the day Alyssa came over after her breakup with Surfer Jeff and how we sent her to the guest room for a private sobfest. Sometimes there is nothing anyone can say or do to ease the pain of a trampled spirit. You just need to cry your little heart out. I love how King David wrote in Psalm 56:8 that God puts all our tears in his bottle. Even in the darkest valleys of life, our Good Shepherd sees. He knows. He cares.

What I saw in Alyssa that sad day and what I still see in her life is a longing to choose God's best. She didn't get angry at God for the way things turned out with Surfer Jeff. Instead she turned fully to God and sought his direction and his will for whatever was next in her life. Alyssa made herself available to God, and he met her right where she was. I watched the days pass and could see how he was a tender Shepherd to her, leading her beside still waters and restoring her soul.

Healing, hope, and true happiness begin when we are available to God. Even when we are shattered and lost, there's no point in trying to run from him. He longs to pick us up and carry us in his arms. So if you need to bleat, little lamb, go ahead. Bleat with all you've got and know that Jesus is there.

> He takes care of his flock like a shepherd.
> He gathers the lambs in his arms.
> He carries them close to his heart.
> —Isaiah 40:11, NIrv

Being called involves God initiating an intimate relationship with us and our responding by going to him. Many times being called involves a deliberate action on our part in which we step away from whatever is holding us back from knowing him more fully.

I have to add, though, that I have seen many situations in which a person was too broken to move from where he or she was to go to God. All that individual could do was cry out and wait. Jesus came and lifted up that person. He carried him or her close to his heart.

My friend Donna told me a great example of what it looks like to be called out and to respond. When she was in high school, she and some chatty girlfriends were standing in a closed circle at lunchtime talking about the guys across the way. One of the football players in the group of guys had his eye on Donna. They were acquainted but didn't have a close relationship.

That afternoon when he caught her eye, he gave her a nod and then a come-here gesture with a tilt of his head. She wasn't about to leave the safety of her group of friends and walk over to the group of guys. What if his subtle message hadn't been intended for her? What if she went up to him and he ignored her? What would her girlfriends say? None of them seemed to have noticed the silent message.

Donna shot him another look. She tried to appear open. Hopeful. Willing.

He read her expression and did a daring thing. He left the cool group of fellow football players and strode across the school courtyard. Going right up to Donna, he reached for her hand and drew her out of the group. He made that deliberate move because he wanted to have a relationship with her. He called her out of the group and drew her to himself.

The daring move worked. They've been married for more than thirty years.

In the same way, Jesus has called us out.

Whether you realize it or not, God is calling you out daily. Every moment of every day. He is waiting. He is there. He wants you. He does not give up. He longs for you to catch his gaze, read his invitation, and come to him. He will go to any length to win your heart. And here's the crazy thing—he did.

He formed you and created you in his image.

But there you were, the girl who wanted to take control of her life and be her own god, thinking she knew better than he did. You were the one who went your own way. Because of sin, God couldn't be in relationship with you, because he is perfectly holy and righteous and can't look on sin. You got what you wanted, but it turned out not to be what you wanted after all. You ended up in a dungeon far away from him. You were the damsel in distress.

That's why God sent his Son to rescue you.

When Jesus died on the cross, he called out to you—you might say he proposed to you—saying, "I love you. I want to be with you forever. I'm taking your judgment, your sin, your shame and guilt, the wrath that you deserve to die for, and I am taking it upon myself. I'm exchanging your clothes of wickedness for my robe of righteousness. Here, you are clothed with a royal gown. I want you. Won't you be mine?"

On the third day Christ rose from the grave, showing that God had accepted his payment for your sin. It is finished. Your sin is no more. Your shame is no more. Your guilt is no more.

Now God is holding his arms wide open to you. He is calling out to you. He is longing for you. He wants to be with you. He wants you to be his beloved—all of you. Your heart, your mind, your soul, your hopes, your dreams, your pains, your fears, your struggles—he wants you.

Will you say yes? The choice is up to you.

> But you are a chosen people, a royal priesthood, a holy nation, God's special possession, that you may declare the praises of him who called you out of darkness into his wonderful light.
>
> —1 Peter 2:9

What Do You Think?

1. What or who is keeping you from being in a fully committed relationship with the Lord?

2. In what ways do you think God might be calling you out of darkness? Think about the friends you have, the sort of entertainment you engage in, your secret thoughts and actions.

3. Recall a time of loss, hurt, or rejection that cut deep into your life. What or who helped you to heal and to be restored?

4. How does it feel when you think about being chosen and called out from the darkness?

5. Is any shame, guilt, or sin weighing you down or preventing you from fully running into the Lord's arms? Read Psalm 103:12; Micah 7:19; and 1 John 1:9. What do those verses say about your sin?

Six

You Are of Great Value

You might have observed by now that the concept that you are *spoken for* sometimes takes awhile to journey from your thoughts all the way to your heart. Embracing who you are and whose you are might include a bit of work, but this is good work. It's the work of letting go, leaving the lies behind, and leaning in closer to the Savior until you can hear his heart beating for you.

Here's a review of what we've looked at so far:

- You are wanted by God.
- You are pursued by God.
- You are deeply loved by God.
- You have been called by God.

And, now, the next truth: you are of great value to God.

The wonderful thing about belonging to Christ is that first and foremost he wants us to *be* with him. He highly values our relationship in the same way we prize our relationships with our closest friends and family, only more so. True friends love being with each other even when they're not doing anything. They don't have to *do*. They can just *be*. They can hang out, sit together on the porch swing, and talk about anything and everything. True friends make each other laugh and comfort each other when hard times come.

Think about how different the interaction is in a relationship between a master and a servant. A servant must continually work to keep the relationship going with the master. Servants have assigned tasks and expectations, and they are compelled to *do;* they aren't free to simply *be*.

A servant would never follow the master into the bedroom, stretch out on the bed slumber-party style, and say, "So, let me tell you what happened. This day has been insane!"

Jesus described the difference in relationships to his disciples in John 15:15. He told them that he no longer called them servants because a servant doesn't know what the master is doing. Instead, he told them they were his friends. He welcomed them into a close, everyday, intimate friendship with him. That is the kind of relationship he wants to have with us.

> I am the vine; you are the branches. If you
> remain in me and I in you, you will bear much fruit;
> apart from me you can do nothing.
> —John 15:5

So many people don't enter into that level of sweet, deep friendship with the Lord because they go through their lives with a master-servant mentality toward Christ. They believe the lie that it's up to them to *do* something important and valuable for God.

The truth is we aren't of any great use to God.

Did you catch that? We aren't of any great use to God. He can do whatever he wants; he doesn't need us to be puppets, servants, or envoys to *do* his work for him. The only way anything happens for his kingdom is when he gives us the power and invites us to come alongside him and to be part of what he is already doing.

God *can* use us, and he does all the time. But in and of ourselves we aren't of any great use to God.

However, we are of great value to him.

Being of great value is different from being of great use.

> You are precious to me.
> You are honored, and I love you.
> —Isaiah 43:4, NLT

Robin

I remember where I was sitting as I was typing the last few chapters of *Love Finds You in Sunset Beach, Hawaii.* The novel is about Sierra Jensen, a character who was friends with Christy in the Christy Miller Series and is the main character in the Sierra Jensen Series.

In the *Love Finds You* novel, Sierra has spent the last five years serving, serving, serving in Brazil. She is a missionary woman, and she would never trade the five years of hard work. However, her position has been phased out, and she is burned out.

I was writing a scene in which Sierra is in the car with Mariana, her friend from Brazil. They are on vacation on the island of Oahu, and Mariana is trying to help Sierra make sense of what her life had been about and what she is going to do next.

The scene is memorable even though I wrote the book a number of years ago. As I sat at the kitchen table typing, I glanced out the window at the swaying palm tree and asked myself the same questions Sierra was asking. My husband and I had just moved to Maui, and I was trying to find my place. I was used to serving alongside my husband in youth ministry and a variety of other ministries over the years. But with the move our lives had changed dramatically. I was praying about what to write next, which speaking events to commit to, and how to be involved in the local ministry at our church.

I felt as if I had given my problem to Sierra and then sat back and kept writing, hoping she would somehow solve the dilemma for both of us.

Sometimes when I'm writing I don't think about the words ahead of time. Dozens of possibilities of what might happen in the story blip through my thoughts like happy fireflies on a summer night in Tennessee. They blink, they flit, they do loop-de-loops, and I chase them all over the place, barefoot and giggling until I catch one. On rare occasions it's as if the firefly perches on my fingertip and rests there contentedly. That's when I know I don't need to scurry after any of the other thoughts. This is the one. I did not go after it. It came to me.

That's how it was with the answer to the dilemma that I shared with Sierra. The truth spilled out of Mariana's mouth:

"I have looked for love for a long time in a lot of places. I know many times over what love is not. And I also know what love is when I see it. You love God. I know that. Now, I think you will be able to love him even better if you can stop trying to make God proud of you."

Sierra felt as if the world had stopped. All was silent. The only sound she heard was the whispered echo of Mariana's last sentence: Stop trying to make God proud of you.

I stopped typing, sat back, and knew that I had fallen into a mind-set of believing I was serving God best with all the things I could *do* for him. Right along with Sierra, at that moment I re-aligned my heart to simply *be* with him, and the pressure I'd been feeling lifted. Instead of leaping ahead of the Lord with all my clever plans, I fell back in step with him, with his timing, with his way of doing things.

That's when I saw that I was of no great use to God, especially when I was busy, busy doing things to make him proud of me. I could see that, instead, I was of great value to him, especially when I was living with him as the vine and me as the branch. Every bit of life-giving hope, joy, and direction flowed from him. All I had to do was *be* connected to him.

Remain joined to me, and I will remain joined to you.
No branch can bear fruit by itself. It must remain
joined to the vine. In the same way, you can't bear
fruit unless you remain joined to me.
—John 15:4, NIrV

Have you ever watched one of those television programs in which people learn that something they own has great value? I heard about one of those shows in which a man was asking for an appraisal of an old oil painting. I think the painting was of a vase of flowers. It was pretty. Not amazing. Not the sort of painting that would make you stop and stare as you admired the details. The frame was old and not in very good shape. As the appraiser took a closer look, his eyes grew wide.

"What is it?" the owner of the painting asked. "What do you see?" For years the owner had seen nothing special about the painting. He just knew it was old and might qualify as an antique.

The appraiser carefully peeled back the crinkled and faded paper affixed to the backside of the painting and caught his breath. Calling several other specialists to come see what he had discovered, the appraiser paused a moment to gaze in awe. The others leaned in. There was a large document on parchment paper.

The onlookers began to murmur. "Could it be? Do you think it's one of the original copies of the Declaration of Independence?"

"If it is," the appraiser said reverently, "it's priceless."

"Priceless?" The owner was stunned. "I thought it was just an old painting."

The document was examined by a round of experts and found to be authentic. It was of great value. In fact, it was priceless.

"How did you know to look inside?" the owner asked the appraiser.

"It was the signature that gave it away. When the Revolutionary War broke out, the important documents were hidden for safekeeping. So, when I saw the name written on the bottom of the painting, I knew who he was. I knew he may have hidden this priceless treasure where no one else could find it."

I just love that story.

It's such a perfect analogy of how we carry around priceless treasure inside us. Others might look at the outside and see only what seems to be an ordinary, average person. Nothing special. But if they look close and see God's signature on our lives, they know that something of great value is hidden on the inside.

In 2 Corinthians 4:7 our hidden value as believers is explained this way: "But we have this treasure in jars of clay to show that this all-surpassing power is from God and not from us." Clay jars were the most ordinary, everyday sort of containers at the time that Paul wrote that verse. They weren't cute like our clay garden pots that have a uniform shape and are often painted with rich colors. Clay jars were easily cracked, and when they were, those were the best ones to hold a candle to shine the light through the irregular slits.

God put his glorious new life inside of us, and all that light shines through the cracks. That way the credit goes to God. All the glory is his.

We can't increase our value by anything we do. We simply are. And what we are is his, with his power tucked inside us. God entrusts to us all his riches—his "love, joy, peace, patience, kindness, goodness, faithfulness, gentleness and self-control" (Galatians 5:22–23, TLB).

I once told some teenage girls that it wasn't a problem if they weren't beautiful by the time they were sixteen. But it was a problem if they weren't beautiful by the time they were sixty. They looked at me with bewildered expressions.

I explained that any young woman can look ordinary and unimpressive based on her outward appearance. She can try all the makeup and makeovers and make-dos to alter the outside. But what's on the inside is what will last forever. When that young woman's true self is in Christ, she is like the painting; she is carrying a hidden treasure.

The thing about carrying that much eternal glory inside your unhindered heart is that it's going to leak through as the cracks and wrinkles start to show. By the time a woman is sixty, if she has spent her days with Christ, as his friend, he has been set free in her spirit to do a lasting sort of makeover. The heart's makeover.

Sixty is the age when true beauty shows up by way of loving touches, eye-crinkling joy, tranquil expressions, patient moments, kind words, and an overall loveliness that radiates from the inside. That kind of beauty can't be replicated by Botox or a face-lift. It's real. It's eternal. And it's of great value.

> Your beauty comes from inside you. It is the beauty
> of a gentle and quiet spirit. Beauty like that doesn't
> fade away. God places great value on it.
> —I Peter 3:4, NIrV

Alyssa

When I was sixteen years old, a couple of years after I started to follow Jesus, I also started to follow the world's view of self-image. Somewhere along the line I forgot that I was of great value to the Lord, forgot who I was in him. Yes, I loved Jesus with all my heart, but I started to be more interested in gaining the attention of guys.

The world tells us that beautiful is skinny. That message is all around us, in movies, magazines, billboards, and television. Lose this amount of weight, be this size, "be the better you." In high school I wanted to fit in, and I wanted a boyfriend. I looked around me, and it seemed as though the skinny girls had boyfriends. So I concluded I had to be skinny to gain a guy's attention. What started out as a desire to be wanted or to have attention slowly formed into a habit that lasted six years.

All through high school and off and on throughout college, I had an eating disorder. I wanted a guy's attention, and I wanted to control my life. As women, we tend to struggle with our desire to be in control. But the Lord never said that's okay.

In fact, his directives are the exact opposite. He commands that we give up control and that we trust in him, the only One who truly has control. His control is not harsh, but rather he maneuvers situations with wisdom, power, and abundant love. He causes events that are for our good and for his glory. All that he does is out of love for us.

For me, eating was one thing I felt I could control. When life was out of my control—studying for a test, not having a boyfriend, feeling lonely—I turned to eating, or the lack of eating, because that's something I could control. I would count every calorie and plan out what I was going to eat the next day. Slowly I began to eat less and less. Desiring to be a size 6 turned into wanting to be a size 0.

I hid this truth from everyone. I was so ashamed, so afraid of people discovering that I had a problem, even though deep down I was crying out for someone to rescue me. I felt as if I couldn't tell anyone because I was the girl who encouraged others, who listened to their struggles. I was the Bible study leader, the mentor, the resident assistant. A few people knew—my parents and a couple of my best friends—but when they said something, I would just push it to the side. Even though I knew what I was doing was wrong, I enjoyed it. I liked pushing myself to see how little I could eat. It was one thing I could control in my life. Except it wasn't right at all, not right spiritually, emotionally, or physically.

During this time I loved the Lord deeply. I walked with him and poured out my heart to him. But I couldn't fully give up this one area. I prayed a thousand times that the Lord would forgive me and help me stop, but I kept running back to my poor eating habits whenever I felt as if my life was just a little out of control.

I remember one day when I was walking up a steep hill to reach my college dorm room. The flowers were in bloom, and the birds were singing, yet inside I felt dark and lonely. I had just come from eating lunch at the cafeteria, where I had managed to put down a salad with a little dressing and a bit of water. My usual lunch. Oh, I had seemed bright and cheery, but inside I cringed with every bite, fearful of gaining weight.

As I walked up that hill, I cried out, *Lord, I'm so tired of this. I know it hurts your heart. I know this isn't of you, and yet I keep doing it. I'm so afraid of gaining weight. I want to fit in. I want to be skinny like the beautiful girls, Lord. I want to be liked and wanted. I want a guy to notice me. I feel as though I'm in a dark prison, with no light, and I can't get out. This has gone on for so long, Lord. No one understands. There's no way I can tell anyone who could help me either. I'm way too ashamed, Lord. Embarrassed. Guilt ridden. God, help.*

I continued like that for a few more years. In fact, my eating problems grew worse each year. Right before I left for Maui, I was visiting my best friend in California, and she asked how I was doing in this area. She walked life with me. She asked the hard questions. And she stayed with me even when there didn't seem to be any progress or healing in my eating habits. I admitted to her that it was the worst it had ever had been and that I needed help. She told me she had been praying that the Lord would provide a mentor in my life in Maui to help me heal, to help me see my value, and to help me be transformed in this area. I began to pray the same.

A month later I became close friends with the woman who would be my mentor, a woman who had struggled with the same issue in high school and who helped me see how to eat well and how I could renew my mind with what God said about me.

When I moved to Maui, I was finally willing to give up. Let go. Surrender. Forever. I wanted to be free, to live as God intended, to be set free by his grace. That came, slowly and beautifully, by digging into Scripture and seeing for the first time how God sees me.

God weaves through Scripture how precious and valuable we are to him, how we are his treasure, his beautiful one, and the one in whom he delights. He tells us from the get-go that we are made in his image, that we are fearfully and wonderfully made, and that we are his temple. His Spirit dwells in us. Our bodies are not our own, but they have been bought at a great price.

If you find yourself doubting that you are precious to God, go back to chapter 2 and review the list "What God Says About You." Draw those truths into your heart, and meditate on them often.

> God paid a high price for you,
> so don't be enslaved by the world.
> —1 Corinthians 7:23, NLT

As I pondered the truths found in God's Word, they slowly displaced the lies I had believed for so long. They wiggled their way into my heart and have stayed there ever since. Truly, he has set me free. I am valuable to him. I have worth in him. I can place all my trust in him and rest in his good control.

> Do not be conformed to this world, but be trans-
> formed by the renewal of your mind, that by testing
> you may discern what is the will of God, what is
> good and acceptable and perfect.
> —Romans 12:2, ESV

When I first met Jeff and then as we started to date, I was in the thick of healing from my eating disorder. I met him when I was at my worst but didn't say anything because I was terrified. Terrified that he wouldn't like me anymore, he wouldn't understand, he wouldn't want me. As I began to heal, I realized that an important step in the process was to confess the issue, to make it known, and to bring it to light. So when I went home for Christmas, I told Jeff I struggled with an eating disorder.

Whoa! There, I said it. It was out in the open.

To my surprise Jeff was gracious and kind. He grabbed my hand and squeezed it. He thanked me for sharing, for being so honest. And he encouraged me in the healing process. After that he asked occasionally how I was doing, and he always encouraged me to eat. Jeff loves food, so it's easy to love it as well when I'm with him.

Jeff showed me that my size didn't matter to him; what he

was after was my heart. He loved my personality, my character, my love for the Lord. Yes, he thought I was beautiful and was attracted to me, but not because I was a certain size.

It wasn't until we started to date our second time around that I discovered the beauty of being completely honest and vulnerable with someone, that it's okay to take risks because ultimately I'm secure in the Lord. But that was the beginning. From the start Jeff showed me that it was safe to be transparent with him, that I had great value and was precious to him. He treated me with respect, honor, and tender love. I didn't have to prove myself; I just had to be me.

In the same way, the Lord loves us because we're made in his image. Before we ever did anything, said anything, or thought anything, he loved us. He died for us while we were still sinners—at the height of our rebellion. He gave his life for us. Whenever you doubt your value or worth, look to the cross. There you will see the ultimate proof that you are his treasure. Not because of anything you have done but because of what he did.

What Do You Think?

1. What would it take for you to believe—really believe—that you are of great value?

2. What lies have you believed about yourself?

3. What does God's Word say about those lies?

4. Pick a favorite verse from the list of "What God Says About You" at the end of chapter 2 and memorize it.

How does that verse help you believe that you are of great value to God?

5. If you're doing this study in a group, turn to the person next to you and speak a truth from God's Word to her. Affirm who she is according to what God says about her. If you're doing this study on your own, send a note or text to a friend and tell her about one of the truths from the list at the end of chapter 2 that you want to encourage her with.

Seven

You Are a Peculiar Treasure

id you know that God has nicknames for us? In the same way that a wife might call her husband "honey" or a sibling might call his sister "Sis," God calls us names. Sweet names. Pet names. Tender names that show once again his enduring affection for us.

Here are a few of God's terms of endearment for us:

- Peculiar Treasure (Exodus 19:5, KJV)
- Chosen (John 15:16, KJV)
- Saint (Romans 8:27, NASB)
- My People (Romans 9:25, NASB)
- Beloved (Romans 9:25, NASB)
- Masterpiece (Ephesians 2:10, NLT)
- Child of God (1 John 3:1, NASB)
- Bride (Revelation 19:7, NASB)

In each of these verses, God makes it clear that we aren't like those who turned their backs on him. We turned to him, and when we did, we were set apart. His Holy Spirit began the work of sanctification in our lives, and this process is making us holy.

It's a very personal process accomplished by a very personal God who comes to us with tender mercy and kindness. He communicates with affectionate names that remind us of what our relationship means to him.

Here's how it works. God calls us, as we saw in chapter 5. When he calls us, he does so with loving names. He then teaches us what is good, right, and true. He changes our hearts and our minds so that we begin to want what he wants.

God has set us apart from the rest of the world. We now have a purpose and a way of life that are different from what's standard in our society. As believers, we live in the world, yes, but we are not of the world. See the difference? If we were of the world, we would value the same things everyone else does and go after the same things they run after. We would talk like they do and act like they do. That's how we lived before we became his. Now that we are his, we experience a new way of life and a purpose that bring such joy because God's way is far better.

What does that process of change look like in your everyday life—school, work, friends, relationship drama, family conflicts, crazy emotions, dreams, and disappointments?

While every person's journey with Christ is different, one constant applies. To fully experience the joys and blessings of a God-directed life, our response to him must always be one of obedience.

> Now if you will obey me and keep my covenant, you
> will be my own special treasure from among all the
> peoples on earth; for all the earth belongs to me.
> —Exodus 19:5, NLT

Robin

Years ago we lived in a house that had two large cherry trees in the backyard. One August afternoon I picked a basket of luscious cherries and dipped them in melted chocolate. Yum!

My nine-year-old friend Natalie came over as I was lining up the dipped cherries on waxed paper so the chocolate could cool and set just right. She plopped down at the kitchen counter, watching me with her head in her hands.

I caught her glum expression and asked if she was okay.

She crossed her arms. "All my friends went to the movies, but my parents said I couldn't go."

"Why?"

"They said it wasn't the kind of movie I should see."

"Oh."

"It's not fair. I hate being the one who is left out. My parents are just way too overprotective. That's the problem."

I thought for a moment how to best respond. I mean, how do you explain to a nine-year-old the blessing that comes from living according to God's standards and not going along with the rest of the world? How do you explain sanctification, being a peculiar treasure, being set apart?

I ended up asking her a question. "Natalie, would you like to have some of these cherries?"

"Really? Sure! I thought you were making them for somebody special."

"I was." Giving her a wink, I added, "They're for you."

She perked up.

I grabbed several cherries by the stems. "Let me put them on a plate for you." I went over to the kitchen garbage and rummaged around until I found a dirty paper plate and then pulled it out.

The flimsy plate was stained with beans and hot dogs from a barbecue the night before.

Natalie looked stunned. "You're not going to use that dirty plate, are you?"

I shrugged, holding the plate in one hand and the cherries in the other, waiting.

"Don't you have any other plates you could use?" Natalie asked.

"Oh yes." I returned the paper plate to the garbage and the cherries to the wax paper. "I have other plates. They're special plates. Clean plates. Plates that I have kept set apart from all the others."

Natalie watched as I went across the room and unclasped the glass door of the antique china cabinet. I lifted out a single fine china plate. Looking at her I said, "You might think I'm way too overprotective of these plates."

A flicker of understanding crossed Natalie's face when she recognized the "way too overprotective" line she had just used in reference to her parents' decision to keep her from going to the movie.

"I'm protective because these fine china plates are very valuable," I said. "Because they are so valuable, I want to keep them clean and set apart. That way they will be kept from harm and will always be ready for me to use to serve others."

I handed her one of the plates. She held it carefully and traced the gold trim around the outside of the plate with her finger.

"It's beautiful," Natalie said.

"It is beautiful. Being set apart can be very lonely, but it can also be very beautiful."

Natalie blinked shyly as if waiting for what I was going to say next.

"Natalie, you have been set apart, just like a fine china plate. You are more valuable than you can ever imagine. And you are so beautiful. Don't you see? You weren't created to be a flimsy, stained paper plate. You are a fine china plate."

Natalie thought a moment. "I guess that's why my parents wouldn't let me go to the movie."

I nodded. "Yes. They see you as being valuable, beautiful, and worth protecting, just like a fine china plate."

"And fine china plates don't go around getting smeared with beans and hot dogs."

"Exactly."

I couldn't stop smiling as I took the plate from her and filled it with chocolate-covered cherries. I watched as she enjoyed each bite.

"How did you come up with that?" Natalie asked. "I mean, where did you learn about being a fine china plate?"

"I learned the secret of the fine china plate from the Bible."

"Really? I didn't know the Bible said anything about special plates."

"It does. I'll show you." I went upstairs to retrieve my Bible. When I returned, Natalie had finished her treat and was at the sink washing the china plate. I handed her a dish towel, and she dried it with care.

"Do you want me to put it back in the china cabinet?" Natalie asked.

"No. I think this fine china plate has a new purpose." I reached for a permanent marker in the catchall drawer, took the plate from Natalie, and wrote on the back of it. I gave it a minute to dry and then handed it to Natalie. She turned the plate over and read aloud:

Natalie,
You are a fine china plate.
2 Timothy 2:21

She looked at me with the sweetest expression. "You're giving this plate to me?"

"Yes, it's yours."

"And is this the verse where you learned the secret of the fine china plate?"

"Yes, it is. Do you want to read it for yourself?"

Natalie reached for the Bible and turned to 2 Timothy 2:21:

If you stay away from sin
you will be like one of these dishes
made of purest gold—
the very best in the house—

so that Christ himself can use you
for his highest purposes. (TLB)

Her eyes grew wide. "You were right! It *is* in the Bible!" She looked at the verse again. "What does it mean about being used for his highest purposes?"

"Well, what is the plate doing right now?"

"Shining?"

"Yes, it's shining because it's clean. You can see its true beauty when it's clean. A little earlier, when I put the cherries on the plate, it was being used to serve you. God's highest purposes for us are to love him and to love others. When we stay clean, we are set apart, ready to do what we were created to do. We beautifully reflect his handiwork as we serve others."

Natalie looked at the plate again and then looked at me with a shining smile on her face. "It feels special to be set apart like a fine china plate."

"Yes, it does. And I hope you remember that the next time your parents make a choice for you that will help keep your heart clean." I leaned down and gave her a little kiss on the top of her head. "Because, as you know, being set apart can also be lonely sometimes."

She nodded and then wrapped her arms around me in a hug.

When Natalie left my home that afternoon, she carried the fine china plate with great care. At her request her mom hung it on Natalie's bedroom wall so that during the hard or lonely times in the years ahead, she could look at it and remember who she was and whose she was.

Just like Natalie, when you came to Christ, he set you apart, like a fine china plate. Like a china plate, you are of great value. You are beautiful. You are easily washed clean when you become soiled by sin, and when you are clean, you shine with his magnificent glory. He takes great delight in using you to serve others.

You have been set apart like a fine china plate.

Alyssa

One of my favorite terms that the Lord calls us has always been *beloved*. It might sound old-school; no one uses that word in normal conversations today except for more traditional weddings when the pastor says, "Dearly beloved, we are gathered here today..." But throughout Scripture that is God's name for Israelites, for Jesus, and also for us, his chosen ones.

God calls us his beloved, meaning we are to *be loved* by him, and we are, every moment of every day regardless of what we do or don't do. He loves us with an unconditional, unrelenting, die-for-you kind of love. He has set his affections on us, and we are marked by his favor. We are precious to him, dear to his heart, held close, and forever wanted.

For the longest time I wanted to get *Beloved* tattooed on my wrist (but I never did because, let's face it, needles freak me out) to remind me of who I am to Jesus. Since the time I started to truly follow him, my relationship with him has been deep, rich, satisfying, and truly a joy, but it also has been hard at times. Following Jesus doesn't mean we get to take the easy way out; rather, it usually involves going against the cultural norm, against the standards of this world, making hard decisions, and standing up for what's right and true. Following Jesus can be hard because it's abnormal from the choices society makes. Often people just don't get it. But see, when we have been saved—when we are set apart from sin and this world and set apart to Christ—we are called to live differently. We are called "holy" (Ephesians 1:4, TLB); we pursue holiness. Not to earn God's love, but because we are already dearly loved—beloved. Knowing and resting in the truth of who we are brings comfort and the strength to face trials.

> Therefore be imitators of God, as beloved children.
> —Ephesians 5:1, ESV

I saw this truth play out in my life when I was a new Christian and a high school freshman. Something was different. Even though I don't think I could define what it was at the time, I was set apart.

That became evident when I didn't like gossiping about friends behind their backs or making crude jokes at lunch. I had lived like that before, but now that I knew Jesus intimately and understood who I was in him, I didn't want to live like that. Something in me was different from my friends. I no longer had a big urge to be popular or flirt with guys to get attention. I didn't want to go to the kind of parties that classmates were rushing off to.

I saw that those things brought a false sense of happiness. But God is the real deal. He brings ultimate joy and abundant life.

However, when I didn't participate in those things anymore, I became lonely. The loneliness forced me to cling to Jesus and to look to him to be my comfort, my portion, and my friend.

During my sophomore year in high school, the Lord opened my eyes to see how my school was the mission field that he had placed me in. Yes, I was different. Yes, I didn't fit in and was lonely, but God had placed me there to be a light. My friends needed Jesus. They needed to see that there was something so much better. I wasn't there to save them, but I was there to love them and to show them Jesus.

May I share a secret with you? When you really love Jesus, when he is everything to you and not just a "Sunday thing," you will face loneliness at times. You may be the only one not to go to that party. The only one not to date because you don't want to settle. The only one not to dress in a revealing way even when it's popular and stylish.

But God promises that you aren't alone, regardless of how you feel. Hebrews 13:5 says, "I will never leave you nor forsake you" (ESV). God is omnipresent, meaning he is always with you. He never leaves your side but in fact is always surrounding you. One Hebrew word translated as *presence* literally means "face." God is always facing you. He sees you. His eye is on you.

You may feel left out at times, especially when you stand up for what's right or when you don't participate in what you know to be wrong. But you are never alone. God is your Father, Friend, Guide, and Shield.

> The LORD did not set his affection on you and
> choose you because you were more numerous
> than other peoples, for you were the fewest of all
> peoples. But it was because the LORD loved you....
> Know therefore that the LORD your God is God;
> he is the faithful God, keeping his covenant of
> love to a thousand generations of those who
> love him and keep his commandments.
> —Deuteronomy 7:7–9

God is faithful to provide you with friends who love Jesus too. Even though I struggled with loneliness in high school, I eventually connected with girlfriends in youth group. I had to step away from the old friends before I could meet these new friends. I soon realized this new group was my support system. They had the same values I did. We would pray together, serve together, and hang out together. And these are still some of my best friends today.

God is all about community. He himself dwells in community as the Trinity: the Father, the Son, and the Holy Spirit. We were created *out of* community *for* community. God didn't intend for us to be islands, isolated and alone. He desires the exact opposite. We are to live life together with others, and in fact, that's the only way we'll flourish.

We can't do this life alone. We need other people, especially other believers, in our lives. I love looking back and seeing God's hand in all that has happened. I can see how he placed friends and mentors in my life to help guide me, encourage me, and call me to a life set apart.

Life is hard. There's a lot of pressure to act a certain way and to do certain things. I especially struggled in the area of dating. I didn't date anyone until I dated Jeff when I was twenty-two. (God's doing, not mine!) I remember how hard it was to long for a boyfriend but not to have any guys knocking on my door. Everyone around me was dating or going to school dances.

My mom was a huge encourager. She felt my pain, she understood my longing, and she walked through it with me. She prayed for me and encouraged me to do fun things like travel through Europe all summer on a mission trip. She stayed up late with me when I would come home crying because I felt lonely or the boy I liked didn't reciprocate my feelings. She prayed for me and pointed me to Jesus.

Then when I was in college, the Lord answered my prayers again and brought a friend into my life. She asked me the hard questions and saw into my heart. She encouraged me with what God was doing in me but also dug down deep to help me see my motives, the lies I was believing, or the habits that weren't what the Lord wanted for me. She did it all with kindness, grace, and humility. She loved me so much that she called me out in love. Calling someone out takes great humility and courage. It's an act of love because it's not for your benefit but for the other person's. It's wanting what is best for the person, regardless of how it may affect you. She showed me what it looked like to be honest, transparent, and humble.

When I lived on Maui, the Lord surrounded me with girlfriends and mentors to walk out that season of life with me. I matured as I put on my big-girl shoes by experiencing dating, breakups, and living in true community.

After I broke up with Jeff and then when Surfer Jeff broke up with me, I was a mess. I cried often, easily got overwhelmed, faced fears and doubts, was angry, and was shakily walking in faith. These women walked with me. They didn't just check in with a text, but they lived life with me.

My roommate held me some nights as I cried. My mentors had me over for coffee, lunch, or dinner and asked how I was doing. They helped me to process. They listened. They came before the Lord daily on my behalf. They pointed out lies I believed and the truth that God declares.

Community is beautiful, and every one of us needs it. Without community we'll sink. And the only way to have true community is to be transparent. To share the stuff you think about at night as you go to bed. To ask the hard questions. To encourage, listen, pray for, and speak truth to.

In some seasons community may be lacking. I feel like that now in my own life. I've felt like that in the past as well. But God has always been faithful. Every time I have prayed for friends who love Jesus or for a mentor to help guide me, he has provided. He has not let me down. It has taken time, yes, but he has always been faithful. Why? Because community is God's idea, and he wants that for you too. A place to be set apart for him yet to belong with others.

> Friendship is one of the sweetest joys of life.
> Many might have failed beneath the bitterness
> of their trial had they not found a friend.
> —Charles Spurgeon

Peculiar Treasure, Treasured Possession, My People, Beloved, Bride, Chosen, Child of God, Saint, and Masterpiece. These are not just any names. These are your names. For you. Given to you. They are you. God looks at you and sees you as his beautiful treasure, his very own, his daughter. Do you believe that? Do you see yourself as God sees you? You are treasured. You are highly esteemed. You are close to the Father's heart.

No, we don't deserve those names. We know deep down that, left to ourselves, each of us is a mess. But because God is merciful, gracious, and forgiving and because Jesus stood in our place, those names ring true about us. They are our identity. We must take these truths and live our lives out of them. Know who you are and then live according to your identity in him.

You are his.

You are beloved.

You are set apart.

What Do You Think?

1. Go through the list of God's tender names for you at the beginning of the chapter. Which one sticks out to you? Why?

2. When have you felt lonely because you were different from those around you? In what ways did you find God during that time?

3. How does knowing that God is present, that he sees you and faces you, affect you and help you to live set apart?

4. What changes do you need to make starting today to live truly set apart? What do you need to walk away from or let go of that's holding you back from this high calling?

5. Choose a name from the list to meditate on throughout this week and to recall when you begin to doubt your value.

Eight

You Are Set Free

Do you remember playing Freeze Tag when you were growing up? You had to stand in place while others ran around you. Remember how your best friend would sprint up to you, slap your hand, and set you free? Free to run wild with the others.

Ah, the joy of running with your hair flying in the wind, playing with the other kids. Remember how special you felt when your friend rescued you? How awesome it was not to have to stay in the same pose anymore? Sweet freedom.

Fast-forward a few years. You turn sixteen and can drive. You can go to and from places without your parents. Mom or Dad places the car keys in your hand, and you're off. You can stay out later, spend more time with your friends, and sing at the top of your lungs when you're alone in the car.

Skip ahead just a bit more, and suddenly you are eighteen and graduating from high school. You leave your nest at home and venture off. You are now officially an adult. You can choose whether to further your schooling, find a job, or travel on a whole different path. You are grown up.

All of these life experiences are steppingstones to freedom. Although they each require more responsibility, they still are sweet.

Now, take that feeling of freedom and apply it to your life with God. The moment you believe in Jesus as your Lord and Savior and begin to follow him, he sets you free. You are set free *from* something and *to* something. Set free from sin, selfishness, wrath, eternal separation from God, mistakes, guilt, shame, and your past. And you are set free to live fully for him. To continue to put off sin and to put on Christ. To love him and the things he loves. To run free from what was holding you down and to live a life of joy, peace, and abundance in him.

The freedom lasts forever. It's not gradual like other freedoms in life often are but comes all at once.

Yet one of the greatest tragedies in a believer's life is when the believer doesn't live as if he or she is set free.

> So if the Son sets you free, you will be free indeed.
> —John 8:36

Alyssa

I recently spent some time studying Hosea. This small book in the Old Testament tells how God calls Hosea, a prophet, to marry a prostitute. Let that sink in. Prophet. Prostitute. Marriage. Scandalous, right!? Here is a man of God, a man who loves the Lord and seeks to make him known, a man who walks in righteousness and integrity.

God has a word for him. A mission. Hosea waits eagerly to hear God's plan. He is ready to obey whatever his Almighty King commands.

"Go, take to yourself a wife of whoredom and have children of whoredom, for the land commits great whoredom by forsaking the LORD" (Hosea 1:2, ESV).

Now, the Bible doesn't say how Hosea reacts to this mission. We can imagine the plan isn't what Hosea was expecting to hear. He may have been shocked. He may have been disappointed. Maybe he had been waiting to marry a woman who loved the Lord as he did. Hosea may have been fearful. "What will people think of me?" Imagine the rumors that would buzz around: "Did you hear? Hosea is getting married—to a prostitute." "A prostitute!? What!?"

We don't know how Hosea feels, but we know what he does.

"So he went and took Gomer, the daughter of Diblaim, and she conceived and bore him a son" (Hosea 1:3, ESV). Hosea obeys the Lord. No questions asked. No matter the rumors or ruin to his reputation, Hosea trusts the Lord. He fears the Lord alone.

That sounds nice. It could make a great ending to a story. There was a prostitute, she found her Prince Charming, who loved and cherished her, and they had a son (and a daughter) and lived happily ever after.

Sounds good to me.

But it doesn't go quite like that. As you read more of Hosea 1–3, you find out that Gomer has another son, but it isn't Hosea's.

Can you imagine the shame you would feel as a husband? Your wife is pregnant again. But it's not your child. Hosea must have felt horror, realizing Gomer had been with another man.

Here's the thing. She doesn't have a one-night stand, repent, and come back to Hosea. No, she leaves him and chooses to be a prostitute again. Even after experiencing freedom and love, she goes back to her old ways. She chooses slavery. She chooses sin. She chooses other lovers over her husband.

God doesn't forget Hosea, though. The Lord speaks once more: "Go again, love a woman who is loved by another man and is an adulteress, even as the LORD loves the children of Israel, though they turn to other gods and love cakes of raisins" (Hosea 3:1, ESV).

So Hosea buys Gomer back. Imagine the scene. He walks into the town square, where he sees his wife on a platform—naked, shackled, up for grabs for any man to buy her, to use her. Hosea shoves his way through the crowd, makes his way to the front, and offers the highest bid. He buys back his bride. His wife. He buys back the woman who left him and chose other men.

Why does the Bible contain this story? Why in the world would God call Hosea to marry a prostitute? Go back to Hosea 1:2 (ESV): "For the land commits great whoredom by forsaking the LORD."

God wanted Hosea to reenact how the Lord saw his relationship with Israel. Israel was God's chosen people. His bride. He was her husband. But throughout history Israel turned her back on God and went after other gods. How many times did the people forget God? Do things their own way? Grumble, complain, and test their faithful and good God? Israelites played the whore. They returned to prostitution even after they had found a love that none can compare to.

But each time, God went after them. He pursued them in their mess. In their shame. In their sin. He got them back.

God says in Hosea 2:14, 19–20,

> Therefore, behold, I will allure her,
>   and bring her into the wilderness,
>   and speak tenderly to her....
>
>   And I will betroth you to me forever. I will betroth
> you to me in righteousness and in justice, in steadfast
> love and in mercy. I will betroth you to me in faithful-
> ness. And you shall know the LORD. (ESV)

If we were to take an honest look at our lives, wouldn't we see that we are just like Israel? We are wanted, pursued, loved, and cherished; yet how often do we forget God? How often do we choose other things, other lovers, over him? How often do we do things our own way, thinking we know best? How often do we pick the things of this world over him? And how often do we forget who we are and go back to the world to find our identity?

> You were bought at a price; do not
> become slaves of human beings.
> —1 Corinthians 7:23

It's easy for us to fall into the same trap as Israel did. We uplift and love the things of this world more than we love Jesus. Even if the things we love aren't anything wicked, the focus on them takes our eyes off our relationship with Christ. When we choose other people and things over Christ, it becomes easy to forget who we are in him.

Halfway through my second year interning, Surfer Jeff ended our relationship, and I was broken. Brokenhearted yes, but also broken over the words that were spoken to me when he ended the relationship. The words went to the depths of my heart and made their home there.

Why did I struggle so much? They were just words. They were only his feelings and thoughts. But I couldn't shake them off. My spirit was taken captive by a lie. Three lies, actually. I started to let these lies tell me who I was.

1. I was too emotional for anyone to love me.

2. I was exhausting.

3. I was not worth it.

Let's be honest—I am emotional. Not just your typical-girl emotional either, but a bit more sensitive than the average girl on the street. I cry easily, get hurt quickly, and feel fragile often. This, of course, would wear anyone out, especially a guy! And because I was too emotional and exhausting, Surfer Jeff was done. It was too much for him. *I* was too much for him.

That's what I believed. That's what I carried around and repeated to myself.

But it wasn't true. They were lies. Three lies that I clenched tightly.

> Jesus said to the people who believed in him,
> "You are truly my disciples if you remain
> faithful to my teachings. And you will know
> the truth, and the truth will set you free."
> —John 8:31–32, NLT

I finally couldn't take it any longer. I went before the Lord and threw those lies before Jesus's throne. I begged him to show me who I was. I needed to remember who he said I was. He led me to Psalm 139, a beautiful song of how precious we are to him. These words especially spoke to me: "For you formed my inward parts; you knitted me together in my mother's womb. I praise you, for I am fearfully and wonderfully made. Wonderful are your works; my soul knows it very well" (verses 13–14, ESV).

In the light of God's Word, I replaced the lies with truth. The Lord formed my body, mind, and heart. He made me with purpose and intention. He fashioned me uniquely and knows my heart, my struggles, and my emotions.

Truth: I am not too emotional for the Lord, nor am I exhausting to him. He made me as I am. He sees all of me, loves me, and receives me with arms open wide. Yes, I am sensitive, but I believe the Lord created me that way so I can have a soft heart that yearns to bear others' hurts and needs. The downside is that I can be overly sensitive when someone says something hurtful, or I can be too emotional. But the Lord is refining me, smoothing out my rough edges. He is at work in me, and he does not give up.

Truth: I am worth it to God. He died for me so he could be in relationship with me. He will go to whatever lengths are necessary to get me. In Deuteronomy 31:8 Moses promises, "[God] will not leave you or forsake you" (ESV). No matter what. Unconditional love. Committed. Secure.

Knowing the truth didn't mean the lies went away with a finger snap. I had to choose to fix my mind on the truth, not the lies. I had to purposefully think of what God said about me and prayerfully believe it. Day by day, moment by moment, thought by thought, I chose to be intentional in how I viewed myself.

> Now the Lord is the Spirit, and where the
> Spirit of the Lord is, there is freedom.
> —2 Corinthians 3:17, ESV

A turning point for my healing came on a gorgeous Maui morning. Janet, one of Robin's best friends, was visiting, and Robin invited me to join them on an outrigger-canoe adventure. One of the nearby resorts offered an early morning paddle in a classic Hawaiian outrigger canoe under the instruction of two locals.

The night before, I had cried myself to sleep. I was still reeling from the pain after the breakup with Surfer Jeff. The vicious lies still entangled my heart.

As the sun rose over the Haleakala volcano, we three women strode onto the sandy beach. The two guides greeted us by blowing into a conch (a huge seashell) and doing a Hawaiian chant to greet the new day. We each grabbed a side of the outrigger, ran into the crashing waves, and hoisted ourselves into the canoe.

Taking a left turn, we headed over to a cove where turtles liked to play. The water was exceptionally clear that day, and I could see to the bottom of the ocean. Today was a new day. A day filled with beauty and joy, I told myself, as I chose not to think about Surfer Jeff's view of me.

> Weeping may endure for a night,
> but joy cometh in the morning.
> —Psalm 30:5, KJV

Robin slid out of the canoe and into the water, and I followed suit. An early dip in the ocean wakes up your soul. We snorkeled around, watching turtles glide through the water and tropical fish weave in and out of the coral reef. When we surfaced, one of the guides pulled up a bright-red sea urchin from the reef. It looked like a bunch of school pencils all connected into the shape of a star. He placed the spiny creature on top of my head as I treaded water. Robin and I giggled about my cute little hat, and her friend snapped a photo from the outrigger before the guide returned the urchin to the coral below us.

I floated on my back and looked up at the bright sky. The rays of sunshine sparkled all over my salty face. I knew in that moment that I was going to be okay. That God was near, that he was caring for me just as he cared for the turtles, the fish, the sea urchin, and all of his creation.

And I was full of hope. I believed that God was with me, healing me, drawing me to himself, and preparing me for something that was beyond what I could ever imagine. He was present. And he was giving me hope, setting me free.

> The steadfast love of the LORD never ceases;
> his mercies never come to an end;
> they are new every morning;
> great is your faithfulness.
> "The LORD is my portion," says my soul,
> "therefore I will hope in him."
> —Lamentations 3:22–24, ESV

We jumped back into the outrigger. (Well, Robin kind of kerplunked; it's tough being graceful when getting into a canoe!) We laughed that deep kind of belly laugh that friends share. As we held our paddles in position, the guide at the back of the canoe gave the command in Hawaiian, and we worked as one, paddling our way back to shore. I knew I was surrounded, front and back, with good friends who would paddle with me through life. Today was a new day. God was going to see me through.

If you're in the same place I was, listening to lies about you rather than the truth, let God set you free by going back to the end of chapter 2 to review the list of "What God Says About You." Don't let the lies bind you. You are free in Christ.

> You are the God who buys me back.
> Every time I run to the marketplace
> And sell myself to a lie
> You show up with a fistful of truth
> And you buy me back.
> Every time.
> I belong to you, Great God.
> You bought me back at a great price.
> May I not run from you today.
> —Robin Jones Gunn

Robin

My husband, Ross, once told me I apologized way too much. "You're always saying you're sorry for things that happened in the past or for things that go wrong that aren't even your fault."

I knew he was right. I felt bound up by a sense of failure. Logically I knew I was forgiven, but my heart still felt heavy.

I told him, "When I mess up, even after I apologize, I still feel guilty."

"That's a trap of the enemy," he said.

"A trap? What do you mean?"

He reassured me that if I apologized or asked forgiveness for my mistake, then that was the end of it. In God's eyes my error, my sin, was tossed into the deepest sea. It was ridiculous for me to paddle out and fish around to pull my failures back up just so I could hold them high to say, "Look at how I messed up. I'm so sorry."

Ross reminded me that God's Word makes it clear we have a very real enemy who wants nothing more than for us to be in bondage. He is the one who accuses us. He's the one who wants us to think we have to do something to pay for our mistakes and somehow atone for our failures. If we could do that, we wouldn't need a Savior.

But we do need a Savior! We need a Savior very badly.

That's what Christ did for us when he took on all our sin and failings. His blood atoned for our sin. He set us free.

Ross asked me, "Do you believe that? Do you believe Christ has really set you free?"

I nodded and said yes wholeheartedly. But inwardly I still felt bad. I continued to beat myself up whenever I messed up.

Then one night I was talking to my sister on the phone and asked if she ever felt the same way, even though she knew she was forgiven.

"All the time," she said. "I know that's not how the Lord wants me to think or feel, but I do. I'm not sure if it's a result of how we grew up or what, but I always feel a sense of shame. It's like a chain around my ankle."

"Me too! That's it; you just named it. Shame. I feel ashamed even when I know I've been forgiven."

We talked some more about how we wanted to know and to feel complete release. We wanted to be free. Free from the shame.

"Okay, then," I said over the phone. "Let's make an agreement. From now on, whenever we mess up, once we've made things right with God and with others, let's tell ourselves, 'Shame off you.'"

She laughed. "I like that. Shame off you, Robin."

I echoed the blessing to her. "Shame off you, Julie. Shame off you, and grace on you."

Neither of us realized what a breakthrough that phrase would become. We were both set free in our thoughts. The enemy no longer had a foothold from which he could pull us down with an imprisoning sense of guilt and shame. We were free in Christ because he had forgiven us and broken off our shackles of guilt and shame.

For years now my sister and I have blessed each other by saying, "Shame off you. Grace on you." We say it to each other, to ourselves, and to any friend or family member who needs to be reminded that he or she has been set free.

God knows us by heart. He knows we're going to stumble. That's why he gave us the directions in 1 John 1:9 to confess our sins. We must tell him right away when we realize we've done something wrong. We agree with him and say, "That wasn't what you wanted for me, was it? I know that what I did made you sad, Father. I'm sorry. Please forgive me."

When we make that confession, he sees us as blameless. Forgiven. We are made right before him. We are set free.

> There is therefore now no condemnation
> for those who are in Christ Jesus.
> —Romans 8:1, ESV

Last fall I taught at an international conference held in Nairobi, Kenya. One of the writers who signed up for a consultation told me he was from a neighboring African nation. He was tall, very thin, and had dark eyes that seemed to go soul deep. We discussed writing disciplines, organization ideas, and deadlines before I asked the twenty-seven-year-old what he was working on.

"I'm translating the Bible into one of the dialects of my country."

I was astounded. His task was monumental. I asked him how it was going.

"I use English translations," he said. "There are many that are easy to understand, and they are all free online."

"But English isn't your first language," I observed. "How did you master English?"

"I learned it a few years ago."

"You're so fluent. I thought perhaps you learned English in school when you were young."

"No," he said. "I only went to school until I was eight."

"Eight? Wow. Why did you stop going to school?"

He lowered his chin and looked away. "I was taken."

"Taken?"

He looked up at me as if I were playing a cruel joke. My innocent expression must have made it clear that I didn't catch the meaning of his phrase. In a solemn voice he spoke five words that sounded like a thunderclap to my heart.

"I was a child soldier."

He watched my face, his deep eyes steady and unblinking.

I held back an aching gasp and stumblingly asked, "Do you ever talk about that?"

He shook his head, and as he did, a slow light seemed to glow in his eyes. "I escaped when I was twelve."

I sat in silence, reluctantly giving way to thoughts of the gruesome injustices that had been acted out on child soldiers to strip them of their humanity. I had read those unspeakable accounts over the years, but I never imagined I would be sitting face to face with one of the lost boys.

Then, as if he knew that my thoughts were headed to a vile place filled with images of the worst sort of depraved behavior, he firmly said, "Jesus delivered me."

I drew in a quick breath. Redemption. Freedom. New life. Yes!

Shame off. Grace on. Yes and amen.

A softness formed around his mouth as ready words rolled out of his heart and covered us both, quelling the awkwardness and pain I felt on his behalf. The words he spoke next were from God's Word.

"One thing I do, forgetting those things which are behind and reaching forward to those things which are ahead, I press toward the goal for the prize of the upward call of God in Christ Jesus."

I recognized the verses as part of Philippians, chapter 3. I had memorized those same verses years ago. But I hadn't taken them to heart the way he had. For my African writing friend, those words were words of freedom. They were his new marching orders. All the atrocities of his past were deliberately forgotten. He had a life purpose. He was reaching forward, pressing toward a noble goal. The upward call of God in Christ Jesus had become a life-giving, truth-bearing reality, and he was free from the past. Completely set free.

The same is true for each of us, regardless of our pasts. We have been set free.

You, my brothers and sisters, were called to be free.
But do not use your freedom to indulge the flesh;
rather, serve one another humbly in love.
—Galatians 5:13

Call out to God. Leave the past behind. Flee. Turn your back on your old life. Run to Jesus. He will deliver you. Then live in that freedom.

Shame off you. Grace on you.

What Do You Think?

1. What thoughts or behaviors has God set you free from?

2. Do you live as if you are free, or do you hold on to the past—to lies, guilt, or shame? Explain.

3. What lies do you currently believe about yourself?

4. What truths counterbalance the lies you wrote down in question 3? Let those truths sink into your heart.

Choose one verse that contains a truth to memorize this week.

5. In what ways does the phrase "Shame off you; grace on you" apply to your life right now?

Nine

You Are Covered

magine that you are at a restaurant with friends. You've finished eating, and the waiter places the check on the table. You're about to go for your wallet, but someone else reaches for the bill and says, "I've got this. You're covered."

What a nice gift that is.

Or what if you were expecting a big bill and knew you couldn't pay it? For days you've been awake at 3 a.m., trying to figure out a solution. The invoice arrives. You cringe as you look at the total, expecting to see the enormous amount you owe. To your sweet surprise, these words are written across the bill: "No charge. This has been covered."

You would be ecstatic. Someone covered a debt you couldn't. You suddenly feel lighter, happier, more blessed than you ever imagined. You did nothing to deserve such extravagant kindness, and yet you got graced. Big time. Life is once again full of possibilities, and hope overflows.

Now let's ramp up the scenario. What if the debt you owed was for your disobedience, selfishness, anger, jealousy, and every secret rebellion against God? The price required for your sin was your very life. Your blood. Jesus enters at just the right moment and says, "I've got you covered. I paid in full with my life."

Do you see what an extravagant, undeserving gift God gave to us when his only Son died? Jesus's love for us, demonstrated on the cross, covered all our sins with God's love, forgiveness, grace, mercy, and peace.

But what does that mean in our day-to-day living?

Above all, love each other deeply, because
love covers over a multitude of sins.
—1 Peter 4:8

Robin

About four years into my marriage I had a meltdown. A whole lot of hidden pain came gushing out of a deep place in my spirit. I crumbled in our home's hallway, curled up across from the open door of the bedroom that was supposed to one day be a nursery. I tried to get as small as I could and drew up my legs to my chest. With my arms wrapped around my knees, I rocked back and forth and wailed.

The front door opened. My husband was home early. I didn't expect him for at least another two hours.

"Hey, I'm home! Where are you?" Ross called out to me, but I couldn't move. I had been weeping so deeply I couldn't turn off the tears. My sobs came in a second wave of anguish.

He came around the corner and spotted me in my miserable state. "What are you doing there? What's wrong? What happened? Why are you crying?"

I had a terrible time trying to form the words to tell him how fearful I was. A long list of anxiety giants had taken me down. My patient husband sat down in the hallway next to me and urged me to talk to him. Just talk. Start with one of the things I was feeling and go from there.

I drew in a deep, wobbly breath.

We hadn't gotten pregnant after four years. He nodded but didn't say anything.

My job was in jeopardy. He knew that and had no new insights or advice for me.

We had bills we couldn't cover that month. He had been thinking about that too.

Nothing in our young married life felt secure or hopeful.

"What else are you feeling?" he asked. "Is there something more?"

There was, but I didn't want to tell him. It was difficult to confess how all the fears had opened the way to the painful memory of how my fiancé rejected me so many years ago. The memory had come at me like a fiery dart in the midst of all my insecurities about our future. The poison in that dart was the fear that one day my husband might also decide that he no longer wanted me. He would reject me too.

I will never forget what he did as I spoke my hideous thoughts to him.

He covered me.

He wrapped his big, strong arms around me and drew me close. He whispered that he would not leave me or reject me. Then he prayed for me. He prayed that the enemy would go away and stop harassing me. He prayed that I would trust in the Lord with all my heart and lean not on my own understanding. He asked God to give me his joy and to show me his truth.

My husband's powerful expression of love lifted me out of a

deep, dark place. I had chosen to let my thoughts go to a prison, locked away from the light of God's truth and love.

Once I calmed down, I felt God's peace covering me. Faith, hope, trust, and joy all came scampering back with renewed strength.

As my husband stood and offered his hand to help me stand up, I realized that none of the circumstances that had knocked me down had changed. I still wasn't pregnant. Things were still precarious where I worked. We still didn't have enough money for the bills that month.

What had changed was my trust in God.

I went from feeling the weight of all the deficits in my life and my faith to fully believing that the Lord had this covered. All of it. It was as if the Holy Spirit was saying to me, "I've got this. Be free. You just do the next thing and don't worry. Trust me. I've got you covered."

Did we eventually have a baby? Yes, two. A boy and a girl.

Did I lose my job? No. I resigned after our son was born.

Did we pay all the bills that month? Yes. Somehow. I don't remember now where the money came from, but it was there when we needed it. God's constant provision.

Did my husband leave me? No. After thirty-six years we're still busy learning how to love each other and serve God together.

Above all, has God been faithful over all the years? Yes, yes, yes!

On that major-meltdown day, I learned that God always has it covered. Everything.

He has every day of your life covered as well. Trust him with your whole heart. Don't let fear sneak in and lock you in a prison of despair.

> Whoever dwells in the shelter of the Most High
> will rest in the shadow of the Almighty.
> I will say of the LORD, "He is my refuge and my
> fortress, my God, in whom I trust."
> —Psalm 91:1–2

Alyssa

Life can be scary at times. We don't know what the future holds. We get hurt. We are let down. We give our heart to someone, and sometimes that person crushes it. Or our unfulfilled expectations and dreams are crushed. Life doesn't go as we had hoped. Our plans fail, no matter how tightly we grasp to have control. Fear can creep in. The what-if question looms heavy. Anxiety can take over.

But God… What a sweet phrase. *But God* is with us. But God is for us. But God is our God and takes over. He is the King, and no plan of his can be changed (Job 42:2). Everything that happens to us must pass through his hands first. He allows it to happen, in his mysterious way, for his glory and our good.

God covers us. He holds us. He protects us. He is our Shield and Strong Tower. Therefore, because of who God is, we can fully rest in him. We can step out and take risks. We can live courageously because we are in his hands.

After Surfer Jeff broke up with me, the last thing I wanted to do was date again. I didn't want to even consider dating or getting to know someone else. I was done.

But the Lord had other ways of healing my heart. Part of my healing process was bringing my Jeff back into my life to show me what true love really was. To show me what kindness, tenderness, and grace looked like.

When Jeff reconnected with me through e-mail two weeks after Surfer Jeff had called things off, I was shocked. I quickly closed my computer, not wanting to talk to Jeff—or any guy for that matter. No thank you. I'm done. Stay away. The pain was so deep; I couldn't go through it again.

When I mentioned Jeff's e-mail to a friend, she encouraged me to pray about e-mailing him back and reminded me that, if nothing else, he was my brother in Christ. As I prayed about it, the Lord gently opened my heart to Jeff. The more I prayed, the more I saw God's kindness through my Jeff. How thoughtful that he had wanted to see how I was doing after my breakup even though I had broken his heart months before.

So I replied to him. And that began frequent e-mails back and forth for months. I asked him to forgive me for how I had broken up with him and how I had treated him since. I was humbled when I thought about how I had ended our relationship, which was so much like how Surfer Jeff broke up with me, and I knew how awful that felt.

Jeff showed me nothing but grace and love. I was overwhelmed by his tenderness, by how he comforted and encouraged my heart. He kept pointing me to Jesus and praying for me.

I eventually confided in my mom and a few mentors and friends that I liked Jeff so much, even though I had ended a relationship only a few months before and was still messy and healing. But each one supported this new direction with Jeff. There were no hesitations, no doubts.

One night in July, Robin and I got together to have a heart-to-heart. She took me to one of the glamorous Maui restaurants to have chocolate fondue and coffee as the sun set. I would soon be ending my time in Maui and moving back home.

She asked about Jeff, and I disclosed all my thoughts, doubts, and feelings to her. By this time I wanted to get back together with him but was terrified. My heart melted for him, but fear of being hurt was taking over.

What if it didn't work out?

What if he didn't want to get back together with me?

What if he had moved on?

What if I opened my heart to him and he realized he didn't want it after all and ditched me?

What if, what if, what if?

Robin listened intently and then spoke words of truth. "Lyss, don't be afraid. God is for you, and you are his. Everything I've heard about Jeff leads me to believe that God is directing you to respond to Jeff's pursuit of you. So what if it's scary? You can take risks. You can take this risk because you are in God's hands. He's got you. Be open. Walk in faith. Trust God's leading. And whatever you do, don't let fear make the decision for you."

As we talked further, she pointed out ways in the past year that Jeff had fought for me. She listed Jeff's actions that demonstrated he had never stopped loving me or given up on me, but instead had waited for me. This was real love. This was the love that I had waited for. Giving. Unending. Selfless. Unfaltering love.

Others in my life saw the same things in Jeff. As I sought counsel from people I respected, they agreed that this was a good thing. This was a God thing. I wasn't forcing it. I wasn't controlling it. No, this was the love story God was writing for Jeff and me. I just had to let go of my fears and step into his work.

So I did. I surrendered my fears to the Lord and trusted in his fatherly care. I knew that the Lord was my portion, that he was faithful, and that he was good. I was covered by the Lord and covered by godly mentors and friends.

I told Jeff that I wanted to date him again. But we didn't officially get back together until after I moved home and he was working at summer camp. Thus began chapter 2 for us.

A big part of taking risks with the Lord and in relationships is our willingness to be vulnerable. We have to open ourselves up. We have to entrust ourselves to the Lord and loosen our grip on controlling the situation. Instead of focusing so heavily on the situation ahead and all that could happen, we need to place our focus on Jesus and follow, one step at a time, where he leads.

Nothing in life is a sure thing. Nothing is safe, perfect, or in our control. But the Lord says not to fear. We have no reason to when we walk in the light of who he is. I love what Mr. Beaver in C. S. Lewis's novel *The Lion, the Witch and the Wardrobe* says about Aslan, the lion that represents the Lord.

"'Safe?' said Mr. Beaver; 'don't you hear what Mrs. Beaver tells you? Who said anything about safe? 'Course he isn't safe. But he's good. He's the King, I tell you.'"

God isn't safe. Life isn't safe. We're not safe as believers. But we are covered. We are secure. We are free. We are protected. God is good, and all that happens is for our good. Not necessarily for our happiness but always for our holiness.

God's goal is to make us more like his Son, and often that involves trials and pain. But those difficulties are opportunities to rely on our Savior, to run into his arms, to nestle ourselves in his embrace, and to walk with him.

To love at all is to be vulnerable. Love anything, and your heart will certainly be wrung and possibly be broken. If you want to make sure of keeping it intact, you must give your heart to no one, not even to an animal. Wrap it carefully round with hobbies and little luxuries; avoid all entanglements; lock it up safe in the casket or coffin of your selfishness. But in that casket—safe, dark, motionless, airless—it will change. It will not be broken; it will become un-breakable, impenetrable, irredeemable.

—C. S. Lewis, *The Four Loves*

What Do You Think?

1. How would you live differently if you believed the debt of all your sins was covered?

2. Think about a time someone covered your debt or paid for something you owed. How did that feel?

3. What areas of your life are you holding back from the Lord? What are your what-ifs?

4. What steps can you take today to entrust these matters to the Lord?

5. On a scale of 1 to 10, how vulnerable would you say you are with the Lord? With others?

Ten

You Are Promised

See if you can relate to this.

You're clicking around online and see a link posted by a friend of your cousin's friend's roommate's sister. It's a proposal video, so of course you click on the link even though you have no idea who these people are.

The hidden camera is slightly askew in a beautiful park setting. As the camera moves to the couple, you see the man holding a guitar. The young woman sits on a bench with a dozen red roses in her lap. The man serenades her with a song that he wrote just for her. As he sings, the tears flow. She is not the only one crying.

His song finished, the young man lays down his guitar. He takes her hands in his and draws her up to stand facing him.

The young woman's smile is radiant and expectant. The young man goes down on one knee. Then with tenderness and confidence, the bridegroom-to-be offers her a small box that holds a beautiful gift—a ring.

"Will you marry me?" he asks.

"Yes! Yes! A thousand times yes!"

The video clip ends and you sigh. Perhaps you smile and watch it again.

That tender moment of promise is something we never tire of witnessing. That's because every proposal, every love story, is an echo of the Great Love Story of how Christ invites us to forever be his. He has offered the Holy Spirit as the "engagement ring" of his eternal promise.

You could almost say that the Holy Spirit "seals the deal" in our eternal relationship with Christ. Here's how it's explained in Ephesians:

> You also became believers in Christ. That happened when you heard the message of truth. It was the good news about how you could be saved. When you believed, he marked you with a seal. The seal is the Holy Spirit that he promised.
>
> The Spirit marks us as God's own. We can now be sure that someday we will receive all that God has promised. (1:13–14, NIrV)

When you see your relationship with Christ this way, it's beautifully romantic, isn't it? You are promised to him. His thoughts of love are continually for you. He is preparing a place for you so that when this life is over, you can be with him forever.

Until that day the Holy Spirit's presence in your life is evidence to you and everyone else that you are spoken for. You are promised. Your affection and loyalties are for your Bridegroom and his kingdom, not for this world. Not for other lovers. This is intended to be an exclusive relationship. No false gods need apply. The hunt for the true love and joy of your soul is over. Jesus made his intentions clear, and you said yes to his proposal of a true, forever-after love.

Let the plans for the wedding feast of the Lamb begin!

I found him whom my soul loves.
—Song of Solomon 3:4, ESV

Alyssa

Even though Jeff and I had some obstacles to work through while we were dating, I knew that I wanted to marry him the first night I saw him after moving back home. We met up for dinner at Red Robin. He was so handsome, with big broad shoulders and his five o'clock shadow. His smile met mine. Big bear hug. Yep, I wanted to spend the rest of my life with him.

After seven months of dating the second time, I was so eager for him to propose to me. We were reading *The Meaning of Marriage* by Timothy Keller and were in pre-engagement counseling.

As the weeks drew closer to the actual proposal, Jeff asked a lot of questions about weddings: "How many people would you want at your wedding?" "Where would you want to get married?" "What all is involved in planning a wedding?"

To say that marriage was on my mind was an understatement! I would fall asleep dreaming of spending the rest of my life with Jeff and would pray daily, surrendering the timing of it all to the One who held our hearts in his hands.

When I look back on that time, I realize that I never really thought about the ring or tried to plan much of our wedding. I just wanted Jeff. I didn't want to spend another day without him. I didn't like being at home while he traveled the world; I wanted to be with him. It hurt when he was gone.

Finally the week of the proposal came.

I had a hunch that this week might be *the* week. I got a manicure just in case. I mean, a girl's gotta have her nails done when the man she loves places a ring on her finger!

The night before Jeff proposed, we were at his friend's wedding. We took a walk after dinner, arms around each other, once again talking about weddings. Jeff commented that he thought it was genius to buy a fake diamond—they're way cheaper and way bigger! I protested, saying that I would like a real diamond, even if it was so small you needed a microscope to see it.

I cried the entire way home, thinking that he hadn't even bought a ring yet; therefore it would be *months* before we were engaged.

The next morning Jeff and I drove to a church where he was scheduled to speak to the youth group. We hurried off when he was done (unusual for Jeff) because he had planned a special picnic lunch for the two of us at a cute beach in Gig Harbor, Washington. We pulled into the park and walked hand in hand through a meadow full of spring flowers.

When we reached a dirt path with a wooden fence, I looked up and saw candles and rose petals that went all the way to the beach. On the fence were pictures Jeff and I had taken together over the past three years. Butterflies danced in my stomach.

This. Was. It.

Jeff and I looked at each photo, reminiscing over our sweet moments together. Haleakala sunrise in Maui. Hiking at Mount

Rainier. Carving pumpkins. Baseball games. Shamu show at Sea-World. Ice skating.

As we made our way to the beach, we came to a blanket spread out on the ground, rose petals strewn about, candles lined up, and more photos. Sitting down, Jeff said, "Before we start, I want to read something from my journal that I wrote before I met you." He had written a letter to his future wife, which he had added to through the years.

This man had thought of me, dreamed of me, prayed for me.

"Alyssa, you are that woman. You are the woman I want as my wife." Then he pulled out a thermos of warm water and a bowl. He washed my feet, sharing with me how he wanted that act to symbolize our marriage: how he wanted to cherish and tenderly take care of me as my husband.

Tears welled up in my eyes.

Getting down on one knee, Jeff pulled out the ring. "Alyssa Joy Fenton, I love you with every part of me. I cannot imagine my life without you—nor do I want to. You are the woman I want to walk life with, to spend the rest of my life with. Will you marry me?"

With tears in my eyes and a huge smile on my face, I whispered, "Yes." We laughed, and I shouted a huge yes. We were getting married! I was going to marry the man of my dreams. The man I had prayed years for.

"Did you even see the ring?" Jeff asked.

Oh right, I get a ring too! I had been so overcome with the joy of knowing I would marry Jeff that I forgot about that part. I looked down, and on my hand was a beautiful diamond shining up at me.

"Is this *real*!?" I asked, remembering his comment about fake rings.

"Of course it's real, Lyss!"

The diamond was his great-grandmother's, and it was stunning.

As we moved through the next three months, the Lord revealed truths along the way about how engagement reflects his love for and relationship with us. That he has set his affections on us is a mystery, just as falling in love is wonderful yet mysterious.

> He put his Spirit in our hearts and marked us
> as his own. We can now be sure that he will
> give us everything he promised us.
> —2 Corinthians 1:22, NIrV

For Jeff and me, the engagement was a sure thing. He had waited to propose until he was sure he wanted to spend the rest of his life with me and was ready to do so. When that man makes a decision, he jumps all in, and there's no going back!

I was ready to commit my life to him. My heart was ready. My mind made up. Mentors and my parents were in support of our relationship, and I had peace from the Lord that this was best for me.

From that day forward, every day on my way home from

work, I would pray for our marriage, and I would stare at my sparkling ring. (I know, not a good idea while driving!) I would think about how much Jeff loved me and how crazy in love I was with him. Those thoughts led me to reflect on the Lord's tender love.

Jesus loves me. Jesus laid down his life for me. On the cross Jesus made a way for me to be with him always. And when he ascended into heaven, he sent his Spirit to dwell in us.

I understood in a more personal way how the Holy Spirit is like an engagement ring. He is the promise that Jesus wants me and is coming back. He will come for me the way a groom comes for his bride. During the waiting time God has given us the gift of his Spirit to be with us, to assure us of his promise, to comfort us until his return. What a gift to have a promise like that from the Lord and to wear it around my heart every single day!

> Deep in your hearts you know that every
> promise of the LORD your God has come true.
> Not a single one has failed!
> —Joshua 23:14, NLT

In Bible times, engagement was a little different from what it is today. When a man wanted to marry a woman, he went to her father to ask for her hand in marriage. He would pay a price for her, and the father and new son-in-law would make a covenant. Then the fiancé would go away to build a home (actually an apartment that was added on to his father's house). The woman never knew when her husband-to-be was coming back, but she made herself ready and waited patiently.

So it is with Jesus. He came to win our hearts. He paid a price to the Father for us, the most costly price—his life. Then he ascended on high to prepare a place for us in his Father's home. We don't know when he will return, but we know that he will. Until then, we make ourselves ready, seeking him daily, growing in our knowledge of him and love for him.

We can set our hopes on Christ, knowing he will return for us. Whenever we doubt, we can go to his Word and remember his promise to come back. He has given us his Helper to be with us until then.

Robin

I love Alyssa's engagement story. My favorite part is the string of photos that lined the way to where Jeff and Alyssa drew close and promised themselves to each other. It's such a lovely parallel to how the Lord is with us all along the way. What if we could look at all the snapshot moments of how God has expressed delight in being with us? If we had any doubts that he loves us and longs to be with us, those images would make it clear that we are his beloved.

> I am my beloved's and my beloved is mine.
> —Song of Songs 6:3

When my husband proposed to me, it was simple and straightforward. We had been talking about marriage in round-about terms, the way many couples do in that tenuous space when they realize they want to spend the rest of their lives together.

Ross knew that I was still cautious about letting myself fall in love. I knew that he had talked with my dad and had sought his blessing in pursuing marriage with me. And, like Alyssa, I had a feeling the proposal would be coming soon.

But I didn't expect it to happen the way it did, and neither did he. We were sitting across from each other, sharing a piece of pie, when suddenly the words "Will you marry me?" popped out of his mouth.

I put down my fork and tried to read his expression. Was he serious? I hoped this wasn't a joke.

The poor guy had a look on his face that suggested he was thinking, *Oh, wait... Did I just say that aloud?*

He reached for my hand and quickly said, "I had plans. I really did. I called a place to see about us going up in a hot-air balloon. And I thought about renting a billboard with 'Robin, MARRY ME!' in big letters. But the hot-air balloon people never called me back, and I'm pretty sure I don't have enough money to rent a billboard."

I had to smile because it was so Ross-like. Creative ideas are always running through that brain of his, but the man has no guile and just says what he thinks all the time. I love that about him. What you see is what you get. No secrets. No hidden agendas.

With sincerity he leaned forward and held my gaze with his steel-blue eyes. "Here it is," he said. "I want to spend the rest of my life with you. I know you don't need the Goodyear blimp to come by right now with my proposal in flashing letters to convince you that I mean it. I know you believe me when I say that I love you. I want to be your husband and learn how to love you the way Christ loved the church and gave himself for her. So what do you think? Do you wanna get married?"

I said yes. Simple, straightforward. An honest echo from my heart. Yes.

We shopped together for a ring later that week, and when he put it on my finger, I felt as if our engagement was official. I was promised to a man of integrity, and soon we would start our lives together as one.

Many years later, when our son proposed to his wife, the event was a carefully organized moment at the beach in Southern California, followed by a surprise party to celebrate with their friends.

Our daughter got engaged at sunset in a gazebo on a bluff overlooking the Pacific Ocean. Her fiancé had selected that location because he had asked her to be his girlfriend in a gazebo, and he knew that her dream was to get married in a gazebo. And they were.

Promises planned. Promises made. Promises kept.

For anyone who has believed a promise that was never kept, it is an even deeper joy to watch as well as to experience a promise made and a promise kept.

Hope deferred makes the heart sick,
but a dream fulfilled is a tree of life.
—Proverbs 13:12, NLT

If you were to ask ten couples how they got engaged, each of them would have a different story. If you asked ten Christians how they came to know Christ, they would have different stories as well. God treats us as individuals. He knows what makes our hearts sing. He knows our love language. Jesus orchestrates his "proposal" moment with us and knows what it takes to woo us. He desires for us to rise up and leave all other pursuers. He wants us to be his alone, knowing that one day he will return when all is ready for the wedding. He will call to us to come away and be with him forever. Until that day, we can live with unwavering confidence, knowing that we are promised to him. We are spoken for.

My beloved spoke, and said to me:
"Rise up, my love, my fair one,
And come away."
—Song of Solomon 2:10, NKJV

God's way with us is so deliberate and creative. We were made in his image, and we have within us the same desire to show love to our spouse in specific ways that are meaningful to him or her. Jeff arranged to have the photos hung and the rose petals strewn along the trail at Gig Harbor before taking Alyssa on their life-changing picnic. My husband knew that a simple and straightforward approach would work best with me. Our son knew the exact spot on the beach and just the right gift he would give his wife-to-be when he asked her to marry him. Our son-in-law knew the moment he saw the gazebo overlooking the ocean that it was the right place to propose.

Lots of different, tender moments. Each of them included an invitation delivered in the recipient's heart language, and each proposal was followed by a jubilant "Yes!"

The proof that something wonderful had taken place was evident by the ring finger of each woman. We knew we were engaged. We were off the market, so to speak. The promise was sealed. Our love for the groom was evident by our glowing faces and exuberant expressions of affection, joy, and celebration.

But for all of us, the ultimate proposal has been offered. Life eternal with the Prince of Peace, who loves us and gave himself for us. Christ has come to us with loving words that speak to us individually. And now the Bridegroom awaits your response.

May you cry out to him, "Yes! Yes! A thousand times yes!"

> Get in the habit of saying, "Speak, Lord,"
> and life will become a romance.
> —Oswald Chambers, *My Utmost for His Highest*

What Do You Think?

1. How does the truth that you are promised to God encourage your heart?

2. Write out any doubts you have that God loves you and wants to be with you forever. Then write God's truth next to each doubt.

3. Think of at least three instances in which God has shown his faithfulness to you.

4. What, if anything, is holding you back from saying yes to the Lord? Maybe you're struggling with being obedient, taking a leap of faith, or surrendering something to him. Ask the Lord to search your heart and to help you say yes.

5. The Holy Spirit is your Helper, your Comforter, and your Seal. How can you apply his three roles to your everyday life?

Eleven

You Are Spoken For

We hope that you've come to see your relationship with God in new ways as you've read this book. The faithfulness of our Relentless Lover is evident through the entire Bible. His tender ways of wooing us are woven through our days.

Let's do a quick review. God wants you. He loves you and is continually pursuing you. He has called you out of this world because you are of great value. You are his Peculiar Treasure. You are set free. You are covered, and you are promised to him.

All these truths add up to one strong and steady conclusion:

You are spoken for.

When you came to Christ, your name was written in God's book. You're on the invitation list to join him when your life here draws to a close. What might you expect when that day comes? A glorious celebration! At long last the Wedding Feast of the Lamb written about in the last chapters of the Bible will commence.

Let us rejoice and be glad
and give him glory!
For the wedding of the Lamb has come,
and his bride has made herself ready.
—Revelation 19:7

Robin

I've always loved Isaiah 62:4: "The LORD delights in you" (NKJV). It's humbling to know what a bumbler I am and how often I've missed the mark of what God desires, and yet he still delights in me.

That gets me every time.

The Lord delights in me not because of anything I do or don't do. He delights in me because I am his.

God doesn't have to do anything. He doesn't have to love anybody. He could have given up on all of us long ago. But his feelings for us are made known when he says that he delights in us. What an extravagantly gracious Savior we have!

That thought in Isaiah is followed by this one: "As the bridegroom rejoices over the bride, so shall your God rejoice over you" (verse 5, NKJV).

Once again the Lord paints a vivid picture of his passionate, romantic love for us by using the idea of a wedding. A bride, a bridegroom. He is the One who watches us come to him down the aisle of life. As we get closer to him, we will see that the look on his face is one of pure delight, joy, and radiant love.

I can't imagine how I would have felt on my wedding day if I had started down the white runner and found that my husband's back was turned toward me or that he was standing there waiting with his fist in the air and a look of ferocious anger on his face.

That wasn't what I saw. My husband was trying to hold back the tears as his eyes were fixed on me and nothing else in the church. Just me, his bride, coming to him at last.

It surprises me whenever someone tells me that their image of God is a vengeful, fierce, and angry almighty being, seated on a huge throne and throwing lightning bolts through the clouds at us.

That isn't the way God describes himself. Yes, he is a jealous God who desires our complete devotion. Yes, his Word tells us of how his anger is ignited when we rebel against him. But through it all he still loves us and woos us, continually inviting us to become his beloved. He compares himself to a bridegroom. He identifies us as the bride. He has done everything he can to communicate the depth of his love as well as the kind of relationship he longs to have with us.

This is your chance to respond with blissful abandon to his goodness. Start living like a woman who fully embraces who she is and whose she is. Begin to see yourself as a confident bride. No wavering. No doubting. Remember, the Bridegroom calls you his beloved. Let yourself be loved by him now and know that the best is yet to come.

Alyssa

The engagement season is so sweet. You and your fiancé are committed to each other, you're planning this awesome party, and you're preparing your hearts to be one. You get to see all your closest friends during the showers and week of the wedding. And best of all, you're planning your future together.

I was glowing the whole time, either from pure joy or from sweat and tears over all the decisions. You're colliding two lives together, which is a beautiful thing but sometimes a difficult thing.

As Jeff and I continued our premarital counseling, we learned more about God's intentions for marriage and our roles, and we talked about practical things like expectations, in-laws, responsibilities, communication, and conflict. I'm thankful we had an older couple who walked through those conversations with us. They had us share our hearts and listen to each other and then helped us work out differing opinions.

For instance, we filled out a worksheet on responsibilities, who will do what in the house. We talked about if we were "clean" people. Both of us were. Who will keep the house clean? We both said we would. However, our definitions of "clean" were different. Jeff's "clean" is organized. He could care less if the toilet is scrubbed and the bookshelves are dusted. He's more concerned if the house is put together: pillows symmetrical on the couch, candles burning, books aligned just right.

My "clean" is deep clean. Toilets scrubbed, sinks washed down, dishes unloaded, carpet vacuumed. If things are a bit out of order, no problem. But if the house is dirty, no way!

Two lives are becoming one. Lots of conversations, lots of discoveries about ourselves and our soon-to-be spouse. Of course, far more important conversations unfold during this season. How will he lead you and love you? How will you honor him and follow his lead? How do you communicate with each other? How do you work through conflict? *Do* you work through conflict, or do you run and hide or forget it happened? Yes, laying out expectations and defining what is "clean" are important, but the bigger issues dominate the prenuptial time.

I loved the engagement season. I loved the time spent with my mom, shopping for a wedding dress, picking out flowers, staying up until the wee hours to make name cards and to address invitation envelopes. I loved talking on the phone with my girlfriends, sharing prayer requests, and asking them marriage advice. I loved going to premarital counseling and learning more about Jeff and how to be his helper in marriage. I loved any chance I had to be with him—registering, finding a place to live, planning the honeymoon, going on dates, and dreaming of our future together.

Most of all I loved what the Lord was doing in our lives during that season.

I had to run to him, to surrender my expectations and dreams, to trust his working, to let him, not me, be at the center of it all. He loosened my grip on my life—how I love to take control— and helped me lay it at his feet. Daily I would draw near to him and lay down all the wedding details, our needs, our future, and Jeff. I would pray for our hearts to be prepared, humble, and seeking the good of the other above ourselves. God made my heart soft, moldable, and open to his working.

Jeff, the man whom I had prayed years for, the man who never gave up on me, who pursued me despite my rejecting him, who patiently drew me out, who made me laugh until my sides hurt, who showed me what true grace is, and who often ushered me into God's presence, was to be my husband. This man who had won my heart was going to enter into covenant with me. Through thick and thin we were choosing to be together, to pursue each other, to walk this life together.

I never doubted getting married to Jeff. In my head it was a done deal, and I was ready. We did, however, get into a couple of arguments during our engagement that made me wonder if I was ready to marry him.

About a month and a half before the wedding, we were looking for a place to rent. Jeff had found this awesome house: three stories, front porch, and wood floors. But it was in the center of a rough part of town.

As we were sitting at Starbucks discussing whether to go for this house, Jeff told me that he wanted to live in the inner city and to minister there, to have our home open to our neighbors and to shelter boys who have no dads at home. I love his heart. I love his dreams and his desire to show Jesus to this world. However, I wasn't ready to live in the inner city where cops came to your door often to make sure you were all right. Not yet. Perhaps one day, but as a newlywed who grew up in the suburbs, I just wasn't ready.

We argued. Then we settled in and talked about where we wanted to live and our philosophies of ministry. I was forced to ask myself, *Am I willing to follow Jeff wherever he goes? Wherever the Lord calls him?*

After a few days of praying and thinking, I realized that, yes, I was willing to go wherever Jeff went because I knew that he followed Jesus, and that ultimately wherever Jeff went was where Jesus was calling him. I trusted Jesus. I trusted Jeff.

When we met for breakfast a few days later to decide on the house, I went willing to go where Jeff wanted but also to share that I didn't feel comfortable in that house.

Jeff concluded the same thing. He knew that wasn't the best place for us at the time.

When I compared that experience to the promises in God's Word, I could see how none of us needs to feel anxious about where we will dwell for eternity. As his bride, we can be filled with hope about our eternal future because Jesus made it clear in John 14:2 that in his Father's home are many mansions (KJV). He said he was going to prepare a place for us. He promised that we would dwell with him. Our hearts stir in anticipation of that day!

As fun as it is to plan a wedding, it's far more important to invest in the marriage. A wedding is one day—a beautiful, special, cherish-in-your-heart-forever day, but it is only one day. Your marriage is a lifetime. The wedding is a bonus, but being made one with your husband is where it's at.

That's how it is with our time on earth, as we are made ready to be united with Christ in heaven. One day we will be with him. How sweet it is to revel in his love during this "engagement" period. How glorious it will be to dwell with him for eternity!

On the day of our wedding, I woke up in my home of twenty-five years, knowing this was the last time I would wake up as a single woman. The wedding party drove to the wedding location, a beautifully restored barn in a field of flowers. The bridesmaids and I got ready in a cute cottage. My hair was curled, the flowers were in place, and my makeup was on. I climbed into my wedding gown with my mom's and my girlfriends' help. Strapless. White tulle. Sparkling beads sprinkled over the bodice. Silver sparkly flats adorned my feet. I was ready to see my man.

The barn held a magical glow as the lights twinkled from the ceiling. The guests were seated as the *Father of the Bride* soundtrack played in the background. Candles were lit; silver vases held baby's breath all the way down the aisle. The wedding party was lined up, ready to begin. I held on to my dad's strong arm, tears already streaming down my face as I realized that this was it. I would forever be my daddy's little girl, but today was the day that my parents would hand me over to Jeff's care, to be my protector, provider, and best friend.

The barn doors swung open. Pachelbel's Canon in D played. There, ahead of me, waited my Jeff, handsome and strong. The rain began to fall softly. All our family and friends who had walked life with us stood before us, supporting our covenant. My dad walked me down the aisle, steady and sure. All I could do was look right at my Jeff, overcome with joy. My parents handed me over to him as we all hugged. Deep breath. *Here we go.*

The pastor gave a beautiful message on marriage, covenant, and God's faithfulness and grace. We looked into each other's eyes the whole time, overwhelmed by God's tender love. We recited our personal vows to each other with sincerity and vulnerability.

We took communion together, humbly coming before the Lord and committing our marriage to him. Jeff gently kissed my forehead before he led me back to the pastor to exchange rings.

Knowing what was next, I was so giddy I couldn't contain it. Any second now I'd be Mrs. Bethke. I squealed and jumped just a bit.

Our pastor then said, "Jeff, you may kiss your bride."

Jeff held me close and kissed me tenderly. He cherished me. I knew it. All his words of love for me over the years came through in his kiss.

"It is my great pleasure to present to you for the first time Mr. and Mrs. Bethke!"

Everyone cheered. Jeff grabbed my hand as our song played, and we danced down the aisle, laughing and smiling from ear to ear.

Some of us spend years dreaming of our wedding day, planning what we would want, pinning creative ideas and beautiful decorations on Pinterest. Others, though, may have never given their wedding a thought but most likely desire to be married one day. Or perhaps the whole wedding-marriage thing terrifies you, or maybe you are doubtful it will ever happen to *you*.

Here's the beautiful truth: it already has happened for you. Regardless of your marital status or hoped-for status, you are promised to the Bridegroom. You already are his. When you surrendered your life to Christ, you became his bride-to-be. And one day you will be with him forever.

It's as though the Lord has sent you a love letter in his Word, and he longs for you to read it and cherish it. To believe his truth of who you are, and to rejoice in the truth of knowing you are his. You belong. You are accepted. You are deeply desired.

Can you imagine what it will be like when we are called into the wedding feast with believers from throughout the ages? One day we will sit down together as brothers and sisters in Christ, with our family, and be joined to God as his beautiful, redeemed bride. We will be clothed in white. He will be wearing a robe of righteousness. The Lord, the One who is faithful and true, the One who has "King of kings and Lord of lords" tattooed on his thigh, will come back for us on a white horse. Oh, what a day that will be! What a wedding feast to end all wedding feasts!

> Then I heard what seemed to be the voice of a great
> multitude, like the roar of many waters and like the
> sound of mighty peals of thunder, crying out,
> "Hallelujah!
> For the Lord our God
> the Almighty reigns.
> Let us rejoice and exult
> and give him the glory,
> for the marriage of the Lamb has come,
> and his Bride has made herself ready;

it was granted her to clothe herself
with fine linen, bright and pure"—
for the fine linen is the righteous deeds of the saints.
Revelation 19:6–8, ESV

As beautiful as weddings are and as awesome as marriage is, they are only a glimpse of our relationship with Jesus. They give us a glimmer of who he is and who he says we are. We are redeemed. We are wanted. We are deeply loved. We are fought for. We are delighted in. We are pursued. We are secure. We are protected. We are held. We are his. We are his bride, his chosen one.

We are spoken for.

But now thus says the LORD...
"Fear not, for I have redeemed you;
I have called you by name, you are mine.
When you pass through the waters, I will be with you;
and through the rivers, they shall not overwhelm you;
when you walk through fire you shall not be burned,
and the flame shall not consume you.
For I am the LORD your God,
the Holy One of Israel, your Savior....
You are precious in my eyes,
and honored, and I love you."
—Isaiah 43:1–4, ESV

A Note from Robin and Alyssa

We have so enjoyed sharing with you from our hearts. Our dearest hope is that you will respond to the invitation of the true Bridegroom and step into the center of his epic love story.

We welcome the chance to hear back from you. Please come visit us at www.robingunn.com and www.alyssajoy.me, where you'll find links to connect with us via social media.

We also want to let you know about other books that are near and dear to our hearts.

- The Christy Miller Series by Robin Jones Gunn—Alyssa mentioned in chapter 2 how these stories drew her to Christ.

- *Praying for Your Future Husband* by Robin Jones Gunn and Tricia Goyer—Robin and Alyssa used this book during a weekly study. It helped Alyssa know how to pray for her future husband before she and Jeff were reunited.

- *Jesus > Religion* by Jefferson Bethke—Alyssa's husband, Jeff, wrote this book during their engagement season. It's a great resource for those wanting to explore basic truths of Jesus.

Now to him who is able to do immeasurably more
than all we ask or imagine,
according to his power that is at work within us,
to him be glory…for ever and ever! Amen.
Ephesians 3:20–21

What Do You Think?

1. When you hear "You are spoken for," what comes to mind?

2. Isaiah 62:4 says that God delights in you. Do you believe it? Why or why not?

3. Are you a confident bride? What does God say about you, as his bride?

4. How does knowing that God is the Bridegroom and we, as the body of believers, are his bride change your perspective or affect your daily life?

5. Is the Lord your all in all? Are you totally satisfied in him, or are you holding things above him? Ask the Lord to search your heart.

CARL F. H. HENRY

Makers of the Modern Theological Mind

Bob E. Patterson, Editor

KARL BARTH by *David L. Mueller*
DIETRICH BONHOEFFER by *Dallas M. Roark*
RUDOLF BULTMANN by *Morris Ashcraft*
CHARLES HARTSHORNE by *Alan Gragg*
WOLFHART PANNENBERG by *Don Olive*
TEILHARD DE CHARDIN by *Doran McCarty*
EMIL BRUNNER by *J. Edward Humphrey*
MARTIN BUBER by *Stephen M. Panko*
SÖREN KIERKEGAARD by *Elmer H. Duncan*
REINHOLD NIEBUHR by *Bob E. Patterson*
H. RICHARD NIEBUHR by *Lonnie D. Kliever*
GERHARD VON RAD by *James L. Crenshaw*
ANDERS NYGREN by *Thor Hall*
FRIEDRICH SCHLEIERMACHER by *C. W. Christian*
HANS KÜNG by *John Kiwiet*
IAN T. RAMSEY by *William Williamson*
CARL F. H. HENRY by *Bob E. Patterson*
PAUL TILLICH by *John Newport*

Makers of the Modern Theological Mind

Bob E. Patterson, Editor

CARL F. H. HENRY

by Bob E. Patterson

WORD BOOKS
PUBLISHER
WACO, TEXAS
A DIVISION OF
WORD, INCORPORATED

Carl F. H. Henry

Copyright © 1983 by Word, Incorporated

Library of Congress Cataloging in Publication Data

Patterson, Bob E.
    Carl F. H. Henry.

    (Makers of the modern theological Mind)
    Bibliography: p.
    1. Henry Carl Ferdinand Howard, 1913-
2. Evangelicalism. I. Title. II. Series.
BR1643.H47P37 1984   230'.044'0924   83-21725
ISBN 0-8499-2951-2
Printed in the United States of America
89801239 FG 98765432

To
Linda Lee
daughter extraordinary

Contents

7

Author's Preface

As editor of this series, "Makers of the Modern Theological Mind," I had to select an (or *the*) outstanding American evangelical theologian about whom to write a book. The choice was simplicity itself—Carl F. H. Henry, of course. Carl Henry is the prime interpreter of evangelical theology, one of its leading theoreticians, and now in his 70s the unofficial spokesman for the entire tradition. In 1978 *Time Magazine* named him Evangelicalism's "leading theologian." With the publication of his six-volume, 3,030-page *God, Revelation and Authority*, he has given evangelical theology a solid intellectual basis for these three doctrines.

At its best, a systematic evangelical theology tries to use reason in the service of revelation to the greater glory of God. It doesn't profess to know all of the truth, but it claims to know *real* truth. Under constant revision, its final appeal is to Jesus Christ given in Holy Scripture. This kind of theology flowered in nineteenth century America in the systems of the Presbyterians Charles Hodge (1797–1878) and William G. T. Shedd (1820–1894), the Baptist Augustus H. Strong (1836–

9

1921), the Lutheran Franz Pieper (1852–1931) and the Reformed Louis Berkhof (1873–1957). But those were the last of the great system builders, and by 1930 evangelical theology had lost its place as an opinion-maker. In the 1960s evangelical theology had become a viable option again, but it was vastly overshadowed in the public news media by more catchy theological fads. As we moved toward the 1980s and a search for stability, conditions appeared ripe for a more conservative faith. Carl Henry has been the prime mover in helping evangelical theology in America reassert its self-respect.

I have deliberately chosen to write this book on Carl Henry (and as editor of this series, who would deny me that right?) for three reasons: to educate myself about the whole evangelical tradition by immersing myself in its literature; to expose myself to Henry's first-rate theological mind and let him pass judgment on some of my own theological ideas; and to share my journey with those readers outside the evangelical tradition who have read the other volumes in this "Makers" series.

Others have shared this work with me and I am grateful. I am indebted to my two graduate assistants, Richard Walsh and Travis Summerlin, both true professionals. And my thanks go to my secretary who typed the final draft of the manuscript, Michael Goodman. My own school, Baylor University, as always has given me unfailing support. If I ever sit down to draw up a list of those good and understanding people who have given shape and meaning to my life, I suppose that even Texas "itself could not contain the books that should be written."

CARL F. H. HENRY

I. The Evangelical Heritage

Evangelicals so dominate the North American religious scene that "evangelical chic" may be impending. Thanks to media visibility they are a talking point everywhere. There is unprecedented interest in many aspects of evangelical activity and outlook. Some secular pundits talk as if evangelicals are about to take over. Their churches are growing—many of the nation's great churches are now evangelical. They have highly visible campus and youth ministries—colleges and seminaries are thriving. They have phenomenally successful publishing and other media efforts—hundreds of Christian radio stations have been established in recent years and sales of Bibles and evangelical books are booming. Numerous conversion stories are being related by people in the public eye—unlikely "twice born" celebrities such as former White House hatchet man Charles Colson, Jeb and Gail Magruder, Johnny Cash, television's "Galloping Gourmet" Graham Kerr, former Black Panther leader Eldridge Cleaver, a large number of athletes, Malcolm Muggeridge, Jimmy Carter and Ronald Reagan. These, among others, have caught the eye of mainline Protestants, Roman Catholics

and the secular news media. The new social and political activism among evangelicals has given encouragement to tired liberals, radical theologians and denominational-ecumenical leaders. Evangelicals are showing remarkable vitality and are being showered with attention.

The Year of the Evangelicals

George Gallup, Jr., the poll-taking monitor of the American religious scene, predicted in his *Religion in America 1977–1978* a continued upsurge of evangelical strength. Gallup says that three out of ten (28 percent) Americans, or over forty million adults, are evangelicals. He points out that this figure may be low since some evangelicals may not be aware of the term. The evangelical population is generally estimated at between forty-five and fifty million, equaled or outnumbered only by the Roman Catholics (forty-nine million). Evangelicals form a conservative minority of about one-third of the thirty-six million Protestants in "mainline" churches belonging to the National Council of Churches. In addition 33.5 million are distributed among scores of orthodox Protestant groups outside the NCC.

Gallup defines an evangelical as one who has had a born-again conversion by accepting Jesus as his or her personal Savior, believes the Scriptures are the authority for all doctrine, and feels an urgent duty to spread the faith. Richard Quebedeaux, America's chronicler of Evangelicalism, defines an evangelical "as a person who attests to the truth of, and acts upon, three major theological principles: (1) the full authority of Scriptures in matters of faith and practice; (2) the necessity of personal faith in Jesus Christ as Savior and Lord (conversion); and (3) the urgency of seeking the conversion of sinful men and women to Christ (evangelism)."[1] Carl Henry defines an evangelical as "one who believes the evangel. The Good News is that the Holy Spirit gives spiritual life to all who repent and receive divine salvation proffered in the incarnate, crucified

and risen Redeemer. The Christian message is what the inspired Scriptures teach—no more, no less—and an evangelical is a person whose life is governed by the scriptural revelation of God and His purposes."[2] The Christian evangel, a person devoted to the good news that God has sent Jesus Christ as Savior, is summarized in 1 Corinthians 15:1–4 (NEB):

> And now, my brothers, I must remind you of the gospel that I preached to you; the gospel which you received, on which you have taken your stand, and which is now bringing you salvation. Do you still hold fast the Gospel as I preached it to you? If not, your conversion is in vain.
>
> First and foremost, I handed on to you the facts which had been imparted to me: that Christ died for our sins, in accordance with the scriptures; that he was buried; that he was raised to life on the third day, according to the scriptures. . . .

For most evangelicals the experience of receiving the Good News is the principal event of any Christian life. Some conversions are dramatic, but the vast majority of born-again religious experiences come simply and quietly. In March 1976, when President Carter decided to tell a press conference how he had formed a personal relationship with God through Christ, he said: "It wasn't mysterious. It might have been the same kind of experience as millions of people who have become Christians in a personal way." In a 1976 survey, Gallup discovered that half of all Protestants—and a third of all Americans—said that they had been "born again." Besides the marks of conversion, reliance upon the Bible, and evangelism, an evangelical will usually place a strong emphasis on a personal relationship with God and adhere to a strict moral code.

According to the Gallup survey, 22 percent of evangelicals prefer the smaller evangelical denominations. Fifteen percent are Methodists, 12 percent are Catholics, and 42 percent are Baptists. Although only 42 percent of Baptists call themselves evangelicals, a large majority indicate they adhere to the definition of what an evangelical is.

It seems likely that the evangelical impact will be felt more

strongly in the nation's churches during the coming years. They
are no longer the silent strangers on the American religious
scene. Almost six in ten Americans give evangelicals a "highly
favorable" rating. As ecumenical Protestants have declined,
conservative evangelicals have gained. While the four churches
that epitomize the cultured Protestant Establishment—United
Methodist, United Presbyterian, Episcopal and United Church
of Christ (Congregational)—have suffered a net loss of 2.7 million members, the Southern Baptist Convention has alone
gained nearly 2 million and is now the nation's largest Protestant body (14 million). Where evangelicals were long ignored
by outsiders they now are on the upswing. They flourish because
the institutions that gave them visibility (denominational head-
quarters, colleges, seminaries, publishing houses, periodicals)
have only lately reached maturity. Ecumenical Protestants (once
known as liberal evangelicals) have lost some of the prominence
that they enjoyed for two or three generations, and conservative
evangelicals appear by contrast to prosper more than they otherwise would. Evangelicals are also growing because they are
modifying their traditional style and approach while still affirming the doctrines at the heart of Christianity. They now make
up a substantial minority of the American population.

Evangelicals are particularly strong among Southern Baptists, and the Baptist tradition is presently the dominant one.[3]
There are four major traditions in contemporary American
Evangelicalism. First, the Holiness-Pentecostal tradition with
its strong emphasis on themes of pietism and perfectionism.
It has historical roots from English pietism, dispensationalism,
and millenarianism. Second, the Anabaptist tradition with its
emphasis on the objective, rational expression of faith as op-
posed to the experiential. It stresses the solidarity of the church
community over the rights of individual believers. Its historical
roots are in Northern Europe, specifically German Protestant
theological and religious movements. Third, the Reformational-
Confessional tradition, which even more than the Anabaptist,
tends to view faith and the salvation process in rational terms.

Like the Anabaptist, this movement descends from Northern Europe. Fourth, the Baptist tradition which has a highly individuated conception of human salvation in contrast to the notion of collective salvation. With its belief in personal volition, faith and salvation are highly subjectivized. The Baptists came from the English tradition. All four groups seek to recover and restore the spirit and truth of New Testament Christianity.

Martin Marty, church historian, says that the Christian world is getting "Baptistificated." But some Southern Baptist officials insist that they have never belonged to the evangelical camp. Foy Valentine, activist head of the SBC's Christian Life Commission, says: "We are *not* evangelicals. That's a Yankee word. They want to claim us because we are big and successful and growing every year. But we have our own traditions, our own hymns, and more students in our seminaries than they have in all theirs put together. We don't share their politics or their fussy fundamentalism, and we don't want to get involved in their theological witch-hunts."[4] Still, most Southern Baptists are sympathetic with the evangelical mind-set.[5]

For four years President Jimmy Carter was the best-known Baptist deacon in America, and for a time he replaced Billy Graham as the honorific "Mr. Evangelical." George Gallup, Jr., in his 1978 survey felt that Carter's open discussion and practice of his faith focused positive attention on the evangelicals. Although Evangelicalism has remained a cognitive minority in America, it is now a sociocultural majority.[6] Carl Henry is a Baptist, holding membership in a church that is aligned both with the Southern Baptist Convention and the American (Northern) Baptist Convention. Evangelicals are so widely accepted that Jeremy Rifkin claims that a second Protestant reformation may be dawning. Rifkin says: "Certainly, in terms of structure and outreach, . . . there is no other single cultural force in American life today that has as much potential as the evangelical community to influence the future direction of this country."[7]

Evangelicals are in the current limelight because there are

so many of them, but this is not the only reason they are
being given attention. They are maturing and communicating
more effectively—they are at every social and professional level
and there is more common ground for communication. They
are cooperating more with each other and fighting less—there
is a growing climate of unity on the basic essentials. As a
theological vacuum has become evident in mainline Protestantism, biblical orthodoxy has again come to the center—theological alternatives have fallen on hard times. Disillusionment over
the results of a humanistic technology has made our society
look for an outside help—humanity cannot be trusted after
all. The two-hundredth anniversary of America recalled the
nation's spiritual roots and helped call attention to the evangelical faith—today's evangelicals are the spiritual offspring of
the Puritans. These factors alone justify the media attention
now being given the evangelical surge.

Spiritual Ancestry

Evangelicals are front page news and Carl Henry is their
outstanding theological spokesman. He best represents the characteristics of evangelical thought, and his recent six-volume
work *God, Revelation and Authority* marks a significant mile-
stone in evangelical thinking. In these volumes Henry attempts
a grand synthesis of biblical, philosophical, and systematic theology. Billy Graham has called him the most eminent of conservative theologians. Louis Cassels, late religion editor of United
Press International, designated him as "probably the most noted
evangelical theologian in the United States." No individual
has provided more intellectual dignity, prophetic insight, and
clarification to the movement than Henry.

If evangelicals are believers who have been converted to
Christ (born again), what of Carl Henry's experience? Conversion implies a salient experience of spiritual decision and
personal resolution. Henry says that he was converted to

Christianity from virtual paganism. He was the son of a Roman Catholic mother and a Lutheran father. He was born on 22 January 1913 in New York City to Karl and Johanna (Vaethroeder) Henry, but he says that religion was a matter of private indifference to his parents. He had felt that God had been calling him for years "but I had never dreamed he would or could call so insistently, nor so inconveniently."[8] Yet he was not without religious training. He says: "In early teens I was both baptized and confirmed in the Episcopal church where I attended Sunday School and became exposed to the vocabulary of the Book of Common Prayer."[9] When he was confirmed in the Christian faith—in fact, on two successive Sundays— he was still very much a stranger to Jesus Christ. As a neo-Christian pagan he soon became a church dropout. He says: "I shed the church in my mid-teens. In the course of my evacuation I had managed to pilfer a Bible from the pew racks, however, and as I opened it now and then upon retiring, one segment of that Book held a special fascination for me: its narratives of the resurrection of Jesus Christ from the dead."[10] After high school graduation in 1929 he began a career in a down-to-earth fashion by selling newspaper subscriptions and earning $12 a week.

By age twenty he had worked himself up to being Long Island's youngest newspaper editor, on the Smithtown *Star*. He later became editor of the *Port Jefferson Times Echo*. He says that in his twenties an assorted volley of religious encounters "impinged upon me: a Seventh-Day Adventist plied me with catastrophic forebodings from the book of Daniel; an elderly Methodist lady stressed my need to be 'born again'; a Presbyterian minister deplored my newspaper coverage for the New York press in contrast to his coverage of Long Island for God; a university graduate in the Oxford Group pushed me to personal decision for Christ."[11] Against this ecumenical potpourri background, he was discussing religion one spring morning with a friend, an ardent layman. They were sitting

in the front seat of a car overlooking Great South Bay. After
three hours, he says, "I made a commitment to Christ. I knew
my life was no longer my own."

As a prelude to that hour of decision Henry notes: "I was
a newspaperman preoccupied with man's minutiae when God
tracked me down; the Word was pursuing a lost purveyor of
words. In this encounter, my own semantic skill meant little."[12]
Locking the doors of his automobile, he and his friend knelt
on the front seat of the car to pray. But Henry did not know
how to pray. He says: "There I was, a Long Island editor
and suburban correspondent quite accustomed to interviewing
the high and mighty of this world, yet wholly inept at formulat-
ing phrases for the King of Glory. Not even the dimly familiar
words from the Order of the Holy Communion . . . seemed
to fit the sheer spontaneity of that occasion."[13] Instead, he
and his friend settled for the Lord's Prayer. "Phrase by phrase
I repeated the words of my friend," he said. "My heart owned
its abysmal depth of need. How blest are those who know
that they are poor; the kingdom of Heaven is theirs—so the
New English Bible translates Jesus' opening words in the Sermon on the Mount. My aching spirit cried out to God for
forgiveness of sins and for new life in Christ. Somewhere in
the echoes of eternity I heard the pounding of hammers that
marked the Saviour's crucifixion in my stead."[14]

Out of this experience Henry has formulated his own definition of conversion. "Incomparable peace, the reality of sins
forgiven, a sense of destiny and direction, and above all the
awareness of a new Presence and Power at the core of life—
this is rebirth. I was now on speaking terms with God, a friend
of the King, a servant of the Saviour."[15] In recounting this
typical evangelical conversion he says that "by the grace of
God on June 10, 1933, I gained firm assurance of spiritual
regeneration, and of divine forgiveness for sin on the merits
of the saving work of Jesus Christ."[16] On that day of his intimate
discovery of Christ, he says, "had the Risen Redeemer com-
manded, I would have gone to China or to any of the uttermost

parts."[17] This unexpected meeting with God was no ordinary, soon-to-be-forgotten rendezvous.

His new faith led him to enter Wheaton College, a distinctly evangelical liberal arts college (the "Evangelical Harvard") at the hub of the evangelical establishment. Like many evangelical colleges, Wheaton affirms the Bible as "verbally inspired by God and inerrant in the original writing." He graduated from Wheaton with a B.A. in 1938 and started theological studies at Northern Baptist Seminary in Chicago. His steps toward a denominational future with Baptists are most instructive of his spiritual pilgrimage. He says that his student days "in the interdenominational climate of Wheaton College propelled me toward Baptistic views as I studied Scripture, interacted with campus associates and reflected on contemporary religious life."[18] In 1937 he was immersed on profession of faith and became a member of Babylon Baptist Church on Long Island "after the local pastor somewhat carefully reviewed the implications of this step."[19] While completing his seminary preparation he was ordained to the Baptist ministry at a student pastorate, Humboldt Park Baptist Church.

Henry says that his persuasion of Baptist distinctives was deepened and strengthened through these student years. Indeed, he says, "I came to wonder at and regret the limited insight of their heritage possessed by many Baptists."[20] What are the Baptist distinctives that so impressed Henry during his collegiate days? Henry lists them in this order: (1) The final authority of Scripture above all creeds and speculation; (2) the priesthood of all believers; (3) believer's baptism by immersion; (4) the autonomy of the local church; and (5) the separation of church and state. Henry says that while "I might not use this precise order of tenets now, I would surely insist on the inclusion of each one."[21] He says that it is obvious that not all Baptist distinctives are exclusively Baptistic. "The priesthood of believers is a Reformation doctrine also; the final authority of Scripture is affirmed by many creedal communions; the Greek Orthodox Church practices immersion, although of

infants. But," says Henry, "the total combination of these tenets
and their special emphasis is unique to Baptists."[22]

Two of the Baptist distinctives seemed to have special appeal
for Henry—personal conviction and religious experience alongside an unchanging biblical inheritance. These features seemed
to parallel his own spiritual growth and thinking. He says
that historically Baptists "are a people of resolution, a people
enjoining spiritual rebirth, a people circumscribing their primary resources within the New Testament revelation."[23]

Respect for the authority of Scripture may be the key to
understanding the Baptist witness, and why this witness so
strongly appeals to Henry. He says: "Reliance upon Scripture
to reveal the saviourhood and lordship of Jesus Christ, and
his plan and purpose for mankind, is more than the first tenet
of authentic Baptist belief; it is the foundation stone for the
other principles which, if unsettled, jeopardize the total Baptist
spiritual structure."[24] Henry finds most appealing the Baptist
confidence that the New Testament revelation is the climax
of divine disclosure. He does not feel that this Baptist distinctive
and ecumenical interest necessarily conflict. He says that while
"the Baptist tradition is for us the preferred medium to communicate the life of Christ in his church, we do not on that account
deny that some measure of genuine Christian status attaches
to other traditions, even as we are quick to admit that something
less than full Christian status often intrudes into our own!"[25]

Henry says that unwavering dedication to the requirements
of the scriptural revelation will best guard and promote specific
Baptist distinctives and ecumenical Christian priorities. "Whatever reinforces the New Testament consciousness is good,"
he says, "both for ecumenical Christianity and the Baptist
witness."[26] Unhappy with some of the trends in his denomination, Henry has warned that any Baptist activity that does
not conform to Bible-relatedness becomes a mere abstraction.
He says that only "though acknowledgment of this scriptural
foundation, and justification of Baptist positions in the light
of this criterion, can Baptists everywhere be impelled to the

conviction that the same concern controls their unity in Christ."[27] Henry still holds that "Baptist distinctives are valid, and that the Baptist mission in the closing decades of the twentieth century is extraordinarily urgent."[28]

By 1943 Henry had married and completed most of his formal education (B.A., M.A., Wheaton; B.D., Th.D., Northern Baptist Theological Seminary). In 1949 he completed his Ph.D. at Boston University. In 1947 he was chosen by Harold Ockenga and Charles E. Fuller (1887–1968) to help start the newly founded Fuller Theological Seminary in Pasadena, California. This seminary, founded with high intellectual standards coupled with evangelistic zeal, was designed as a counterpart to the major liberal Protestant denominational and ecumenical graduate schools of theology. Henry helped launch Fuller on its road to becoming one of the most outstanding seminaries in America. During his nine years there, 1947 through 1956, he wrote nine of his books.

In 1956 Henry began a twelve-year term as the first editor of *Christianity Today*. He was chosen for this position by Billy Graham and Graham's father-in-law, L. Nelson Bell (1894–1973), the executive editor of *Christianity Today*. When Sun Oil board chairman J. Howard Pew (1882–1971) and other conservative businessmen formed the journal, Henry agreed to become its first editor—for one year. Henry said that the *Christian Century* "always spoke out of the left side of its mouth, whether on theological, political, or economic matters," and he wanted to create an evangelical publication that would compete with this liberal journal. The circulation of *Christianity Today* grew to over 160,000, and through Henry's lengthy editorials, essays, and interviews in its pages he emerged as the arbiter in defining and defending conservative Protestantism.

Under Henry this journal became the biweekly voice of the evangelical message. Designed primarily for clergy and seminarians and deliberately cast in a scholarly and intellectual style, it was to become the "official" mouthpiece for three organiza-

tions: the National Association of Evangelicals, the Evangelical Theological Society, and the Billy Graham Evangelistic Association. Henry had much to do with shaping the message that reached thousands through its pages, and he became Evangelicalism's foremost journalist and strategist.

But Henry wanted more opportunity to write in the area of systematic theology. His editorial chores had become a "miserable routine" and he wished to move more broadly into "the modern theological scrap." He resigned and became "professor-at-large" at Eastern Baptist Theological Seminary in Philadelphia. He taught for one semester each year, which gave him free time to write, speak, and travel. He has taught or lectured on America's most prestigious campuses and in countries on every continent. His teaching and lecture ministries have been worldwide. He has written twenty-seven books (some have been translated into Korean, Norwegian, German and Spanish), and he has edited numerous significant symposium efforts. Frequently quoted by the national press and news magazines, he is widely recognized as a leading evangelical opinion-maker, and he continues to shape the evangelical theological perspective. He makes his home in Arlington, Virginia.

Christian Orthodoxy

Carl Henry feels that part of his intellectual task is to restore an approach to religion that has been lost. Henry is trying to restore the traditional orthodoxy that was rooted in the mainstream of the nineteenth-century American Protestant experience. This orthodoxy was the gilded age of American Protestantism, and was then called Evangelicalism. It held as a norm the core of religious beliefs of reformational orthodoxy, and its theologians said that they were a direct link with the New Testament age as reaffirmed by the Protestant Reformation.

Carl Henry, then, takes a restorationist approach to religion. To understand what he is attempting to restore, we need to

look at what was lost. Between 1890 and 1920 American Protestantism was disestablished. But what was this pre-1890 "orthodoxy" that Henry labors to see restored? To understand that complex of ideas and people is to grasp the framework of Henry's theological system. To that story we now turn.

In the wider sense evangelicals are not new since they have their theological roots deep in patristic, medieval and especially Reformation thought.[29] Evangelicals are most often associated with the doctrine of salvation by faith in Christ alone. Martin Luther's (1483–1546) followers, stressing this singular belief, were generally called evangelicals, and a good number of Lutheran synods both in Europe and the United States still prefer this term in their official nomenclature. Henry and evangelicals are in near uniform agreement with the Reformer's theological stance. They agree with Martin Luther, John Calvin (1509–1564), Huldreich Zwingli (1484–1531), Farel (1489–1564), Bucer (1491–1551), Melanchthon (1497–1560), Cranmer (1489–1560), and so on, in their theological differences with the Roman Catholic Church.

The Reformers set the Bible above Catholic tradition. They said that the Bible did not need the approval of the Church to be authentic. They turned away from the Apocrypha as sacred Scripture. They rejected the authority of Church councils. They taught that sinners were saved by God's grace through faith acceptance alone, and they held that the church is an instrument of grace but not a controller of grace.[30] Henry and evangelical theology are in harmony with these opinions. Where the Reformation placed the priority of Word and act of God over any experience or philosophy of men, the evangelicals agree. The Reformers accepted explicitly or implicitly the great creeds of the patristic period of the church: the Apostles' Creed, the Nicea-Constantinople Creed, the Chalcedonian Creed, and the Athanasian Creed. Henry and contemporary evangelicals accept the substance of these same creeds. Post-Reformation orthodoxy produced a massive literature in the seventeenth century, and contemporary evangelicals are dependent on this

heritage. "One of these great Reformed orthodox theologians
was Franciscus Terrettinus (1623–1687), whose work, *Institutio
Theologiae elencticae* (1688 and 1700) was the textbook for
many years at Princeton Seminary. Out of it came Charles
Hodge's *Systematic Theology* and the work of his son, A. A.
Hodge (1823–1886), *Outlines of Theology*. No other works
have been as influential in shaping the general contours of
evangelical theology in America as the works of the Hodges."[31]

The eighteenth-century Evangelical revival was represented
by Pietism in Germany, Methodism in England, and the Great
Awakening in America. Pietism was originally a movement
started by Philipp Spener (1635–1705) in the German Lutheran
Church to infuse new life into the official Protestantism of
the time. Spener reminded the church that Christianity concerned life as well as doctrine—the truth of faith called for
personal involvement. This movement was to influence the
American Puritans, the Great Awakening (Jonathan Edwards
[1703–1758], George Whitefield [1714–1770], John Wesley
[1703–1791], Charles Wesley [1707–1788] and the holiness
movement of the nineteenth century—Charles Finney [1792–
1875] and others).

Evangelicals have close affinities with the heritage of Pietism.
In Pietism the new birth and the new life were prominent
themes, as they were among evangelicals. And just as Pietism
tried to avoid spiritualism—an appeal to inward experience
over the external Word—so did evangelicals. In the nineteenth
century, especially in England and America, evangelicals have
been thought of as those Protestants who affirmed salvation
through faith in the atoning death of Christ while denying
any saving efficacy either in good works or the sacraments.
In England an evangelical group developed in the Anglican
church and joined forces with the Nonconformist churches that
grew out of the eighteenth century revivals to cooperate both
in social welfare and the missionary endeavors of that century.
These two groups also placed heavy importance upon the reading of Scripture and evangelistic preaching in worship, the

more or less symbolic nature of the sacraments, man's inherent depravity, and the inspiration and authority of the Bible.

During the same period, similar alliances took place in the United States among the Protestant churches to help shape American culture and pose as the religious establishment. Viewed in the perspective of a century ago, evangelicals embodied some of the most deeply rooted traditions and characteristic attitudes in American culture. Evangelicalism's influence on national priorities, cultural outlook, education, and social legislation was enormous. In the period between 1830 and 1860 evangelical Protestantism, led principally by theological conservatives, dominated American religion. The periodic revivals which coursed through the land gave its life impulse. Through their voluntary organizations, the evangelicals sponsored a vast range of missionary and relief programs to promote "Christian liberty, Christian equality, and Christian fraternity." Disputes in the ranks were effectively glossed over by these evangelicals who were restraining vice, making America a decent place to live, and civilizing the world. But the Civil War split the ranks, North and South went their separate ways, and black and white evangelicals divided as the country went through the Reconstruction Era (1865–1877).

In spite of the growing split, Protestant orthodoxy still characterized the theological outlook of the evangelicals. This included a belief in the doctrine of the Trinity, the two natures of Christ, the Virgin Birth, the bodily resurrection and second coming of Christ, salvation by grace through faith, the sinfulness of man, the sacrificial death of Christ for sin, the Bible as the inspired Word of God and the final norm for doctrine, evangelism as the main task of the church, and the Christian life as one of holiness and godliness. These same beliefs today structure the theology of Carl Henry and most evangelicals. But in the period between 1870 and the end of World War I a pattern of evangelical decline was established which would not be reversed for decades. Between 1870 and 1920 revolutionary changes in the basic intellectual assumptions, values, and social

patterns eroded or removed the evangelical version of Christendom. Henry has given his intellectual life to restore this version of religion.

The aftereffects of the Enlightenment dealt orthodox Protestantism a near-fatal wound from which it has never fully recovered. The Enlightenment (characterized by German rationalism, English deism, and French skepticism in eighteenth-century Europe) was that period in modern history when learned men turned their backs on the authority of the past and began to trust in their own abilities. They believed that truth could be obtained only through reason, observation, and experiment. It was a period of science, religious skepticism, tolerance, humanitarianism, historical research, and literary criticism. This movement removed Protestant orthodoxy from the center of life in Europe and America, and a specific Christian outlook is no longer the official belief of the Western world.

One scholar, Friedrich Schleiermacher (1768–1834), represents to Carl Henry and contemporary evangelicals all that is wrong in theology. Schleiermacher did not believe the Enlightenment was fatal for Christianity. He felt that Christianity could profit from the best in the Enlightenment, restate itself, and still be believable to intelligent minds. What traditional doctrines could not be restated in a modern acceptable way could be discarded. Schleiermacher said that Christianity was not dogma or creed (Orthodoxy), moral conduct (Immanuel Kant [1724–1804]), or a reasoned system of thought (Friedrich Hegel [1770–1831]), but a living experience of God. Faith is an internal subjective experience before it becomes an external objective belief. He said that all people (including the "cultured despisers" of religion, the Enlightenment thinkers) were in communion or unity with God, and this unity was mediated by an absolute feeling of dependence on God. This feeling of dependence is the basis of all religion. Religion as a psychological state, a God-consciousness, is universal. Sin is lack of God-consciousness and redemption is restoration to God-consciousness. The Bible tells us that Christ had a perfect God-consciousness, and he can become our Redeemer by pulling

us away from our sinful, sensuous consciousness back to God-consciousness. Schleiermacher was condemned by the orthodox as too radical, but no one else more influenced religious thinking in Protestant circles in the nineteenth century. The branch of theological liberalism that spread to America came from Schleiermacher. In Europe, Schleiermacher's method in the hands of the unfriendly philosopher Ludwig Feuerbach (1804–1872) yielded atheism.

As the Enlightenment ideas moved to America, the established theological community was hit by a barrage of bewildering philosophical and scientific concepts. Biblical criticism eroded confidence in the biblical text, and Charles Darwin's (1809–1882) hypothesis of evolution and natural selection eroded confidence in biblical ideas. The most prominent response to the situation was the emergence within Evangelicalism itself of Protestant liberalism. Liberalism came into existence as a strategy to preserve the Christian faith from the blows of the Enlightenment. This movement intended to restate Christianity in such a way that modern man could believe it without the sacrifice of his science, intellect, or scholarship. In America the pioneer liberal was Horace Bushnell (1802–1876). Notable twentieth-century Americans in the liberal tradition were Walter Rauschenbusch (1861–1918), William Adams Brown (1865–1943), William Newton Clark (1841–1912), Shailer Mathews (1863–1941), and Robert Lowry Calhoun (b. 1896). Liberalism is *the* primary foe of Carl Henry and contemporary evangelicals.

The liberals, impressed with the "givens" of biblical criticism (basically a German import) and evolution, and not too concerned with orthodoxy, began to change the whole tenor of the Protestant community by adopting the "modernist" principle of assimilation of Enlightenment assumptions and values into the Christian tradition. Liberalism originally meant a spirit of inquiry to which nothing was sacred, while modernism spoke of critical and scientific achievements. Modernist and liberal today are interchangeable terms, though liberal is most frequently used.

In varying degrees the liberals emphasized God's immanent

work through natural, historical, and evolutionary forces, the development of Scripture out of natural processes, the continuing revelation of God through inevitable human progress and social change, and the perfectibility of man through the application of Christian moral teachings. (The principles of liberal theology are outlined in Kenneth Cauthen, *The Impact of American Religious Liberalism*, New York: Harper & Row, 1962.) Liberals erased the distinction between the natural and the supernatural. They held that man's reason and religious experience could get along without a divine self-disclosure, and they taught that the world, man, dogma, and the Bible are open systems subject to dynamic change and growth. They also emphasized personality as the key to reality, experience and reason as the final authorities in religion, and the moral teachings of Jesus as the key to understanding Christianity.

Liberals showed a willingness to lay aside as unimportant some traditional orthodox doctrines; in fact, they showed tentativeness about all doctrinal affirmations. They were driven to the social gospel (the attempt to apply the ethic of love to corporate man) by the desperate plight of the poor in the larger industrial cities, and the social gospel movement became the most characteristic expression of liberal theology in America. The differences between liberals and conservatives were institutionalized in 1908 when the Federal Council of Churches was formed to bring together the social endeavors of the more liberal congregations. The conservatives counter-organized and began to harden into the fundamentalist movement. Carl Henry came into theology just in time to revolt against this hardening process.

America was confused in its reaction. While theological liberals remained churchmen within the main denominations, an important element of evangelicals left the denominations in a separatist move. These conservative evangelicals frequently accented a premillennial eschatology (belief in a one-thousand-year period of blessedness after Christ returns to earth) and a high view of Scripture (biblical inerrancy). Some rejected

the social implications of the gospel as well as the whole domain of learning. In Dwight L. Moody (1837–1899) and later in Billy Sunday (1862–1935) they formed a new coalition of faith with a new zeal. Another group that retained the essentials of the revivalist tradition were the Holiness and Pentecostal movements that developed out of the Methodist-Pietist tradition, emphasizing the supernatural transformation of converts by the power of the Holy Spirit and a complete separation from the world. Only recently have these groups merged again with evangelicals.

But most evangelicals remained in the major denominations, rejecting the liberal emphases of immanentism, naturalism, and progressivism, and asserting instead transcendentalism, supernaturalism, and fixed factors in Christian teaching. This coalition of denominational conservatives tried to arrest the spread of liberalism in other ways—by emphasizing the supernatural origin of the Bible, emphasizing the supernatural aspects of Christ's person and work, promoting revivalism, and teaching dispensational-premillennialism (an antiliberal, antiprogressive scheme of history that postpones most of the social and political benefits of Christianity until Christ returns to earth).

These conservatives did not object to every position of the liberals, but they did object to this movement as a whole and its scorn of orthodox doctrine in particular. The first "heresy" trial over liberal teaching took place in the Chicago Presbytery in 1874, and liberals began to be forced out of various positions in the church. These conservative evangelicals formed the basis of fundamentalism in the subsequent era. The broad evangelical community was being pulled apart, and the historical fundamentalists-liberal collision was underway.

One of the most dramatic events in American Protestantism took place shortly after the turn of this century. Hostility toward theological liberals by evangelical conservatives had its roots in nineteenth-century opposition to Darwinism, popular revivalism, and the Niagara Bible Prophecy Conferences, and had long been brewing. It finally exploded with the publication

between 1910 and 1915 of a series of pamphlets called *The Fundamentals: A Testament to the Truth*. The Fundamentals became virtually the definitive handbook of the fundamentalists. These booklets were eventually bound into four volumes and more than a million copies were distributed.

Five of the theological ideas in these volumes came to be known popularly as the "fundamentals of the faith," namely: (1) the verbal inspiration of the Bible; (2) the virgin birth of Christ; (3) his substitutionary atonement; (4) his bodily resurrection; and (5) his imminent and visible second coming. Princeton Seminary Professors Charles Hodge, B. B. Warfield (1851–1921) and other writers contributed to the pamphlets in an attempt to regain control of seminaries and some major denominations (especially the Northern Baptists and Northern Presbyterians). Many of the later fundamentalist groups became so strict that some of the original writers would not have been welcome in their circles.

At the outset of the liberal-fundamentalist conflict, there were conservative theologians of genuine academic ability who do not fit the popular stereotyped image of the fundamentalist as a flailing and wailing pulpiteer. Respectable scholars such as Hodge, Warfield, James Orr (1844–1913), Abraham Kuyper (1837–1920), and J. Gresham Machen (1881–1937), rejected liberalism as authentic Christianity, but to view these theologians as obscurantist is to see them askew. After 1920 the term "fundamentalists" was often used to describe the somewhat diverse, militant theological conservatives in their crusade against modernism. A fundamentalist, then, was an American evangelical who had added the element of opposition to his credo. This battle within mainstream Protestantism to control not only the churches but the culture generally was of decisive importance for much of subsequent Evangelicalism. Carl Henry and the neo-evangelicals are a direct product of that battle.

J. Gresham Machen, a respected scholar at Princeton, became the reluctant but best-known spokesman for the fundamentalists in the theological debate. He said that orthodoxy and liberalism

were two incompatible systems of religion, and that the liberals should withdraw from the denominations. Machen's style of restrained debate was soon overwhelmed by the acrimony of ecclesiastical politics and the growing conservative tendency to separate from theological error and evil in society by withdrawing to establish "purer" organizations which in turn sponsored "purer" educational institutions.

The bitter fight against the liberal enemy was nowhere better exemplified than in a courtroom in Tennessee. The Scopes Trial of 1925, ostensibly an effort to suppress the teachings of biological evolution in public schools, was in fact an attempt by conservative Christianity to repulse the challenge of "modern" science. Tennessee had a statute forbidding the teaching of evolution in tax-supported schools of the state. John Scopes (1900–1970), a mild-mannered school teacher, had been arrested for violating that law. William Jennings Bryan (1860–1925), the silver-tongued orator and three-time presidential candidate of the Democratic party, was the acknowledged spokesman for the conservatives. Bryan was aging and ill at ease in questions of a scientific nature. He was frequently caught off balance by John Scopes' brilliant defender, Clarence Darrow (1857–1938). Bryan inadvertently left the impression that fundamentalism was the final outcry of an outdated, intellectually repressive religious establishment. Instead of modernism being excluded from the denominations, fundamentalism was exiled. The very word *fundamentalism* thereafter suggested to many people a rancorous theological weed which they wished would die off. The only heresy became conservative orthodoxy.

The fundamentalists, losing the war on all fronts, made a disheartened withdrawal. Machen's growing militancy caused him to leave Princeton Theological Seminary in 1929, and fundamentalism became but a shadow of its former strength, edged out of the mainstream by liberalism. In 1935 Machen and others were expelled from the (United) Presbyterian Church, U.S.A., for "violating their ordination vows." Thus the original purpose of the fundamentalist movement was dead.

The fundamentalists now had the choice of remaining in the denominations as a minority, or separating and forming new independent local churches and denominations. Since it saw only apostasy in the historic denominations, fundamentalism chose to defend itself by withdrawing and institutionalizing. It either created or joined the following: Bible conferences; permanent largescale evangelism (R. A. Torrey [1856–1928], Billy Sunday); Bible institutes (Moody Bible Institute, Bible Institute of Los Angeles); publishing houses; fellowships (World's Christian Fundamentals Association); radio broadcasts (Charles E. Fuller's "Old Fashioned Revival Hour"); faith missions that bypassed the denominational missionary boards; and the Scofield Reference Bible. The doctrine of separation was often a test of fidelity. It was just at this crucial time that the young Carl Henry was converted to Christ and started on his educational pilgrimage in theological training.

Theologically fundamentalism especially emphasized the supernatural origin of Scripture and the supernatural aspects of Christ's person and work. The "inerrancy of the Bible in all its details" became one of their favorite expressions. Rejecting the optimistic teachings of liberalism, many of them instead began to espouse dispensational-premillennialism, a very anti-progressive scheme of history that postponed most of the benefits of Christianity until Christ returned to earth. This doctrine provided a rationale for a separatist stance against both church and world. It became so popular that it was often considered a test of orthodoxy. Dispensational-premillennialism was originated by J. N. Darby (1800–1882), a Britisher and founder of the Plymouth Brethren, and it was popularized among the fundamentalists largely by the Scofield Reference Bible. The prophetic sections of the Bible were literalized and no other form of interpretation was allowed. This approach to eschatology divides history into time periods (usually seven) in which God relates to sinful man in a different way in each "dispensation." Before Christ returns permanently to establish a literal thousand-year reign on earth, he will return secretly to rescue

("rapture") his church. The Antichrist will then perpetrate seven terrible years of destruction (the "tribulation") before Christ returns in power to establish the kingdom of God.

Other important positions among the fundamentalists were emphases upon godly living (the deeper life movement), prohibition of alcohol, and a rejection of the legitimacy of the natural sciences. Revivalism remained a part of fundamentalism as it shifted from the North to the South, where revivalism was a long accepted practice in the denominations. Common to many fundamentalists were affinities to political conservatism in which the gospel and the American way of life were not only correlates but almost synonymous. These militants, quite popular during the 1930s and 1940s, would be represented, for example, by Carl McIntire, Bob Jones University, the periodical *The Sword of the Lord*, and J. Frank Norris (1877–1952).

Once the initial noise from the theological collision had quieted and it was seen how lonely a position fundamentalism was, new and different currents began to flow in conservatism. Carl Henry and most evangelicals did not move in a separatist direction with the fundamentalists. Many evangelicals continued to work within the denominations, and during a period that began around 1940 there emerged a group of evangelicals who deliberately distinguished themselves from the older fundamentalists. Henry soon emerged as a leader in this group. The self-conscious new Evangelicalism made such a clear division with fundamentalism that two major movements came to be spoken of—Evangelicalism and separatist fundamentalism. After 1940 these new evangelicals became recognizable in the United States as a strong force within traditional orthodoxy. Liberals and the secular press were a long time in recognizing the distinction, and facetiously said that an evangelical was merely a fundamentalist with a college education.

Henry and his colleagues held firm to biblical beliefs but repudiated the theological and cultural excesses of fundamentalism. Harold J. Ockenga, a seminary student under Machen, was perhaps their most significant leader. In 1942 he became

the first president of the National Association of Evangelicals
and in 1947 the first president of Fuller Seminary and the
first to use the term "neo-evangelical." These theologically conservative Protestants (they came to be known for a time as
neo-evangelicals) objected to the extreme ecclesiastical separation of the fundamentalists. Since the 1920s the fundamentalists
had refused to cooperate with apostates or the friends of apostates, fearful of compromise of any sort even on minor points.
By contrast, Henry and the newer evangelicals sought to cooperate through an intelligent discussion of differences. Many new
evangelicals came from traditions that had had little contact
with organized separatist fundamentalism, and what heritage
they had from fundamentalism was perceptibly modified.

The new evangelicals had separate organizations but did
not insist on them. Again, where the fundamentalists expected
conformity and feared academic liberty, the new evangelicals
rejected anti-intellectualism by emphasizing scholarship in their
own colleges and seminaries. In their schools they continued
to oppose liberal theology but dropped militancy as a necessary
feature. They allowed debate on the question of the inerrancy
of Scripture and were willing to reevaluate some of their own
theological heritage. The evangelicals used much of the scholarly apparatus inherited from the Enlightenment. Bernard
Ramm, a leading evangelical theologian, put it this way: "Fundamentalism attempts to shield itself from the Enlightenment.
It attempts to do its theological and biblical tasks as if the
Enlightenment had never happened. On the other hand, the
evangelical believes that the Enlightenment cannot be undone.
He must use the valuable tools of research developed during
the Enlightenment, and he cannot ignore the entire change
of the intellectual climate of Europe and America that the
Enlightenment produced."[32] They usually tolerated theological
differences, including Pentecostalism.

Again, Henry and the new evangelicals rejected the fundamentalists' flight from cultural involvement by insisting that
Christianity has important social aspects. The new evangelicals

remained predominantly conservative and patriotic, but they took seriously the need for more radical social application (they often dropped dispensationalism, though not usually premillennialism). The new Evangelicalism wanted to return to its former role as a shaper of culture. While evangelism remained their central activity, the new evangelicals were characterized by ecclesiastical cooperation (Billy Graham insisted on the need for "cooperative evangelism"), growth in scholarship (Carl Henry earned two doctoral degrees, a doctor of theology and a doctor of philosophy), and a more sophisticated political understanding to express their renewed social concern. The fundamentalists became a strict subculture within orthodoxy, while the new evangelicals became *the* evangelicals to the American public at large.

The new evangelicals benefited during the 1950s from the general "revival" in religious interest in the nation—Billy Graham and his crusades received a national hearing, conservative seminaries enjoyed a growing enrollment, Bill Bright's Campus Crusade for Christ recruited a growing staff, and Youth For Christ reached out to high-schoolers. Although evangelicals continued to grow, they moved out of the spotlight with the end of the Eisenhower period. Curiosity and media attention shifted elsewhere: to the Catholicism of President John F. Kennedy (1917–1963) and the Second Vatican Council of Pope John XXIII (1881–1963); to the social turmoil of the civil rights struggle; to the Viet Nam war and the loss of hope by the young; to the secular theologians and the "death of God" enigma; and to the emergence in the late 1960s of the passive rebel. But during this period an unnoticed resurgence of evangelical faith was continuing. The news media focused on one flamboyant evidence of this biblical Christianity—the Jesus people. The Jesus "freaks" were bizarre and newsworthy and were exploited commercially. Their attempts to express a valid faith in the midst of the ruins of both secularism and the counter-culture was soon passed off as a fad. Yet an enormous expansion of conventional Evangelicalism had been going on—

the kind that alarmed Dean Kelly in his *Why Conservative Churches Are Growing*, and the type which Richard Quebedeaux had carefully followed in his *The Young Evangelicals* (1974) and *The Worldly Evangelicals* (1978).

This current resurgence of evangelical Protestantism constitutes a near revolution. It was assumed, both in the popular imagination and in the academic mind, that once the evangelical decline was established, it could not be substantially reversed. But George Gallup, Jr., called 1976 the *year of the evangelical*, the new mainline expression of Christianity in America today.

The Rejection of a Theological Relative to the Right: Fundamentalism

Fundamentalism grew out of the attempt by conservative American Protestants between 1870 and 1935 to keep the denominations from becoming liberal—a grass-roots resistance primarily in the northern churches to preserve orthodoxy by rejecting modernism. After 1935 the fundamentalists became separatists, refusing to have fellowship with any but other separatists. During the late forties and early fifties, however, a new alliance of theological conservatives formed with their own distinct emphases and concerns.

Positively, Henry and the new evangelicals wanted to affirm traditional evangelical theology (Protestant orthodoxy linked with American revivalism), and negatively, to reject fundamentalist separatism. To the new alliance, separation was primarily a matter of individual conscience. Years later, in looking back upon his initial rejection of fundamentalism, Carl Henry wrote, "What distressed the growing evangelical mainstream about the fundamentalist far right were its personal legalisms, suspicion of advanced education, disdain for biblical criticism per se, polemical orientation of theological discussion, judgmental attitudes toward those in ecumenically related denominations, and an uncritical political conservatism often defined as 'Chris-

tian anticommunism' and 'Christian capitalism' that, while politicizing the gospel on the right, deplored politicizing it on the left."[33] It was during this period that Carl Henry came on the scene as an important theologian and a major interpreter of the new Evangelicalism.

An important first public step in the formation of the new evangelicals took place in 1941–43 with the formation of the National Association of Evangelicals. Henry, professor of Philosophy of Religion at Northern Baptist Theological Seminary, was an early and enthusiastic supporter of the NAE. The NAE had a nucleus of highly skilled intellectuals for its theological leadership, and Henry was eventually to emerge as one of their most articulate spokesmen. For years he has labored to promote the NAE ideals of unity, education, evangelism, social ethics, and the intellectual defense of traditional American orthodoxy (apologetics). The new evangelicals became a self-conscious movement in 1947 with the founding of Fuller Theological Seminary and the publication of a significant book by Henry.

Better than anyone else, Henry has articulated the weaknesses of fundamentalism and firmly repudiated them. In 1947 he published a book, *The Uneasy Conscience of Modern Fundamentalism*, to point to the "harsh temperament, a spirit of lovelessness and strife," that had brought about the bankruptcy of fundamentalism. The fundamentalists had seen heresy in liberal untruth but not in fundamentalism's unloveliness. In this "manifesto" of the new evangelicals Henry did two things that the fundamentalists had been unwilling to do: he criticized the fundamentalist theological tradition and he pointed the conservatives in some new directions. The fundamentalists' primary interest was in the preservation of the orthodox doctrine of salvation, and they chose to make the errorless Scriptures their first line of defense. Coupled with this insistence upon the final authority of Scripture was their rejection of extraneous philosophical systems, a "social gospel" without individual regeneration, a philosophy of history without an eschaton, and

an ecumenical movement that minimized the absoluteness of Christianity (as the liberals taught). They tried to maintain the status quo by negation. Because they failed to develop an affirmative world view, they lapsed from a religious movement to a religious mentality.

Henry and the new evangelicals inherited the concerns of orthodoxy and continued to defend and develop them, but they did have distinctive new theological concerns. Harold Ockenga had originally said that fundamentalism had the wrong attitudes, the wrong strategies, and the wrong results. Martin Marty put the difference this way: "To those wholly unfamiliar with the American lay of the land it often suffices to provide a first clue: the Evangelicals are people who find evangelist Billy Graham or his viewpoints acceptable. The Fundamentalists would agree with most of his doctrine but separate from him on most other grounds."[34] Henry, then, was not so much in disagreement with fundamentalism as a theology, but with the character of fundamentalism as a temperament. And yet, the way of looking at orthodox Christianity is so differently held by the new evangelicals and fundamentalists that the distinction between the two is finally a theological one. To ignore the right theological materials and to elevate secondary doctrines to cardinal ones is ultimately to be in theological error.

What were the elements in fundamentalism that Henry examined and rejected? First, Henry rejected the attitude or "mood" of fundamentalism—its lack of love for fellow believers in Christ. Many fundamentalists were guilty of a divisive spirit of discord which led to isolation and ineffectiveness in evangelism. This lack of love led to militant, intemperate attacks on both friend and foe, a dogmatism of personal ethics and experience, and schismatic strategies as the normal strategy. Henry was especially severe on the fundamentalist strategy of hyperseparatism. He was in the American Baptist Convention and fully intended to remain there. He felt that splitting off from the major denominations was a futile enterprise.

To show that the fundamentalist "mood" (a harsh and in-

dependent spirit) leads to fragmentation, Henry pointed to Machen's original independent denomination. In 1935 the American Presbyterian Church separated from the mother denomination. In 1937 it split into the Orthodox and Bible Presbyterian denominations. In 1956 the Bible Presbyterian Church split again and many of its members joined the Reformed Presbyterian Church, Evangelical Synod. For Henry, the fundamentalists did not successfully combine love and independency.[35]

By contrast, Henry positively proposed unity and fellowship among evangelicals, a liberality over minor issues, a strategy of influencing the major denominations from within instead of from without, the rejection of a "thou shalt not" Christianity, an informed attitude toward newer forms of liberal theology, and love for all believers in Christ. He urged cooperation and unity among all evangelicals for the purposes of evangelism and of educating believers in orthodox theology. Evangelicals have responded to this appeal and are showing a willingness to converse with non–evangelicals (liberals) for common purposes of scholarly pursuit, to cooperate with churchmen from the Holiness movement, to welcome the charismatics, and to be tolerant of differences in eschatology.

Second, Henry rejected the antieducational program of the fundamentalists. During the twenties through the forties the militant fundamentalists disregarded scholarship, were antiintellectual, failed to produce academically competent books and journals, were reductionistic in theology (the "good news" was little more than the biblical plan of salvation), lacked intellectual honesty in dealing with problems in science (e.g., evolution), had an obscurantist attitude toward the natural sciences, and had a general disregard for all scholarship. Henry labored to correct this situation among the new evangelicals with his emphasis upon an educated ministry, scholarly research and writing, the careful clarification of theological issues, the intellectual defense of the evangelical stance, and a Christian approach to private and public education.

The new evangelicals are greatly concerned to get the best
education at every level from the elementary grades through
graduate school. They have a friendlier attitude toward scientific
studies and an increased emphasis on scholarship. This emphasis on intellectual respectability has had profound theological
consequences for the new evangelicals: it has moved them toward articulating a Christian view of science and an honest
handling of specific scientific–biblical problems; it has given
them a greater openness to some aspects of biblical higher
criticism and a new desire to locate the nature of biblical inerrancy; and, it has made them study the nature of history to
see how it relates to the Christian faith. Of course, this new
willingness to reopen the matter of the total inerrancy of Scripture is viewed by fundamentalists as the main weakness of
the new evangelicals. The fundamentalists charge that the new
evangelicals are no longer "pro-Bible."

The third characteristic of fundamentalism which Henry examined and rejected was its failure to apply Christianity to
the whole of life. Fundamentalism did not insist on a thorough
statement of and concern for personal and social ethics. Henry
chided the fundamentalist tradition for being extremely dogmatic on minor points of eschatology while failing to produce
any adequate system of social-personal ethics based on Chris-
tian-biblical resources. If liberals depreciated the prophetic element in the Bible and misconstrued its historical message,
the fundamentalists depreciated the legitimate demand of the
gospel upon every area of culture.

The liberals were right in their conviction that there is not
a problem of human existence but that Christianity somehow
has implications for its solution, and the fundamentalists were
right in assuming that history has a last chapter. Henry says:
"Fundamentalism was not wrong in assuming a final consummation of history, but rather in assuming *this is it.*"[36] A properly
balanced Evangelicalism can learn from both liberals and fundamentalists. "While the Lord tarries, the gospel is still relevant
to every problem that vexes the two billion inhabitants of an

apprehensive globe. While he tarries, the news of His coming again is equally relevant."[37]

Henry has been especially active in the area of social-ethical concerns, making it one of his doctrinal priorities. He has insisted that orthodox theology is not complete without a thorough system of personal and social ethics. The new evangelicals came of age with Henry's 1947 attack on fundamentalism's ethical indifferentism, its aloofness in a distraught world. Henry charged that "a predominant trait in most Fundamentalist preaching is this reluctance to come to grips with social evils."[38] Rather, he said, "the sin against which Fundamentalism inveighed, almost exclusively, was individual sin."[39] In this connection he also faulted their eschatology. "It was the failure of Fundamentalism to work out a positive message within its own framework, and its tendency instead to take refuge in a despairing view of world history, that cut off the pertinence of evangelicalism to the modern global crises," he wrote.[40] (To this the fundamentalists have replied that the new evangelicals have relegated eschatology to a lower doctrinal status than that of centrality.)

Feeling that the fundamentalists did not have the redemptive word in proper temporal focus, Henry made a proposal. "Contemporary evangelicalism needs," he said, "(1) to reawaken to the relevance of its redemptive message to the global predicament; (2) to stress the great evangelical agreements in a common world front; (3) to discard elements of its message which cut the nerve of world compassion as contradictory to the inherent genius of Christianity; (4) to restudy eschatological connections for a proper perspective which will not unnecessarily dissipate evangelical strength in controversy over secondary positions, in a day when the significance of the primary insistences is international."[41] Henry's evangelical "formula of protest" against the fundamentalists was "(1) predicated upon an all-inclusive redemptive context for its assault upon global ills; (2) involves total opposition to all moral evils, whether societal or personal; (3) offers not only a higher ethical standard than

any other system of thought, but provides also in Christ a dynamic to lift humanity to its highest level of moral achievement."[42]

Nearly four decades after Henry's original criticism, extreme separatist fundamentalism still has no social conscience. Influenced by dispensational theology, it remains totally pessimistic about the present world situation. It is firmly committed to the political status quo. With Billy James Hargis and Carl McIntire, for example, conservative political action is as important as theology. "Christian anticommunism" is an integral part of their theology and as significant to them as the "dictation method" of biblical inspiration and the literal interpretation of Scripture at all points. Even those dispensationalists who are less extreme in their separatist posture (Richard Quebedeaux in his book, *The Young Evangelicals*, calls them the "open fundamentalists" in contrast to the "separatist fundamentalists") still fall under Henry's criticism. Although they may repudiate the alliance with ultra-conservative politics, their theology prevents them from developing a program for reconciliation even among Christians. Hal Lindsey, for example, wrote the best-selling book *The Late Great Planet Earth*. This book popularized the dispensational theology taught by Dallas Theological Seminary, but the dispensational view of the present human situation deprives the book of any meaningful social ethic.

Henry and the new evangelicals propose a new combination of priorities as well as a new theological alternative. In a 1948 article in *Christian Life* Henry set forth five aims of the new evangelicals in their search for a new sense of proportion: (1) to clarify the philosophical implications of biblical theism; (2) to develop a valid social ethic; (3) to promote a more open attitude over points of eschatology; (4) to promote a new spirit of love and ecumenism among evangelicals; and (5) to find a way back from dogmatic theology to biblical theology.[43]

From Carl Henry and others the new Evangelicalism took its shape and form as a distinct theological movement. Both

new evangelicals and fundamentalists hold to a belief in the inspiration and authority of the Bible, the necessity of the "new birth," and the need for evangelism. But evangelicals do not like to be called fundamentalists and fundamentalists do not like to be called evangelicals, because they differ dramatically in their basic postures.

The Rejection of a Theological Relative to the Left: Neoorthodoxy

In affirming the veracity of one evangelical tradition, Carl Henry points to the illegitimacy of two other traditions—fundamentalism and neoorthodoxy. We have seen that Henry advocates an intelligent recommitment to the orthodox heritage which fundamentalism had lost by a too narrow theological understanding. Henry may have shared some of the same theological grounds as fundamentalism, yet he differed widely in many respects. But Henry is not fully understood until it is seen how he also differentiates himself from the neoorthodox kind of evangelical. He feels that neoorthodoxy retains too much of the liberal theology on which it was nourished.

Neoorthodoxy, succeeded where fundamentalism and the evangelicals had failed—it brought down the house of liberalism. But neoorthodoxy as a theological attempt to correct the errors in liberalism was in the long run unacceptable to Henry and the new evangelicals. Neoorthodoxy made much the same criticism of liberalism as did the evangelicals, and the evangelicals learned from and were influenced by the luminaries of neoorthodoxy. Yet Henry and the evangelicals would finally have no part of this school of Christianity. Some evangelicals branded neoorthodoxy as "neoliberalism"—merely old liberalism in a new form.

As a new, more theologically conservative reaction to liberalism, neoorthodoxy was spearheaded largely by the thinking of scholars like Karl Barth (1886–1968) and Emil Brunner (1889–1966) in Europe and Reinhold Niebuhr (1892–1971)

in America. These extraordinary men were trained in the liberal
tradition, and a chief reason why their attack on liberalism
was so devastating was that they understood it so well. Paul
Tillich (1886–1965), Rudolf Bultmann (1884–1976), and
Friedrich Gogarten (1887–1967) eventually so distanced themselves from the movement that they cannot be classified strictly
as neoorthodox. In 1918 Barth published a commentary on
St. Paul's Epistle to the Romans in which the theme was "God
is God." By this Barth meant three things: (1) between God
and man there is an infinite qualitative difference; (2) sin is
man's attempt to obscure this difference; (3) only God can
bridge the gap, and for man to acknowledge this is saving
faith. These three points mounted a full-scale attack on Protestant liberalism. It was in the 1930s that neoorthodoxy as a
theological revival in the United States began in earnest. It
was also the time when Carl Henry was beginning his theological
studies.

Neoorthodoxy was a vigorous reaction to the optimism of
old liberalism. The Western world was most optimistic about
its future between 1890 and 1914, but the manifest horrors
of World War I gave impetus to the neoorthodox stance. First,
the neoorthodox felt that liberalism had not taken the power
of sin seriously. The inhumanity of man in two world wars
was enough, they felt, to shatter the naive optimism of the
liberals that society was innately perfectible. Hope had to be
located beyond a culture in crisis. The kingdom of God, brought
about by man's unaided efforts, was not just around the corner.
Even the best of people or programs are guilty before God,
and God's judgment falls on the inherent pride in any human
endeavor. Liberalism was a dead-end option, because in stressing the autonomy of man it lost the majesty of God and therefore
made theology impossible. Neoorthodoxy felt it was the true
heir of Luther and Calvin, and it tried to retain through rein-
terpretation what the Reformers meant by original righteousness, original sin, Adam, and the Fall. Genesis 3 was not a
historical event (as Henry and the evangelicals claimed), but

a historical condition under which all men exist and which is continually repeated.

Second, the neoorthodox said that God was more transcendent than the liberals had imagined. God was not to be immanently localized in the goodness of the world or the accomplishments of the social gospel. God was Wholly Other than man and the created order. There are sharp boundaries between man and God, but the liberals were too influenced by idealistic philosophy to catch the spirit of the biblical doctrine of the transcendence of God. Because of this distance between heaven and earth, time and eternity, theology is best expressed in the logical form of a paradox. Rationalistic and empirical approaches to God are wrong, if not wicked. In agreement with Sören Kierkegaard (1813–1855), the nineteenth-century founder of the existentialist movement, the neoorthodox said that theistic proofs for God's existence are unnecessary—the experience of the gospel is self-validating.

Third, God had indeed revealed himself, as the liberals claimed, but not through abstract eternal ideas grasped by the intuitive genius of man outside any historical context. On his own, man knows nothing about God. Through God alone is God known. God has revealed himself through "mighty acts in history," and that primarily through Christ. Christ the God-man is the central figure of Christian revelation. The Bible is indispensable because it is the written testimony of those who saw the mighty acts of revelation, believed in them, and reported them to the community of faith. The best place to encounter Christ, the living Word, is through the Bible, the written Word. The liberals lost the significance of the Bible when they identified revelation with the best in man. But the Bible is only a witness to revelation, not the revelation itself. Revelation is God dynamically giving himself to man in Jesus Christ as disclosed through the power of the Holy Spirit. The words of Scripture are special words in that they witness that this God-man encounter of revelation has happened, and they promise that it will happen again.

Henry and the evangelicals appreciated and learned from the neoorthodox criticism of liberalism and used some of its ammunition for their own attack. But many evangelicals felt that neoorthodoxy was just another expression of liberalism and equally dangerous. Neoorthodoxy, Henry felt, was wholly inadequate in its appreciation of the Bible. The neoorthodox were right in insisting that the liberals had rejected the historical element in the Bible through their earlier biblical criticism, but neoorthodoxy was wrong in not recognizing the words of the Bible as revelation itself. The Bible is not merely the testimony of God's revelation, it *is* revelation. Henry felt that neoorthodoxy had a nebulous view of Scripture—it undercut the reliability of the Bible, it left final decisions to the subjective discernment of individual congregations, it gave no criteria as to how the "mighty acts of God" were to be distinguished from the general flow of history, and it left no firm biblical base from which to operate in the moral realm.

The neoorthodox spoke much of God's revelation in "mighty acts," but very little about the inspiration of Scripture, the testimony of those "acts." "To Barth, inspiration is the willingness of the writers of Scripture to be witnesses of revelation. To evangelicals, inspiration is the process whereby the revelation or Word of God is cast into written form."[44] Even Barth, who looked upon the biblical writers as inspired, was reluctant to say that inspiration guaranteed a fully reliable Bible in all matters of science, history and philosophy.

The neoorthodox view of Scripture was the prime reason that Henry and the evangelicals refused to embrace this group, but there were also secondary differences of opinion. Henry and the evangelicals said that the neoorthodox emphasis on God's transcendence (a correct emphasis) had led them to neglect God's immanence. Henry and the evangelicals held that God intervenes in the processes of nature, that miracles did and do happen, that one can make a conscious personal commitment to Christ, and that God comes to the believer in Christ and dwells in him. They said that regeneration and sanctification

can take place in the inner life, that social service results from a disciplined inner life, and that the experience of faith is an integral part of faith itself. According to Henry and the evangelicals, the devil is real, evil is a dire threat to the world, and since faith has profound metaphysical implications, apologetics is a legitimate enterprise of the theologian. Further, just as Christ came the first time, so he will have a personal, visible return.[45] Again, Henry and others felt that neoorthodoxy, by sidestepping the biblical injunction to be "born again" as an individual, undercut both personal evangelism and any program for social reconstruction. The neoorthodox movement never became a school and Henry was not sorry to see it pass off the scene as a theological option in the mid-1960s.

In spite of important differences with neoorthodoxy, many evangelicals (including Henry) have drunk deeply at the neoorthodox well. They have learned from Reinhold Niebuhr, who said that justice is the social expression of Christian love. They have learned from Karl Barth, probably the most profound and influential Christian theologian of our age. Some evangelicals dismissed Barth as a "new modernist" (Cornelius Van Til, John Warwick Montgomery), but others have valued his contribution (Colin Brown, Bernard Ramm, Klaas Runia, G. C. Berkouwer, and Donald G. Bloesch). Many of the younger evangelicals are members of the Karl Barth Society (a colloquy of scholars who meet annually to study Barth's works). Although Barth has not been fully accepted in the evangelical world, a reassessment and new appreciation for him is currently taking place.[46] American evangelicals recognize a fellow evangelical (as Barth called himself in his book, *Evangelical Theology*) in Barth's call for a theology of revelation, his emphasis on the authority of the Bible, his insistence on the sovereignty of God, the triumph of the grace of God, the substitutionary atonement of Christ, his defense of the Virgin Birth doctrine and the bodily resurrection of Christ, his doctrine of the Trinity, and his understanding of prayer as heartfelt supplication before a holy and merciful God.

But Henry along with other evangelicals still have reservations about what they label as "nonbiblical and even philosophical elements" in Barth's theology. Henry does not like Barth's contention that there is no natural knowledge of God apart from the event of revelation. Henry fears that Barth teaches universal salvation by separating faith from salvation. He is afraid that Barth's doctrine of evil is more Platonic than biblical, since Barth traces evil to nonbeing rather than to demonic sin. For Henry the world is enemy-occupied territory and the warfare between God and the devil still continues. Many evangelicals charge Barth with not taking man's willful unbelief seriously enough. The world is not already redeemed. But Henry and most evangelicals are most disturbed over Barth's doctrine of Scripture. They find Barth to be saying that the Bible is essentially reliable and trustworthy, but that it is not necessarily dependable in everything that it reports. Evangelicals prefer to say that the divine Word is not only witnessed to by the human word of the Bible, but is embodied in it. They applaud Barth's effort to avoid bibliolatry, but they insist that the Bible truly presents God's Word. Barth does not quite hold in balance various emphases in the Bible as Henry and the evangelicals would like to see them held.

Karl Barth considered himself an evangelical holding the true faith of the Reformers and the New Testament. When Cornelius van Til's book, *The New Modernism,* was published in 1946, Barth began to get a bad press among American evangelicals. Van Til's thesis was that neoorthodoxy was really neomodernism. In Carl Henry the bad press given Barth continues. Barth is one of Henry's favorite targets. Henry constantly warns that Barth's views of inspiration and revelation are defective, and that Barth is an irrationalist. But the charge of irrationalism cannot be sustained if one reads at length in Barth's *Church Dogmatics.* Barth always denied that he was an irrationalist. He honored logic and consistently argued that revelation is rational.

Evangelicals Today

Carl Henry was one of the original shapers during the '40s and '50s of a thoroughly classical Christian orthodoxy and has helped guide it to its present status. Quebedeaux says that "it is now quite possible to talk about Evangelicalism as *the* established expression of Orthodoxy in the United States, if not the world."[47] Quebedeaux says that this original evangelical revival (which he calls "establishment evangelicalism") had three important public symbols that gave it national attention— the National Association of Evangelicals, Billy Graham, and the periodical *Christianity Today.* Henry was intimately associated with all three.

He was a charter member of the NAE when it was organized to provide a meaningful fellowship among evangelicals in cooperative witness. At the 1943 constitutional convention in Chicago, the thirty-year-old Henry was one of the most enthusiastic supporters of the NAE. He was one of the several teachers and ministers whose sympathy for a new alliance of theological conservatives led to the organization. He wrote for its official journal, *United Evangelical Action,* and actively promoted it. These early efforts at theological unity led to the founding in 1949 of a Theological Society for evangelical debate. Henry has served as one of the Society's presidents and continues to attend its annual meetings. But Henry has not been satisfied with the scholarly products of the Society. He has said: "Those who declare that unabashed commitment to biblical inerrancy guarantees theological vitality have the past twenty-five years of meager production by the Evangelical Theological Society to explain."[48] Henry's discontent shows that there is progressive movement in Evangelicalism and he has been prodding it along.

Billy Graham has become the most eminent evangelistic symbol of the evangelicals and for years their public spokesman. Graham achieved national fame through his success in the Los Angeles Crusade in 1949. Henry was in that crusade and

encouraged Graham to be more theologically precise in his preaching. In 1957 Graham conducted a crusade in Madison Square Garden. His cooperation with "ecumenical liberals" angered many conservatives and threatened to divide and discredit evangelical understanding of evangelism, cooperation and unity. Henry was the chairman of the 1966 World Congress of Evangelism which met in Berlin and was sponsored by the Graham organization.

In 1956 the biweekly magazine *Christianity Today* became *the* official voice of the new evangelicals, with Carl Henry as its first editor. The journal made an honest effort to break away from the separatist impulse and social unconcern of fundamentalism. At the same time it tried to avoid the lack of a solid biblical-theological foundation for action in the world that it saw in its two "liberal" counterparts—*The Christian Century* and *Christianity and Crisis.* Unfortunately, social caution has characterized the journal, and a new generation of evangelicals has clamored for a greater demonstration of prophetic action.

Broadening has occurred within evangelical Christianity since 1947 and Henry has been one of its most influential advocates. He has helped respectable orthodoxy in its intellectual transformation—its fresh understanding of the reliability and authority of Scripture, its new friendliness to science, its willingness to reopen dialogue with theological liberals, and its combined rejection of dispensationalism and concern for social ethics.

The conscience-rending decade of the 1960s has made many evangelicals even more eager to get on with the task of reconciliation among Christians and prophetic action in the world. Quebedeaux calls this quest for renewal "nothing less than a *revolution* in Orthodoxy."[49]

By 1970 Henry pointed to eight things that these evangelicals want to see in their churches: "1. An interest in human beings not simply as souls to be saved but as whole persons; 2. More active involvement by evangelical Christians in sociopolitical affairs; 3. An honest look at many churches' idolatry of nationalism; 4. Adoption of new forms of worship; 5. An end of judging

spiritual commitment by such externals as dress, hair style and other participation in cultural trends, including rock music; 6. A new spirit with regard to ecumenical or nonecumenical attitudes; 7. Bold and, if need be, costly involvement in the revolutionary struggles of our day; and finally, 8. A reappraisal of life values."⁵⁰

Henry remains an active leader as the evangelicals energetically attempt to renew and maintain the spirit of early Christianity. His books have in certain major respects paced the changes in evangelical theology and ethics. He is dealing with a new generation of evangelicals who are interested in a greater intellectual openness, a more tolerant view of the permissive society, a heightened awareness of this world, and a spirit of ecclesiastical cooperation. They have a new religious consciousness and show that Evangelicalism is no monolithic entity. To the younger among them the fundamentalist-liberal conflict is their parents' memory and not a matter of their own personal experience. They have moved away from a propositional approach to the Bible and are not absorbed by such issues as inerrancy. They are open to biblical criticism, evolution, and sociopolitical theology. Henry is speaking for and speaking to a much wider spectrum of evangelicals than he did over three decades ago.

In the late '70s Henry observed that evangelicals were in the throes of an identity crisis. He said: "Twenty-five years ago there were signs that the long-caged lion would break its chains and roar upon the American scene with unsuspected power. . . . While he is still on the loose, and still sounding his roar, the evangelical lion is nonetheless slowly succumbing to an identity crisis. . . . Having burst his cage in a time of theological default, the lion of evangelicalism now seems unsure which road to take."⁵¹

Evangelicals are in transition, calling for vigorous alternatives, and increasingly discontented with the status quo. Their theology and social concerns are broadening. Henry says that in a decade of mounting internal tension, persistent "criticism has come especially from two groups, those who have switched

to a somewhat more critical view of Scripture and those who
deplore evangelicalism's seeming cultural captivity and lack
of sociopolitical engagement."[52] The National Association of
Evangelicals, the Billy Graham Evangelistic Association, and
Christianity Today no longer serve as the symbol for all evangelicals. "Among them are the National Black Evangelical Association, Evangelicals for Social Action (and whatever new
organization will descend from it), the Evangelical Women's
Caucus, the Wesleyan Theological Society, the Society for
Pentecostal Studies, Evangelicals Concerned, and a number of
prominent evangelical magazines and newspapers like *Sojourn-
ers, Radix, The Other Side, The Wittenburg Door, The Reformed
Journal, Vanguard, Faith at Work,* and *Catholic Charismatic.*"[53]

These discontented evangelicals still believe in biblical authority, conversion, and evangelism, but they are desperately
eager to see evangelicals get on with the job of applying these
three beliefs to modern secular society. Quebedeaux says that
their priorities can be separated roughly into four areas of
concern. "First, there is an interest in developing a richer
understanding of the inspiration and authority of Scripture
as the basis for action in the world. Second, it is felt that
evangelism must always be the proclamation of the Gospel in
its *entirety*—relevant to the whole man or woman and *all* of
his or her needs. Third, there is a new emphasis on discipleship
and on discovering values appropriate to the transformed life
in Christ. And finally, it is believed that the institutional church
should function corporately not only as the community of the
saved but also as an instrument of reconciliation—calling alien-
ated men and women to be reconciled to God, to one another,
and to their own true selves."[54]

The dominant trend of these evangelicals is to stress the
functional power of the Bible to transform man and his social
structures. They charge that the traditional evangelical understanding of the Bible has been that of Scripture as a depository
of divine revelation and propositional truth in words alone.
Discontent among these evangelicals became most evident over

a Thanksgiving weekend in 1973 when they hammered out the now famous Chicago Declaration of Evangelical Social Concern. Guided by Carl Henry and a few other elder statesmen, they confessed in this document the evangelical complicity in the racism, sexism, militarism, and economic injustice of U.S. society.

This is only one example of the ferment taking place in the evangelical vat. Where is Evangelicalism going? Even the most far seeing of our prophets seem reluctant to forecast the future of the identity crisis. Evangelicals are both growing and changing. What once seemed an unbending rigidity now appears to be a busy waterfront of ideas and issues, each tugging and pushing for a choice berth at the dock. Theologically a fierce debate is going on and a number of evangelicals are beginning to sound like the neoorthodox of thirty years ago. No longer can an evangelical theologian be identified as white, male, middle-class, Baptist or Presbyterian, and a rational Calvinistic scholastic. Socially the evangelicals are beginning both to criticize our secular culture and to accommodate themselves to it. Just at the time when the majority of evangelicals are making compromises with culture and becoming typical middle-class Americans, their "social gospel" theologians are wrestling with the proper use of political power and economic pressure.

Ecumenically evangelicals are beginning to probe the old liberal establishment to see if some kind of fellowship in Christ cannot be reestablished. Both liberals and evangelicals are groping toward each other; both are uncomfortable with their continued separation; both hope that some modest form of reconciliation is within reach.

Experientially the evangelicals are opening themselves to learn something new from the charismatics. In the 1960s the charismatics (neo-Pentecostals, a transdenominational middle-class expression of "classical" Pentecostalism) burst on the scene as a particularly energetic, enthusiastic, very experiential, major subculture within evangelical Christianity. Their theology was orthodox (even fundamentalist) on the authority of the

Bible, the necessity of conversion, and the imperative of evangelism. Traditional evangelicals were at first suspicious of the
charismatics because they were too unpredictable. Evangelicals
like to reach doctrinal agreement before they share a unity
in experience, whereas the charismatics say that experience
and witness precede doctrine. But evangelicals now seem to
welcome the charismatics and their grassroots kind of ecumeni-
cism of experience.[55]

Carl Henry has said that what "evangelicals need most amid
the present tide of irrationalism and cultural decay is to enlist
all the movement's rational and moral energies for a comprehensive confrontation of the religious, philosophical, and social
arenas. By sharing in such a vision, the somewhat lame and
halt evangelical forces in all enterprises—from Southern Baptist
and Missouri Synod quarters, from ecumenical conciliar quarters, from evangelical establishment sources, from the more
radical social activist groups, from among isolated independent
spirits who labor with a sense of messianic individualism—
could together forge fresh conviction and brilliant truth for
redeemed society to proffer a despairing world."[56]

Through his writings, Carl Henry has helped the evangelicals
emerge from the exile of the 1930s, regain a sure theological
footing, and overcome the shocks of the harsh fundamentalist-
liberal religious war. Alongside his own numerous books, Henry
has edited a series of composite works which drew authors
from both American and European Evangelicalism (*Contemporary Evangelical Thought*, 1957; *Revelation and the Bible*, 1958;
Basic Christian Doctrines, 1962; *Christian Faith and Modern
Theology*, 1964; *Jesus of Nazareth, Savior and Lord*, 1966).
"In much the same way as *The Fundamentals* had done, these
volumes competently restated the basics upon which evangelical
theology was constructed."[57]

Now Henry is helping evangelicals to present an attractive
and well-reasoned case for orthodoxy. His steadying hand is
needed now as much as ever. Evangelicals are a force to be
reckoned with in American life, but America has not draped

itself at the feet of these Bible believers. "Eighty million Americans are essentially unrelated to churches. Secularism shows no sign of giving up its hold in the public schools where a deterministic humanism prevails as often as not. The evangelical message seems to have made little impact on the American legal system, which, for example, often treats criminals and victims with equal callousness. Few Evangelicals have contributed distinctly Christian insights to the crises of energy and ecology or to the ongoing debate over the moral strengths and weaknesses of the American economic and political systems."[58]

Internally the evangelicals are divided into charismatics, fundamentalists, confessional evangelicals and neoevangelicals with various conservative, progressive and militant sub-groups. A complex and rancorous debate on the nature of the Bible is fostering distrust and discontent. Differences among evangelicals that have existed since the Reformation will not go away. Whether evangelicals will live up to their potential remains to be seen.

II. Philosophical Apologetics: Is Christianity Rationally Defensible?

Apologetics is the task of one branch of theology to arrange answers to the question, "Is Christianity rationally defensible?" In 1946 Carl Henry tossed the apologetic hat into the ring for the evangelicals with his book, *Remaking the Modern Mind*. He was fired by several convictions.

First, he felt that striking reversals had taken place in modern philosophy (secular humanism or naturalism) because it had given non-Christian answers to the cardinal problems of God, man and the universe.

Second, he was convinced that Evangelicalism's biblical theism could fill the void left by philosophy's retreat. "Contemporary philosophy's extremity is historic Christianity's opportunity."[1]

Third, theological liberalism had failed to meet the onslaught of naturalism because it was inconsistent, disunited, and had turned from an authoritative revelation to become a psychology of religious experience. The only unity among liberals was the negative unity of rejecting biblical Christianity.

Fourth, theological fundamentalism, although accepting an

authoritative revelation, had paid no respect to philosophy and consequently had developed no apologetic. Fundamentalists cared nothing about the intellectual perplexity of their college students attending secular universities.

Henry was sure that evangelicals could and should win what fundamentalism had lost by default—study all phases of intellectual interest, call a secular generation into disputation, prove that hostile attacks to the biblical message are based upon errors, show that a critical attitude need not be a skeptical one. He sought to point out that modern naturalism is guilty of self-righteousness in the area of knowledge, and to show that orthodox Christianity is able to answer the fundamental questions of life as adequately as, if not more adequately than, any other view would.

Historical supernaturalism was thought to be in intellectual disrepute at the end of the liberal-fundamentalist fight. Carl Henry and other evangelicals started a literary movement in the late '40s to defend and articulate, to make intellectually respectable, to develop a definitive philosophic grounding for, the orthodox position. Henry was a leader in this activity and has remained one of its guides.[2] He has written several important volumes in apologetics. In his earliest books he was particularly eager to show that evangelical theology could hold its own against both secular and liberal thinking.[3] He has edited the famous seven volume evangelical series on apologetics and theology (see the bibliography on page 178). In his latest six volumes on God, revelation, and authority, he has returned to the apologetic challenge.

Christian apologetics has a twofold task: to set forth the truthfulness of the Christian claim (to verify truth), and to show that Christianity has a right to claim a knowledge of God (to demonstrate a knowledge). But how is one to go about this task? The matter of strategy is crucial. Any apologist will work from a basic assumption of a group of closely related assumptions. In the history of Christian apologetic systems there have been three families or types.[4]

First, some systems stress the uniqueness of the Christian experience of grace—the apologetic of one's personal testimony. The experience of God's grace is so profound that it is self-validating. Blaise Pascal (1623–1662) and Sören Kierkegaard built apologetic systems on this type of argument.

Second, other systems stress the power of human reason to discover the truths about God. Religious truths are verified in the same fashion as scientific truths. Faith in God is just as credible as faith in confirmed scientific laws. Thomas Aquinas (1225–1274) and Joseph Butler (1692–1752) built apologetic systems on these assumptions.

Third, there are some systems that stress God's Word of special revelation as the foundation of apologetics. This system believes that faith in God comes first (the mind is enlightened by the Holy Spirit), and then the reason is to seek understanding as comprehensively as it can. It believes the first school is too subjective (man's experience is put before God's truth), and the second school underestimates man's depravity (sin distorts the thinking process). Augustine (354–430) and John Calvin built apologetic systems on these assumptions.

Carl Henry is closest to the third school in his approach to apologetics. He makes three basic affirmations. First, only orthodox *theism* can meet the intellectual needs of the modern world. Second, orthodox theism is grounded in a *special revelation* of God, "an all inclusive explanation of reality which answers the most problems and leaves the smallest residue of unsolved problems."[5] Third, given revelational theism, the evangelical approach is the most *reasonable* explanation of the many competing views of the world. "For," says Henry, "from the very first, Christianity appealed to the intellect. Revelational theism has never offered itself as an escape from rationality: rather, it has insisted on the subrationality or irrationality of all other views of reality."[6] The world can only be explained adequately from the perspective of the self-revealing Christian God.

Presuppositionalism

Perhaps the best name for Henry's approach to apologetics is *presuppositionalism.* Every system, whether secular or religious, begins with certain presuppositions or assumptions. Before we can think, some things must be taken for granted. Long ago Augustine saw that all thought depends on original assumptions—we must believe something before we can know anything. These absolutistic assumptions are seldom expressed, sometimes unrecognized, and most often unprovable.

Basic assumptions are most significant because they determine the method and goal of thought: axioms determine theorems. Once assumed, an ultimate principle becomes the foundation for all other patterns of thought. In the strictest sense, ultimate principles cannot be proven, but they can be indirectly verified. Some assumptions are more probably true than others, and all assumptions are subject to consistent investigation by reasonable minds. This is possible since there is a common rationality among all men. One's faith assumption (or hypothesis) at the beginning of an investigation should be a reasonable one and give a coherent picture of the world. If one's original faith assumption is false, then its falsity will become evident if it is pursued far enough. A scientist, for example, tests his hypothesis by various experiments; if the hypothesis is consistent with the experiments, then it is assumed that the hypothesis is verified (or "workably true"). In fact, says Henry, modern science cannot act without faith assumptions. "Science continually works within undemonstrable postulates; without them the scientific enterprise would collapse. At point after point, the scientist *believes* in order to *know*. He believes in the continuity of personal identity; in the evidence of his senses; in the reliability of the laws of thought; in the value of honesty in research; in the dependability of the laws he charts. These beliefs make demonstration possible, yet they are not demonstrable beliefs."[7]

If a basic assumption leads to a true world view, then the world view reflects reliably back upon the basic assumption. But how does one test for a *true* world view? Generally, philosophy has graded a world view as true if it can meet four tests.[8] First, any world view must be free from internal self-contradiction: it must be consistent. Second, its various parts or principles must harmonize: it must be coherent. Third, it must illumine or explain some experience more thoroughly than any other basic assumption: it must be applicable. And fourth, it should be applicable to *all* possible experience: it must be adequate. The world view that most adequately satisfies these four tests for truth is the one we should choose, even though still incapable of a strict demonstrative proof. Rival hypotheses are eliminated by showing that they do *not* meet these four tests. If alternatives to the Christian faith can be eliminated, then there is sufficient logical ground to say that Christianity is true. In Carl Henry's opinion only one world view finally meets the test—Christian theism.

Among the four tests, Henry is especially keen on the first one, consistency, i.e., the priority of the law of noncontradiction. Both Christians and non-Christians use logic as a test for truth. No one meaningfully denies the laws of logic—they are universal and necessary. All significant speech and knowledge are based upon them. Further, the laws of logic are not created by man; they are given by God. The principle of contradiction became a law of logic because it was first a law of being. God has so created the universe that two contradictory statements cannot be true of the same object at the same time. This is the only route that avoids final and complete skepticism, makes truth possible, and provides a philosophical grounding for orthodox theology.

Henry's guiding instrument for separating truth from error is the law of noncontradiction. He freely admits that he was drawn to this position by Gordon Clark, an evangelical philosopher under whom he studied at Wheaton. He says: "To no contemporary do I owe a profounder debt . . . than to Gordon

Clark. . . . Since the thirties when he taught me medieval and modern philosophy at Wheaton, I have considered him the peer of evangelical philosophers in identifying the logical inconsistencies that beset nonevangelical alternatives and in exhibiting the intellectual superiority of Christian theism."[9] Clark's approach is that a position and its denial cannot both be true at the same time. Henry has adopted this stance and has relentlessly applied the law of noncontradiction in separating truth from error.

Dr. Henry insists that the most promising first principle is Christian theism, and he proposes to begin by assuming (not proving) the existence of God revealed in Scripture. One must begin with God, he says, not only to get to God, but to get to anything. "From a certain vantage point, the concept of God is determinative for all other concepts; it is the Archimedean lever with which one can fashion an entire world view."[10] All systems begin with presuppositions, and Christian theism begins with the presupposition of revelation. "Where God has spoken, revealed truth becomes the starting point of consistent knowledge; revelation is the test of truth, furnishes the framework and corrective for natural reason, introduces consistency into fragmentary human knowledge," Henry asserts.[11]

Special revelation is the best starting point for any world view. Man's sin has so affected his natural reason that he cannot recognize God in the created universe. To exclude the principle of revelation is to end up with a false picture of deity. Presuppositionalism attempts to promote biblical theism as the most adequate basic assumption, while trying to unmask the prejudices of those who reject biblical theism as well as pointing out their inadequacies as a substitute for Christianity. These two threads, then, run through all of Henry's thinking: God has given us a revelation of himself in the Bible which, when examined by the laws of reason, stands up better than any other basic assumption; and, by using the law of noncontradiction, all nonevangelical stances can be shown to be contradictory and therefore false.

Revelation: the Source of Truth

In two succinct sentences Henry has stated the method of knowing and the manner of verification in presuppositionalism. "Divine revelation is the source of all truth, the truth of Christianity included; reason is the instrument for recognizing it; Scripture is its verifying principle; logical consistency is a negative test for truth and coherence a subordinate test. The task of Christian theology is to exhibit the content of biblical revelation as an orderly whole."[12] Given the naturalistic temper of our times, Henry feels that apologetics has no choice but to carefully delineate the method and criteria of theology and call secular agnosticism to account. The first task of evangelicals is to insist upon the truth, and the second task is to identify truth and indicate how one can recognize and be assured of it.

The first principle of Christian theology is God in his revelation. All doctrines are judged by this revelation. Only after God has disclosed himself can man make legitimate statements about him. God's revelation of himself is a universal reality "even where men disown it and other religions distort it."[13] Schleiermacher influenced liberal Protestantism to turn from God's objective revelation to man's inner experience as the source of Christian faith. Ernst Troeltsch (1865–1923) was the liberal who rejected any possibility of transcendent divine revelation. "Troeltsch relativizes God's revealing activity, and thus renders the reality of a special divine revelation not only improbable but inconceivable. Transcendent revelational disclosure is philosophically suppressed, and the truth and value of all that is distinctively biblical is obscured."[14] Liberalism substituted anthropology for theology when it turned from revelation to man's inner psychological state. Without the solid authority of objective revelation, liberalism logically fell back toward agnosticism and skepticism.

Championing rationality, the presuppositionalist avoids the problems latent in alternative views of knowledge. "More than

this," says Henry, "on the basis of revelation and its implications he can adduce some specific and highly significant epistemic considerations. Evangelical theology is not only ready to debate any and all rival axioms proposed for an understanding of reality and life, but is also more eager than its rivals to do so, as attested by its evangelistic initiative and missionary expansion. To support its own claim and to contest competing claims, revealed religion is fully prepared to adduce criteria and principles for verification."[15]

Human reason, although not a creative source of truth, is a divinely fashioned instrument for recognizing truth. Since God created man for intelligible relationships, reason should never be downgraded, even though the mind cannot unravel all the enigmas of life. Human reason does not fashion revelation, but it is capable of recognizing and elucidating it. Man's estrangement from God does not destroy man's ability to reason. "There are but two ways of thinking—not regenerate and unregenerate, but valid and invalid," Henry writes.[16] Logical thinking is a common ground between the believer and the unbeliever. God uses truth as a means of persuading and converting the non-Christian.

The Bible is the Christian's principle of verification and it is universally accessible to believers and unbelievers. Christians contend that the biblical revelation is intelligible, expressible in valid propositions, and universally communicable. The "new birth" is not a prerequisite to a knowledge of the truth of God found in the Bible. Henry says that the "truth of revelation is intended for sinners, and the unbeliever can indeed examine the content of theology."[17]

Logical consistency is a negative test of truth and coherence a subordinate test. Faith and logic belong together, and tests of truth are wholly appropriate. Whatever violates the law of contradiction cannot be revelation. All that God does is rational: he cannot contradict himself. Henry says: "Logical consistency is not a positive test of truth, but a negative test; if it were a positive test, logical consistency would accredit all views, how-

ever conflicting, that consistently follow from differing starting points. . . . As a test, logical consistency disqualifies any serious contender whose truth-claim is characterized by logical contradiction."[18]

Scripture is implicitly systematic, and the task of theology is to exposit and elucidate its content in an orderly way. The arrangement of biblical axioms and theorems is a worthy goal of the theologian even though it has not successfully been done as yet. Axiomatization is the best means of demonstrating the logical consistency of the biblical revelation. Henry facetiously remarks: "One polemicist has proposed that this task of axiomatization be the first assignment to neo-Protestant theologians in hell."[19] No systematic theology is revelation, but the revelation does lend itself to systematic exposition.

Finally, the theology of revelation requires the apologetic confrontation of non-Christian theories of reality and life. By applying the laws of logic the Christian apologist will force the abandonment of secularism by showing that it has inconsistencies in its axioms. At the same time he will show the consistency of the evangelical stance and point out how it far better accounts for the facts. Theology dare not overlook unbelief and the special difficulties it has with Christianity. "Over against the truth of revelation all speculative theories shelter some marked internal lack of consistency and self-contradiction; non-revelational viewpoints are all prospects for illogical exposure and reduction to absurdity. If the Christian system of doctrine is true, then deductions derived from contrary axioms must be false."[20]

Competing Ways of Knowing

Utterly convinced of the reasonableness of Christianity, Henry and other evangelical presuppositionalists show only scorn for irrationalism. Henry observes: "So much has the leap of faith been exaggerated into a virtue that contemporary religionists have become more noted for their ingenious hurtling

over rational objections than for their intelligible confrontation of the issues."[21] The basic assumption of presuppositionalists is Christian theism (God in his revelation), but this cannot stand alone. Unless the theologian is to "speak in enigmatic tongues," he must submit this basic assumption to the test of truth which embraces "some agreement on rational methods of inquiry, ways of argument, and criteria for verification."[22] Being a revelation, Christianity must reject three sharply differing ways of knowing—mysticism, empiricism, and philosophical rationalism.

Mysticism fails as a way of knowing God because it inexcusably shrouds the self-revealed God in ineffability and paradox. Mysticism (intuition or immediate apprehension) finds God in one's own inner experience as an instant awareness of the religious Ultimate. Henry divides the proponents of religious intuition into three categories. First, rational mystics such as Plato (427–347 B.C.) view human reason as secretly divine. Plato held that human beings know certain things are immediately true on the basis of the soul's preexistence, i.e., all men possess certain underived truths (*a priori*) without resort to inference. The difficulty with this approach, says Henry, is that the preexistence of the soul is a shaky proposition, and what Plato claimed as universal intuitive knowledge is not intuited by all humans. Second, sensuous mystics such as David Hume (1711–1776) ascribe all knowledge to inference from observation. Hume insisted that all knowledge consists solely of sense perceptions and memory images: sensation is everything. The categories of thought are derived from experience; there are no innate truths. The difficulty with this approach, says Henry, is that it gave up any hope of knowing God and lapsed into skepticism. Third, personal illumination (religious) mystics such as Schleiermacher held that God is to be felt, not conceived. He assumed in man's self-consciousness a secret latency for God-consciousness. As a result, Schleiermacher wrote not of God as the Religious object, but of his own religious sentiments. The difficulty with this approach, says Henry, is

that it cannot vindicate as truly objective anything beyond its own inner feelings. Or if it does try to verbalize its feelings about God, it violates its devotion to the principle that God is not knowable in terms of criteria applicable to daily life (ineffability).

Empiricism fails as a way of knowing God because it cannot arrive at truth since it is committed to an unending search. Empirical conclusions are always so tentative that empiricism can never be sure it has found the truth. All truth is derived from perceptual experience, say the contemporary empiricists, and sound conclusions are verifiable in the lives of all persons. John Dewey (1859–1952), for example, held that experience is the all-inclusive criterion of truth, and he applied this principle to revelational theism with an agnostic outcome. In the absence of demonstrative empirical proof, belief is unreasonable. The tentative character of the empirical method requires that not even the concept of God has any absolute right, since all definitions are liable to revision in the light of continuing human experience. When empiricism is so narrowly tapered that what is unverified by sense observation remains merely a hypothesis, it unwittingly destroys its own base of credibility. This method leaves no certainty about anything—the supernatural, moral norms, or past events in history. Many theological liberals defected to humanism when they saw the skeptical consequences of empiricism. God could hardly be pleased, Henry says, with only a commitment to empirical tentativeness about his reality. Further, "does not an insistent reduction of all knowledge to empirical factors become a prideful—that is, worldly wise—justification of unbelief in a transcendent revelation?"[23]

Philosophical rationalism failed as a way of knowing God because it subordinated revelation to its own alternatives and has speculated itself into exhaustion. This method insists that truth can never be self-contradictory, that the mind of man possesses an inherent potentiality for solving all intellectual problems, and that the intrinsic power of the mind can establish

all of man's beliefs. Until the time of Immanuel Kant rationalists often assumed the infallibility of their own postulations. But Kant had learned from Hume's skepticism and wrote that the categories of thought are correlated only with empirical data. All thought is time-bound and space-bound and man is cut off from any immediate knowledge of God. There is no objective, cognitive knowledge of God. The trust in reason has been deeply shaken in the modern period, and our age has turned toward philosophical naturalism. Confidence in reason has been put to rout, and this has left an open invitation to despair. "Impartial truth" was more elusive than the rationalists supposed. Yet, Henry says, the "strength of philosophical rationalism lay in its insistence that the principles of logic and the mathematical sciences are not derived from experience, but make experience possible, and that truth is self-destructive unless noncontradictory and governed by the canons of reason."[24] Like philosophical rationalists, evangelicals insist that reason is the test of truth. But unlike the rationalists, evangelicals do not believe in comprehensive schemes or grandiose theories about the interrelationships of all existence. Henry feels that evangelicals can restore reason to indispensable importance without falling into the error of rationalism. He and other evangelical presuppositionalists are proponents of rational intuition, a position they carefully distinguish from the philosophical rationalists who depicted human reason as an immanent source of ultimate truth.

Neo-Augustinian

Since Henry and the presuppositionalists are, in a sense, following the footsteps of Augustine, a brief reference to Augustine may help make their position clearer. Augustine hungered after certainty. He was deeply influenced by the philosophical skeptics of his day who taught that neither the five senses nor the mind of man could be trusted to lead to truth. The skeptics advocated universal doubt; sensible guesses were the

best they would allow. Further, Augustine felt that sin had
weakened his will and excited his passions, and he was afraid
that sin had also clouded his mind about truth. "Augustine's
apologetics is really tracing out the answer to the skepticism
suggested by both sin and philosophy!"[25]

But how did Augustine get from doubt to certainty? He
began where the skeptics began, with universal doubt, but he
did not end where they did, in universal skepticism. Doubting,
Augustine said, implies a self (the doubter) who can use his
mind to think (doubting implies laws of logic, thinking, remembering, judging). "I doubt, therefore I am." Doubt implies
three things: the reality of the doubter, the reliability of the
faculties involved in doubting, and the truthfulness of the propositions these faculties work with.[26] The doubter possesses truth.
The doubting self knows these things with certainty and assurance.

Augustine located this certainty in the self with a thinking
mind rather than outside the self in the world of the five senses.
Truth was located within the thinking self (inward) and not
within the senses (outward). Doubt may destroy the evidences
of the five senses, but it cannot eat away the evidences of
the mind (laws of logic, wisdom, noncontradiction, and so on)
which are not based on the senses. Truth is found primarily
in the intellect. This position is often called *Apriorism*, meaning
unmixed with anything empirical and validated independently
of all impressions of sense.

For Augustine the laws of the mind, the principles of thought,
the standards of right and wrong, numbers and beauty, were
inborn. They had a real existence in the order of things, they
were innate, they were a priori, they were a part of the created
order of the cosmos, they were given and sustained by God.
They were not invented by man, they were discovered by man.
Augustine, then, moves from doubt, to knowledge, to truth,
to God. The knowledge of God was implicit within the self
all the time. The self that begins by boasting of God's nonexis-
tence unexpectedly ends up by discovering Father, Son, and

Holy Spirit—the God of all truth and the Creator of the cosmos. Since man is created in God's image, he can recognize the things of God.

God, who created truth and implanted it in the world, illumines the mind to all truth. The perception of truth, whether by the mind of the sinner or the saint, is always by illumination. Man's sin has robbed his mind of truth, so man must depend upon God to be properly enlightened. To put this another way, to know God, man must have a divine revelation. Revelation is the guide for reason, and even the external revelation (Scripture) needs an internal revelation within the self (the Holy Spirit) for the sinner to appropriate salvation.

But just how does sinful man come to the truth of revelation? The sinner, with his mind in a state of unbelief, is not disposed to learn anything from God. Augustine taught that God graciously comes to man, touches man's will, teaches man to forsake his rebellious pride and self-sufficiency, and moves man toward moral obedience.

God must first deal with man's will, the most powerful of the human faculties. Man then develops faith, or a friendly disposition toward God. Faith is a species of the will, and until the friendly disposition of faith is present, no learning from God can take place. Faith is a trusting disposition, an openness to receive revelation. God's grace softens the hardened will. The intellect makes a preliminary sifting of the evidence and finds it convincing. Faith begins to think with assent, and the self becomes favorably inclined to learn the truth of revelation.

Faith leads the intellect because no learning can take place without a favorable disposition. "I believe in order to understand." Unbelief closes the door on the things of God: faith purifies the unregenerate mind. Faith without the scrutiny of reason is superstition; reason without the support of faith is unproductive. Faith always brings us to the most reasonable conclusion. Since faith frees the intellect to do its proper work, there can be no final conflict between faith and reason. Augus-

tine sees theology and philosophy as mutually supportive and working in harmony.

Why is Carl Henry attracted to Augustine? First, Henry was disenchanted with the empirical method of theological liberalism. Liberalism was caught up in the Western drift toward empiricism to account for religious experience. Empiricism teaches that the sole source of religious knowledge is experience, or that no knowledge of God is possible independently of experience. It usually denies that there are any necessary and universal (a priori) truths. But, Henry says, empirical theories "are weak because they cannot evince either the universality or the necessity of religious experience, nor can they show any ultimate reason for permanently distinguishing as they do one aspect of experience as religious from another as nonreligious. . . . The empirical explanation of religious experience is unable to reach any universal obligatory conclusions about God."[27]

Second, Henry, like Augustine, hungers for certainty, for an objective standard possessed already in the approach to experience. Henry does not want "a merely inferred God," to rise to God from the not-God. He wants religious experience to involve direct apprehension of God in the inner human spirit. This emphasis on direct knowledge of God links Henry with Augustine and apriorism (or presuppositionalism or rational intuition). Henry feels that the time is ripe for evangelicals to reassert the conviction of man's primal cognitive relationship to God. Man is incurably religious and always will be, and "in the long history of religious philosophy and theology Christianity has frequently been associated with rational apriorism."[28]

Henry rejects the idea that theology and philosophy operate in different spheres. He is afraid of no man, and he is willing to encounter all the significant thinkers whose writings bear on the issue of man's primal religious experience. He has a masterful grasp of the history of men and ideas and this is evident as he comes to grips with the a priori issue.

Besides Augustine, says Henry, representative thinkers have assigned significance to the religious a priori throughout the course of philosophy of religion. Plato represents one characteristic type and Kant another.[29] Plato placed reason ahead of experience in the knowing process. Also, Plato taught that the soul had preexisted in an eternal world of changeless ideas before it became imprisoned in the human body. As the mind recollected this preexistent world, it could make judgments of apriorical validity. "Unable by perception alone to come to any real knowledge, human beings can make judgments of general validity only because experience of the timeless Ideas in a prior existence conditions man's present experience through recollection."[30]

Plato's mistake, Henry points out, was to assume that man's mind was secretly divine, standing in unmediated relationship to the divine mind. Plato's position, Henry adds, taught that the human mind was "capable of unraveling all the mysteries of reality and life by philosophical reasoning independent of transcendent revelation. This rationalistic view denied man's and nature's dependency upon the divine Logos of God for the forms of thought and ontic structures that make human knowledge possible. The reality, order and meaning of all existence was held to be penetrable by disciplined human speculation, the mind of man being regarded as directly expressive of or contiguous with the Divine Mind."[31] Augustine the Christian knew what Plato did not—that the mind was bent by a sinful will. Plato felt no need for a special revelation, so his apriorism assumes that man has final and true knowledge of spiritual truths apart from a revelational grounding. Henry says that human thought is more complex than Plato imagined "since the fact of creation and the moral predicament of the knower enter significantly into the knowledge situation."[32]

Immanuel Kant tried to establish the validity of a priori knowledge by wholly divorcing it from special divine revelation or metaphysics of any kind. For Kant, the typical function of reason was to harmonize the data that come to the person

through his five senses. The principles of harmony in the mind
(causality, space, time, quantity, and so on) do not come from
the senses, so they must be logically prior to the materials
they synthesize (they are "a priori"). However, the principles
of the mind relate only to the world of the senses; they cannot
be employed to say anything about God, the immortal soul,
or the world conceived as a totality.

According to Kant, God may be postulated, but he cannot
be proven. God is necessary only as a postulate to support
the moral governance of the world and man's hope in immortal-
ity. Kant so limits man's mind that he rules out divine special
revelation in a religious a priori, and this precludes his seriously
approaching Augustine. Kant was on the right track, Henry
says, when he emphasized that religion was a necessary part
of the moral conscience, but he was wrong to so skeptically
reduce human experience. Henry goes on: "This ruinous sacrifice of intelligible knowledge of God and external reality Kant
would have avoided had he espoused the biblical view of man
as God's created image and of a Logos-structured universe."[33]
Kant's latent agnosticism had its baneful influence on theological liberalism. The liberals forfeited objective revelation and
cognitive truth about God, says Henry, and they connected
divine revelation instead with novel theories of internal confrontation and subjectivity.

For Henry the Bible holds special historical redemptive revelation at the center, but apriorism of the Augustinian kind is
a support for Christianity in its apologetic task. All men are
created in the image of God (*imago Dei*) which explains the
general religious consciousness. A knowledge of God is a factor
in all knowledge. For the Christian the religious a priori is
grounded in the scripturally attested imago Dei alone. "Evangelical religion discusses man's primal experience only in the
context of a universal revelation of God which directly engages
man as a carrier of the created image of God in both mind
and conscience, and confronts him intelligibly in external nature
and history."[34] Henry stated: "Christianity grounds the possi-

bility of human knowledge solely in the agency of the transcendent Logos of God. By creation and preservation the divine Logos supplies and sustains all the forms and structures of finite existence, and fosters reliable human knowledge of God, of man's self and of other selves, and of the cosmic order."[35]

Grounded in revelation, then, the Augustinian apriorism is superior to its alternatives. It is superior to Plato's view which was dependent upon the soul's preexistence in the supernatural world, assuring validity only through the recollection of that world. It is superior to Kant's view which relegated religion to a mere reflex of morality, schematized in a theory of knowledge so restricted that no personal contact with God was possible.

Naturalism

Stated in a quite general way, naturalism is that view which denies the existence of any reality transcending nature. It is antisupernatural, opposing any deity or being apart from nature. Naturalism holds that the universe is self-existent, self-explanatory, self-operating, self-directing, purposeless, and deterministic. Western philosophy has always had a naturalistic element, but its contemporary hallmark has been its identification of reality with that which may be investigated by the natural sciences. Naturalists believe that all reality is temporal and spatial, but they by no means deny that there are many rich things in life such as beauty, value, consciousness, mind, and even religion. A number of liberal Protestants (e.g., Henry Nelson Wieman, 1884–1975) argued that God is the name for the eternal factor in experience which pushes man toward the good. This approach excludes Being as such from religious significance. Henry says: "Kant had argued that because man's mind is limited he cannot know the supernatural; the naturalists argue that there is no supernatural to know."[36]

The Western world is now deeply steeped in a secularistic outlook, says Henry, the result of the naturalistic conviction

that nature is man's widest and deepest environment. "The contemporary conceptualization of reality is deliberately anti-theological and antisupernaturalistic. The cultural *Geist* is tied wholly to natural processes and events; no category of transcendence is admissible except on naturalistic presuppositions. Notions of the eternal and divine, of revelation and spirit, are shoved aside as strange and shadowy."[37] Henry says that this replacement of biblical theism by naturalistic scientism represents one of the most radical restrictions of cultural mood in the history of human thought. Secular man has four theories about his world.[38]

First, he holds the theory of comprehensive contingency. That is, all reality has a provisional character. God is in exile, and there is no decisive reason for man or the world. "Comprehensive contingency means, in short, that reality is inherently irrational, nature is blind, history is unpredictable and chaotic."[39]

Second, secular man holds the theory of the total transiency of reality and experience. The temporal process is everything.

Third, he champions the radical relativity or interrelatedness of the entire historical process. Since everything is relative, no ultimate truth, morals, or authority can be ventured.

Fourth, he holds the theory of the absolute autonomy of man. Man does not need God: he is self-sufficient.

Henry uses the example of mass media (television, radio, and so on) to illustrate his point that contemporary Western life shows a growing distrust of final truth. Audio-visual technology is conditioning the public to an acceptance of moral decline and the eclipse of God by catering to the secular spirit. The media tends to focus on secular issues alone as being important, fostering an almost purely sensate misunderstanding of reality. "That God is a nonsensory reality is not what gives him 'a poor press'; justice, love, human rights and much else that makes the news are also nonsensory."[40] The media so batters the public with the sensate that it dulls the desire for the transcendent.

But, says Henry, when secular man tries to live consistently by his four convictions, "he drains his own life of meaning and worth and progressively empties his existence of everything that makes human life desirable."[41] The existential stress on the secularist is enormous. He cannot feel at home in a universe that is uncaring. Secular man talks about universal justice, neighbor love and cosmic duty, but these are norms of truth and value which his four theories cannot validate or accommodate. He can hardly reconcile his lifestyle with his view of the relativity of reality. The values that he associates with home, work, and society have no basis to exist if life is ultimately meaningless. "The dilemma of secular man is this:" Henry points out, "In order to escape the nihilism and personal worthlessness implicit in naturalism, he invests his life with sequestered meanings and values that naturalism cannot sustain."[42] To escape the God of the Bible secular man turns his finites into ultimates.

The secularist is caught in a self-contradiction: the four theories that he publicly professes are contradicted by the private life that he lives. He is guilty of a double standard: by the naturalistic credo which he affirms and reveres when it serves his purpose, and by hidden alternatives for action that he readily accepts whenever he prefers. Secular man privately knows that God exists, Henry says, so his naturalism is not a demand of reason but reflects an arbitrary conceptualization of reality. God is known in his creation (general revelation), and the secularist is secretly aware of this. The secularist knows that his conception of reality does not account for all his experience. Henry says: "Secular man does not miss out on general revelation, but he misses out on the joy of God and the goal of life."[43]

The "naturalistic temper," as Henry calls it, has reduced the choice for modern man to Christianity or nihilism, between the Logos of God and the ultimate meaninglessness of life. "The task of Christian leadership," he says, "is to confront modern man with the Christian world-life view as the revealed

conceptuality for understanding reality and experience, and to recall reason once again from the vagabondage of irrationalism and the arrogance of autonomy to the service of true faith."[44]

The Rise and Fall of Logical Positivism

The earlier empiricism and positivism led to the contemporary secular mentality. Logical positivism grew out of this earlier empiricism, but its emphasis on logical analysis of language distinguishes it from that movement. The characteristic features of logical positivism are emphasis on scientific attitudes, the unity of science, and every knowledge that is factual is connected with experience in such a way that verification or direct or indirect confirmation is possible. The task of philosophy was defined as analysis of knowledge, especially of science; the chief method to be used was the analysis of the language of science.

This school of philosophy was founded in the early 1920s and was first known as the Vienna Circle. A group of professional philosophers, mathematicians and natural scientists would gather periodically to apply the scientific method to their fields of specialization. The Vienna Circle "propounded a criterion for verification that recognized as 'meaningful' only statements that are either analytic or in principle supportable by observation. All other assertions were considered 'nonsensical'—although in some cases perhaps important nonsense."[45]

This school elevated the problem of the verification of beliefs from a threshold issue to central concern. These thinkers made the point that unless statements can be known to be either true or false, nothing either true or false is expressed by them. The statement, "God exists," was meaningless to them because it could not be observationally verified. They finally rejected as false all metaphysical statements since such statements had no literal significance.

Henry says that the evangelical apologist is always grateful

when attention is given to the canons of verification because the truths of Scripture are the bedrock of his faith. "If these theological assertions were shown to be not factually true, orthodox believers would be the very first to abandon their faith."[46] Evangelicals welcome the call for verification. The verificationists were right, Henry says, to demand conditions that validate or invalidate theological statements. But they were wrong when they recognized only empirical or sensory verification as meaningful. They were arbitrary in their rejection of theological statements: "they prejudicially narrowed the scope of meaningful cognitive statements."[47]

Positivism was logically vulnerable, and the verification principle as the sole arbiter of truth was doomed to an eventual death. It eventually became clear that when the positivist said that statements about God were cognitively meaningless because empirically unverifiable, he was being self-destructive. If statements about God are to be rejected, then the claim so dear to the positivists ("moral integrity in scientific research") is also without meaning. If theological and ethical statements are mere speculation, says Henry, then "all statements about past historical events, because empirically unverifiable, are shorn of truth-status. Assertions about past memories or about present subjective psychological desires and intentions lose cognitive validity for the same reason."[48]

The fatal blow for the positivists came when it was seen that their basic thesis—that only empirically verifiable statements are true—could not be accepted because it was empirically unverifiable. The positivists' claim that God-talk was nonsense itself became recognized as nonsense. Henry observes: "Logical positivists were convinced that they had leveled statements about God, sin and salvation to sheer nonsense; now they found themselves at the mourner's bench, lamenting the death of their very own dogma. Theologians had been accused of speciously presuming to have knowledge about an invisible spiritual world. Now positivists were indicted of arbitrarily vetoing all metaphysical assertions except their own unverifiable

epistemological bias. The searching questions about confirmation and verification were now turned back upon the positivists, who had sought unsuccessfully to guarantee their own solvency simply by bankrupting all rivals."[49]

The failure of logical positivism pointed up the spreading decline of trust in science. Henry points to the countercultural revolt as an example of the loss of faith in the legend of technocratic scientism that has beguiled Western secular man. The countercultural youth of the mid-1960s denied that the secular empirical world view told the truth about the ultimately real world. Henry observes: "Yet the profound significance of the countercultural revolt lies in its radical critique and rejection of the reigning scientific-mechanistic view which reduces reality to the empirically observable, in its protest against defining the real world only in impersonal technocratic categories, in its challenge to the reductive naturalism which, as Roszak well puts it, assimilates to technological civilization 'the whole meaning of Reason, Reality, Progress and Knowledge.' "[50]

Evangelicals can appreciate the counterculture's revolt against the reduction of external reality to impersonal categories, but they deplore its alienation from reason, its revolt against the rational revelation of God. "In welcoming the growing youth protest against merely technocratic reason, Christianity dare not accommodate a massive transition to contemporary irrationalism."[51] The reason that the protest movement failed, says Henry, lay in its lack of doctrinal logic and its lack of resources adequate to cope with human unregeneracy.

Mushrooming from within the youthful counterculture, the "Jesus People" took up the revolutionary fervor of the movement and gave it a missing spiritual and moral dimension. The Jesus People brought to the movement a personal fellowship with the risen Christ while boldly identifying with the protest against racial discrimination, wanton pollution of the environment, indifference to personal values, and technological totalitarianism. "But," says Henry, "the Jesus movement declared that sin, and not technocracy, is the root of all evil,

and disputed the countercultural assumption that man is basically sound and needs only to be liberated."[52] Henry warns, however, that the Jesus movement is characterized by theological sterility. He says that the Jesus movement "expressed evangelical fidelity not by affirming the Apostles Creed but by shouting Jesus cheers ('Give me a J! Give me an E! . . .')."[53] The Jesus movement seems hardly distinguishable from any other religiously motivated ideological rebellion, and its future is uncertain.

Henry argues that Christianity is a logically consistent system of revelational truths which, like any logical system, depends on undemonstrated axioms. Yet to demand verifiability of any system is proper. He pointed out that the verification principle of logical positivism could not verify itself, so positivism failed. But "public" verification by the scientific method is most attractive to the modern mind. What place, then, does Henry give to empirical considerations in verifying or falsifying theological statements? He says that scientific verification is virtually indispensable to modern life, and the evangelical Christian would be foolish to call it useless. We all see, hear, taste, and smell the same thing, he goes on. The difference comes in what we *think* about reality (our presuppositions). "The positivist thinks that sense data alone can relate us to the real world; the Hindu thinks that sense data are illusory and lead away from the real world; the Christian thinks that the phenomenal world is a real creation that witnesses to its Creator."[54]

Henry says that evangelicals are under ever-increasing pressure to use experiential validation for religious claims. The practical achievements of science have produced an empirically oriented culture; still, science is not a totally reliable guide in its objective description of nature. For example, the most basic laws of physics are subject to constant revision, and what scientist can be certain that the laws of this century will survive in the next century? In science, even a false theory may be highly useful for a time. Henry warns against shifting theology from logical consistency to an appeal to experience. He says:

"To make religious experience—whether the feelings, or volition, or moral sentiment, or even empirical arguments from
the world—the rationale for Judeo-Christian beliefs leads invariably and inevitably to a dilution of the biblical view."[55] Logical
consistency does not disregard experience, but it lifts the discussion of verification to a higher plane than the empirical. Some
questions simply cannot be tested by sense observation: science
has no final truth about light and electricity, let alone about
God.

When Henry's fellow evangelicals turn to historical empiricism to accredit Christian core-claims, he is sharp in his reply.
For example, the evangelical theologian John Warwick Montgomery promotes an empirically oriented apologetic: (1) The
historical method proves the Gospels to be trustworthy sources
of the life of Christ; (2) Christ's claim to be God rested on
his future resurrection from the dead; (3) Christ's resurrection
can be empirically validated; and (4) the Bible is revealed truth.
Henry says that Montgomery's "evidence" would needlessly
invalidate Christianity for the person who was unimpressed
with the empirical data. Empirical data means nothing without
presuppositions. The basic question remains: which presupposition is true? The final meaning of Christ is derived from supernatural revelation, not distilled from historical phenomena.

Henry's position is that empirical evidence should be presented in correlation with the Christian revelation-presupposi-
tion, and not independently of it. He says: "Although given
in the context of the space-time continuum, knowledge of God
must be gained—even if in concrete experience—from its own
proper ground, that is, from God's revelation in his Word."[56]
The Christian, armed with reason, never evades the question
of verifiability. For public verification and validation the evangelical apologist such as Henry turns to the authoritative witness
of scriptural revelation. "Scripture is grounded in the speaking
God as its inspiring source; it illumines Christ the living Logos
whose historical incarnation, atoning death, and resurrection
ministry crown the dramatic testimony of redemptive promise

and fulfillment; it is attested by the Holy Spirit's assurance in the believer's inner life."[57] Scripture is the Christian's ultimate principle of verification, and the logical consistency of revelational data the test of Christian truth.

III. Revelation: The God Who Speaks and Shows

For Henry, *the* crisis in modern theology is over the nature and reality of divine revelation. In volumes II, III, and IV of *God, Revelation and Authority* he attempts a comprehensive overview of revelation in biblical terms—the God who shows himself and speaks for himself. Fifteen theses, supplying a framework for the three volumes, summarize what he wants to say about divine revelation.

A Supernatural Initiative for Man's Benefit

Henry's first thesis is that revelation "is a divinely initiated activity, God's free communication by which he alone turns his personal privacy into a deliberate disclosure of his reality."[1] Only because God reveals himself is God-talk possible. If God had chosen to remain incommunicado we would know nothing whatever about him. Hence revelation is not only new, it is unexpected, apparently impossible, startling, an unannounced intrusion, and an awesome intervention. When God unmasks himself, man can only stand in wonder. *The* primary biblical

idea is that God makes himself known. "The essence of revelation is that God steps out of his hiddenness to disclose what would otherwise remain secret and unknown."[2]

The biblical view is that God reveals himself to man; the speculative view is that man unveils God. Outside of revelation the divine is an ontological inference from the physical world, as from human psychology. Our modern period, says Henry, is characterized by a rejection of the self-revealedness of God by "how I found God" explorers. For more than a century philosophy of religion has tried to argue the case for theistic personalism while ignoring the question of whether God himself has addressed revelation to man. Henry remarks: "Nowhere is the repudiation of Christian belief in recent modern learning more insistent than in the rejection in philosophical and theological treatises of the very idea of transcendent divine revelation."[3] Henry is scornful of both those inside and outside the church who evade the centrality of revelation because, he says, they are doomed to intellectual inconclusiveness. It is impossible to teach anything about God except on the basis of divine revelation; the world does not know God through its own wisdom. Theological vacillation on the subject of revelation is spiritual rebellion. There is no rational basis for unbelief in God's self-manifestation. "Erecting the case for theism apart from divine disclosure is like venturing to hatch a live chicken from an empty eggshell, a highly imaginative but futile project."[4]

Henry's second thesis is that God's "revelation is given for human benefit, offering us privileged communion with our Creator in the kingdom of God."[5] Out of his will and grace, God offers man a place in his kingdom. God discloses himself in order that we may know him as he is, have personal fellowship with him, accept his forgiveness and offer of new life, and escape the catastrophic judgment for our sins. God, as the Creator and Ruler of all, has graciously enlisted us in the historical expansion of his kingdom from heaven to earth.

Just as God has personally given himself, he must be person-

ally accepted. God's revelation is not automatically saving; good news alone does not redeem. The unbeliever, confidently persisting in his own ingenuity and good works, misses God's kingdom both now and later. Revelation is for the sake of reconciliation. Modern philosophy, says Henry, has been preoccupied with the knowledge of God as a theoretical problem but disinterested in reconciliation between a holy God and sinful man. The modern theory assumed that to be aware of revelation was in itself redemptive, substituting the problem of ignorance for the problem of guilt. Henry says: "But knowledge of the truth of God is by no means synonymous with personal salvation."[6] Without personal appropriation, revelation brings salvation to no one. "The immediate correlate of divine revelation is not salvation but knowledge; the consequence of that knowledge is either salvation or judgment."[7]

Transcendent, Coherent Disclosure

Henry's third thesis is that God's "revelation does not completely erase God's transcendent mystery, inasmuch as God the Revealer transcends his own revelation."[8] God is both hidden and revealed. What God has not chosen to reveal about himself we can never know. What God has revealed about himself does not exhaust his being or activity. God has revealed himself truly though not exhaustively. God speaks and acts intelligibly, and his revelation falls inside the sphere of the rational and true. The biblical writers were wholly dependent upon God's self-disclosure (they were not divine themselves), and their knowledge of God was true though partial. There is no divine spark in man that qualifies him permanently to be a means of divine revelation. Humility, therefore, is very becoming to the evangelical who often, because of his confidence in rational revelation, assumes that his theology is as trustworthy as Scripture. Henry says: "The inspired Scriptures remain unique and normative over against even the most devout evangelical expositions of the revealed Word of God."[9]

Henry's fourth thesis is that the "very fact of disclosure by the one living God assures the comprehensive unity of divine revelation."[10] An incomplete revelation does not imply an incoherent revelation. What God has revealed is trustworthy and consistent, or it would not be revelation. Since God is one, sovereign, the Creator and Lord of all, the comprehensive unity of his revelation is assured. Polytheistic paganism was schizophrenic, playing off one god against another and frustrating the possibility of a unified revelation. Biblical monotheism did away with a divided disclosure. God's revelation of himself has been progressive (from Old Testament to New Testament), but it has remained a unity. The full unity will not be disclosed until the climactic end-time, the eschaton.

An Amazing Variety

Henry's fifth thesis is: "Not only the occurrence of divine revelation but its very nature, content and variety are exclusively God's determination."[11] God in his sovereign freedom determines both the form and content of his self-disclosure. He has given himself in a variety of ways: in both general and special revelation, in nature and in history, in the mind and conscience of man, in multiple ways in the Bible, and in Jesus of Nazareth. Each manner of disclosure has been different, and in the eschaton he will reveal himself in still another way. God seems to have already ventured almost every pattern of disclosure short of his final eschatological revelation. God alone sets the terms by which we know him. "Even evangelical orthodoxy," says Henry, "by extreme fundamentalist statements that identify God's revelation exclusively with the Bible has at times obscured the full range of divine disclosure."[12] But, he warns, no theologian has the right to prize and proclaim only certain facets of divine disclosure while eliminating one or another.

Karl Barth, for example, was wrong to deny that God had revealed himself in nature (a general revelation), because by

so doing he denied the basis of moral and spiritual accountability, nullified the biblical witness, and obscured mankind's original relationship to God. In a famous controversy with Emil
Brunner during the 1930s Barth so reduced the scope of revelation that he claimed that any knowledge of God not derived
from Christ is antichrist.

The scholastics were equally wrong when they demoted special revelation to an inferior position within general revelation.
For Thomas Aquinas the existence of God rested solely on
sense observation from the universe. Again, modern naturalism
errs when it sees nature only as mechanical and nonteleological.
Naturalism's impersonal nature arbitrarily eclipses the supernatural, falsifies the natural world, and shuts out purpose, meaning
and value. Henry says that general revelation is the presupposition of redemptive revelation, and that special revelation clari-
fies general revelation. " 'Hear God!' is the biblical message,
not 'Listen to nature!' Nature is God's created order, and in
nature God presents himself."[13] Special revelation presupposes
a general revelation, but not a natural theology (a faith in
God established solely on the basis of general revelation).

Henry says that although the Bible does not define for us
the precise content of the image of God, it does teach that
man bears God's image. Traditionally God's image in man
has been identified with a cohesive unity of rational, moral
and spiritual aptitudes. For Henry, the rational or cognitive
aspect has logical priority. He states: "Only if man is logically
lighted, and not simply morally or spiritually involved independent of intelligence, can he be meaningfully aware of responsible relationships. . . . All distinctively human experience
presupposes the law of noncontradiction and the irreducible
distinction between truth and error."[14] Any beclouding of the
reason will confuse the other elements in the *imago*. Man's
sin hinders his psychological and moral activity, and hinders
his ability to think correctly, but it does not invalidate the
law of contradiction. Man's rational competence survived the
Fall. Henry says: "However serious its consequences and how-

ever far-reaching its effects, the fall of man, therefore, did not involve man's total loss of knowledge of God, nor his rational competence or ethical accountability. Although sullied by the fall, the divine image in man was not totally shattered."[15]

God Names Himself

Henry's sixth thesis is that "God's revelation is uniquely personal both in content and form."[16] God as personal subject originates revelation and intends it for persons. The formula for divine self-presentation is the naming of God's proper name—"I am Yahweh." By the audible self-disclosure of his name, and by the strict prohibition of any visible material representation of himself, God declared his unrivaled incomparability. Israel understood this to mean that all other gods were unworthy of worship. The supernatural appearances in which God directly communicated himself and his message in the Old Testament (theophany) were but preparations for his monumental presentation in Jesus Christ. In giving himself in his name, God gives intelligent, rational, propositional truth about himself.

Unfortunately, says Henry, neoorthodox theology has left the impression in modern theology that God's self-disclosure is "nonintellectual and nonpropositional; that God is never an object of conceptual thought; that theological assertions are nonobjectifying; that personal faith in God excludes mental assent to theological doctrines."[17] Neoorthodoxy, he says, distorted God's self-presentation and made revelation uninformative. This led neoorthodoxy to exile God from nature and history, to lose the supernatural, and to cast doubt on man's significance in the cosmos.

God names himself; unbelief misnames God by calling him names—"sometimes blasphemous, sometimes ridiculous, always somewhat derogatory—indeed, as a refusal to identify him by his true name."[18] The misnamed god of speculative philosophy and of nonbiblical religions is the history of man's

refusal to allow God to name himself. Philosophy has wavered between calling God the "nameless one" and ascribing specific names to him. Modern naturalism rejects a personal God and introduces him—if at all—in terms of impersonal stuff. Nonbiblical religions have not censored God's name, but they have misread and mispronounced it, remodeling it into patterns of polytheism and pantheism.

The biblical names for God are synonyms for his essential nature, perfections, and activity. Henry says that "biblical theology and lively interest in God's names stand or fall together."[19] In the Bible, God's name and nature are identified. "The name audibly introduces or presents a person whose character would otherwise be unsure or unknown."[20] God gives his true self in his name. The many names that God uses for himself give an enlarging revelation of his nature. Through the diversity of divinely authorized names God discloses his full name. "Since God has stipulated the biblical names, they afford knowledge which, although incomplete, is nonetheless true and adequate," says Henry.[21] In giving his name, then, God gives authentic, intelligent information about his nature and ways. God progressively disclosed the inner secrets of his being in the long historical sweep of the biblical epochs. Finally, in "sending his beloved Son, YAHWEH discloses his holy intimacy as Father."[22]

God has disclosed himself historically and progressively, giving both a literary and theological unity to the Bible. God's later disclosures of his name never contradict his earlier disclosures, and the differences in divine names provide no justification for a theory of different documents. Henry says that evangelical expositors of progressive divine revelation have no need of a documentary source theory such as the so-called J-E-D-P hypothesis. (This theory, for example, says that the Old Testament is made up of divergent literary strands, and that later editors correlated and synthesized its content. Thus the statement that God was known to Abraham by the name YAHWEH in Genesis 15:2,7 can be harmonized with the statement

in Exodus 6:3 that he was not known to Abraham by that name.) Henry holds that the theory of editorial revisers is not needed to give religious unity to the Old Testament; rather, progressive divine revelation is its real source of unity. He says that "the evangelical counterassault on higher critical documentary views holds that a proper understanding of Exodus 6 is consistent with the patriarchal use in Abraham's time of YAHWEH."[23] Abraham, he says, knew the name Yahweh, but not its significance; its significance became known only at the exodus. Mosaic history supplements patriarchal history, but does not contradict it. Modern scholarship misses this only because it is biased against transcendent divine revelation.

The proper name *par excellence* for God in the Old Testament is Yahweh. Of the five main interpretations for the name, Henry chooses the following: "In our view, YAHWEH is the revelation of the Eternal, the independent sovereign of all, who pledges in free grace to come to the redemptive rescue of his chosen people. *The God who is*, who is *eternally there*, will personally manifest his redemptive presence in Israel's midst."[24] The other principal name for God in the Old Testament is Elohim, the creator and ruler. "The double name YAHWEH-ELOHIM correlates the comprehensive work of God in creative power and redemptive grace, even as the New Testament depicts the LOGOS as the agent both in creation and in redemption."[25]

The New Testament understands the name of God and Jesus Christ to be one and the same. Christians replaced the variety of Old Testament names by the simple term God (Theos), and the meaning of the divine name is related to the revelation in Christ. More than a hundred names and titles are applied to Christ's work and person. Christ becomes the historical redeemer Yahweh—past, present, and future. "By the realities of New Testament revelation the apostolic community is impelled to stress not simply God's proper names, but also the personal names that disclose the inner secret of the divine triune God in whom the God-man is now forever present and forever active in glorified human nature."[26]

Historical Revelation

Henry's seventh thesis is that "God reveals himself not only universally in the history of the cosmos and of the nations, but also redemptively within this external history in unique saving acts."[27] Evangelicals, he says, insist that certain specific historical acts are integrated to revelation, that sound historical method and intellectual honesty are expected, and that a negative verdict concerning historical revelation, if justified, would invalidate the Christian religion. Evangelicals claim that not only does the God of the Bible reveal himself in history, but that biblical religion gave rise to the idea of history, that Christians have always insisted that history is the arena of God's revelation, that Christians have traditionally espoused the relevance of the historical method in approaching the Bible, and that only since the Enlightenment have certain theologies become antihistorical. Evangelicals believe that divine revelation is historically given and historically investigatable.

Modern historiographers, essentially positivist, have excluded the supernatural as a significant explanatory referent. Henry quotes with approval the thesis of his former teacher, Gordon H. Clark, that what distinguishes Christianity from all other religions is that God, who is independent of the world, is personally active in history. Clark has three principles in his philosophy of history: God controls history; God is directing history to a final climax; God personally acts in history.

To those positivists who say that biblical events cannot be verified, Clark replies that no event of history whatever is subject to absolute verification, whether it be biblical or nonbiblical. To put biblical events in a separate category from secular events (and thus reject biblical events) is wholly arbitrary and unjustified. The existence of secular historical personages is not assuredly certain. But, Clark holds, the denial of absolute historical certainty does not lead to skepticism: the historical aspects of Christianity can be defended. What both Henry and Clark object to are those modern theologians (existential and

neoorthodox) who apply a skepticism to the biblical accounts that they do not apply to secular history. Henry says: "It is impossible to apply less stringent criteria to secular history than to the biblical writings unless one is prejudiced against the historical representations of the Bible."[28]

Unlike the laws of logic, historical events do not lend themselves to final proof. Final certainty about events is not derived from historical investigation. Events must be interpreted: facts cannot speak for themselves. History is not written without presuppositions; history writers reflect their presuppositions by what they select to serve as evidence. Henry says: "Evangelical Christianity in no way presumes to regard historical investigation, now or in the past, as the sufficient method of knowing the truth of revelation."[29] The meaning-scheme that one imposes on history is an act of faith. The Christian gets his meaning-scheme from the Bible, the secularist gets his from a positivist philosophy. The Bible tells the Christian which historical events give the clue to interpret all events. "What secular historiography cannot do, inspired Scripture can do and does: it declares the direction and goal of history and identifies the great events and their redemptive meaning. Divine revelation is the epistemic source and Scripture the methodological principle of the Christian interpretation of history."[30]

Scriptural truths are historical revelation in the sense that they were revealed at a certain place and time. Scripture is a record of historical events divinely interpreted. "The biblical context sets historical acts and their meaning in an intelligibly consistent framework that includes prior knowledge about the nature, purpose and promises of God."[31] The biblical writers were concerned about historical precision. Thus historical evidence is congruous with revelational truth, although it is not the source of faith. Historical positivism is inherently incapable of coping with transcendent supernatural concerns because it has a covert commitment to practical atheism. A redemptive historical act plus its meaning constitute biblical revelation; historical research alone cannot guarantee that the event hap-

pened or give its theological meaning. "Revelation is the act plus its communicated meaning; both historical act and its interpretation belong to the totality of revelation."[32]

Modern theology has seen a fierce debate over the relation between revelation and history. The positions range from those who claim that all history reveals God to those who claim that no historical event has any revelational value. Henry reviews and examines a number of these theologians and their claims, e.g., Karl Barth, Rudolf Bultmann, Oscar Cullmann, Jurgen Moltmann, and Wolfhart Pannenberg. Henry says that evangelical theology welcomes several of their emphases: God's revelation is given in external, objective history. All history is open to God's activity, and revelation is a quality of all historical events. Revelation can be grasped by normal reason and investigated, even Christ's resurrection, even though it cannot be demonstrably verified by historical research. And history will climax with the final judgment of Christ.

At the same time, Henry says, evangelical Christianity must reject other of their correlative emphases: that history excludes the supernatural, thereby making knowledge of God indirect, miracles suspect, and relegating God's self-revelation to the eschatological future; that revelation is not conceptual-verbal; and the contradictory assertions that the burden of proof for revelation rests upon the historian or that the historian cannot investigate revelation. Henry says that evangelical theology, rather, affirms: revelation is not dependent upon historical investigation, and that God discloses himself in other ways than in history; historical revelation and biblical interpretation are a unity; sinful humans need the Bible to understand revelation; revelation through the Logos is direct, objective, and cognitively valid information about God and his purpose.[33]

God's Personal Incarnation

Henry's eighth thesis is that the "climax of God's special revelation is Jesus of Nazareth, the personal incarnation of

God in the flesh; in Jesus Christ the source and content of revelation converge and coincide."[34] God's mystery is no longer concealed because God has revealed it. Unlike the ancient mystery religions which promoted the notion that the divine secrets were only for the initiated few, God's secret is now an "open secret." This revealed mystery "is that the historical mediator of Salvation, Jesus of Nazareth, intrinsically carries the dignity of the personal cosmic creator and of the only mediator of redemption, and as Risen Lord makes the lives of redeemed sinners—Jew and Gentile alike—his dwelling place."[35] Christ has fulfilled the Old Testament prophetic hopes, replacing the past days with the last days. The very *last* day remains future but draws ever closer, placing our world on alert that the coming Judge of our race is at hand.

Jesus agreed with the Jewish view of his day that the Old Testament was sacred, authoritative, normative, and permanent. But, says Henry, Jesus altered the prevailing Jewish attitude toward the Old Testament in at least five ways. First, he judged tradition by the Scripture. Second, he claimed to be the personal fulfillment of the messianic expectations. Third, he claimed an authority equal to the Old Testament and he expounded the inner significance of the Law. Fourth, he inaugurated a "new covenant" and taught that the Holy Spirit gave an internal moral power. Fifth, "he committed his apostles to the enlargement and completion of the Old Testament canon through their proclamation of the Spirit-given interpretation of his life and work."[36]

Henry will have nothing to do with that contemporary branch of critical biblical scholarship which skeptically disowns the originality of Jesus. He says that there is no contrast between the trustworthiness of Jesus' word and the word of the biblical writers about Jesus. This kind of distinction cannot be made because only unitary revelation is given in the Bible. Some critics are inclined to cross out the words of Jesus as alleged literary innovations of the early church. This, Henry says, is to replace the words of Jesus with the deforming theories of

twentieth-century critics. "It is fruitless to contemplate Jesus and the apostles as rival foundations or authorities; in affirming the Christian faith, moreover, some things (not all) that Jesus said, and some things (not all) that Paul said, are central."[37] No rigid boundary can be placed between the revelation in the person of Christ and the written word of the Bible.

The church has always held that "the Old Testament is Christian": the apostles were right to find Christ in the texts. "Nowhere does the New Testament assume or allow a breach between itself and the Old Testament. The disciples and apostles comprehend the coming and ministry of Jesus as a fulfillment of the ancient prophecies."[38] But since the world obviously remains unredeemed since Jesus came, modern day Jewry rejects the messianic claims of the church for Jesus. Contemporary Jewry considers the Christian appeal to prophecy on behalf of Jesus to be a misguided use of the Old Testament.

Henry says that evangelicals through a lack of concern for public justice have contributed to this attitude in Jewry. "While evangelicals avoid internalizing religion completely, they have not in the present century escaped largely privatizing it; by making individual renewal the dominant concern, they lessen interest in the messianity of Jesus among those who stress that the prophetic vision of Messiah embraces universal justice and peace as irreducible concerns of the righteous community."[39] But, says Henry, the New Testament insists as vigorously as Judaism that not all the Old Testament promises have as yet been publicly fulfilled. Many of the predicted blessings of the messianic age await a future fulfillment. Judaism rejected the Christian two-stage nature of messianic fulfillment—suffering and salvation for the Gentiles before a final messianic glory. Evangelicals fault contemporary Jewry for ignoring the predicted suffering of the coming Messiah, for devaluing inner spiritual aspects of the messianic ministry, and for blurring the substitutionary work of the Messiah.

Jesus grounded his predictions of his resurrection from the dead in the Old Testament Scriptures, and the disciples, failing

to understand this grounding, missed the force of Jesus' sayings about his crucifixion. "Jesus related his references to impending crucifixion and resurrection to a divine necessity shown in the fulfillment of prophecy concerning God's purpose of salvation."[40] Jesus taught that Good Friday and Easter were known in advance to the ancient prophets. The disciples failed to understand because they did not comprehend the prophetic writings. Even the most technically qualified of Jesus' enemies (scribes, Pharisees, Sadducees) conceded that his tomb was empty. The disciples of Jesus admitted that they were inexcusably dull in heeding Jesus' warnings about crucifixion-resurrection. Contemporary objections to his resurrection "stem from metaphysical requirements arbitrarily imposed by those who cannot, apart from revelation, know either the entire course of history or the whole secret of the cosmos."[41]

The Mediating Logos

Henry's ninth thesis is that the "mediating agent in all divine revelation is the Eternal Logos—preexistent, incarnate, and now glorified."[42] He is the sole and unique mediator of God's revelation, the giver of creation life, redemption life, and resurrection life. He carries out the executive will of God in revelation, creation, incarnation, redemption and judgment. The Logos as the coordinator of divine revelation is no novelty but has the fullest biblical sanction. The term Logos as a title for Christ is not peculiar to the prologue of John's Gospel but is consonant with the orientation of the entire Bible. The Logos is the mind of God incarnate in Jesus Christ. The Logos is central to the Godhead.

Ontologically, the Logos is decisively centered in the incarnate and now exalted Christ. In general revelation (in history, nature, and reason) every man is confronted with some truth of the Logos. Scripture comprehensively and objectively states this truth to judge and correct man's intellectual and moral truancy. The Logos is experienced daily by secular man as a

fact of life. "Despite the naturalistic relativization of life, secular man prizes perspectives which link him obliquely yet inescapably in relationships to the Logos of God."[43] This emphasis upon the Logos as mediator of revelation guards against two errors: that of reducing all revelation to the revelation found in Jesus of Nazareth; and that of treating general revelation as independent of the Logos who became incarnate in Jesus of Nazareth.

Any alternative to this revelation-giving Logos Henry labels a "phantom logos," a defunct counterfeit born merely to die. The intellectual history of the Western world has seen many conjectural alternatives to the Logos of revelation based on structures immanent in nature or a priori inherent in man. This long succession of imposter-*Logoi* has finally reached the contemporary period which is resigned to a truant or absentee-*Logos.* This desertion of the Logos of revelation, says Henry, has led to an intellectual disaster, the loss of the fixed meaning of existence, and the giving up on the enduring worth of man. "If we can learn anything from these speculative or mythological logoi of rationalistic philosophy and religious theory, it is simply that each and every such phantom-*logos* has its day and is soon spent."[44] The alternatives are either nihilism or the Nazarene.

Neoorthodox theology (one of Henry's favorite targets) falls short of evangelical adequacy in its formulation of man's knowledge of God. Neoorthodoxy focused on the Word of God in divine confrontation of man, only to develop this emphasis, says Henry, in a way patently alien to the Bible. It pitted the Logos against the Scripture and refused to allow the Word of revelation to be known as an object of reason. Neoorthodoxy would not relate logic to the Logos, and on that basis demeaned propositions as carriers of truth. This has finally led to the American "death of God" theology which proclaimed the total irrelevance of the transcendent, leaving only private truth to establish all truth. Henry insists that if theology places a logical gulf between human conceptions and God as the object of reli-

gious knowledge, the end result will be skepticism. Either the law of noncontradiction is necessarily true of the externally real world, or we cannot assert any belief at all. "We are therefore back to the emphasis that the laws of logic belong to the *imago Dei*, and have ontological import."[45] The language of redemption and revelation is subject to the same laws of logic as all other language. Any kind of thought that has truth as its aim—whether prescientific or scientific, religious or non-religious—must conform to the laws of correct thinking. The logic of Christian theism is not formulated upon a special "exotic" or peculiar language but upon the ultimate context of the Logos of God.

Revelation As Rational-Verbal Communication

Henry's tenth thesis is that "God's revelation is rational communication conveyed in intelligible ideas and meaningful words, that is, in conceptual-verbal form."[46] Evangelical orthodoxy teaches that God reveals himself intelligibly in a variety of modes: "in his objective disclosure in nature and history, in his disclosure also internally to reason and conscience, in the entire content of this general revelation along with that of God's special redemptive disclosure—consummated in Jesus Christ—stated authoritatively and perspicuously in Scripture."[47] Neoorthodoxy drifted away from this understanding, putting the emphasis instead on divine noncognitive self-disclosure consummated either in the present or in a past event such as the resurrection of Christ. Neoorthodoxy pitted personal revelation against propositional revelation (a personal but noncognitive confrontation between man and God) that became the almost universal understanding of revelation in contemporary Protestant theology. Henry observes: "The theory that revelation conveys no information but is only a perspective-altering phenomenon supplies no rational basis for distinguishing between true and false, good and evil, normal and abnormal perspectives."[48] The device of embellishing myth as a revela-

tional concept does not ultimately solve the problem, says Henry, because the modern mind takes myth to be devoid of intellectual claims. Neoorthodoxy's separation of historical revelation and rational revelation was a disaster for the recent doctrinal fortunes of Christianity. Evangelicals, on the other hand, hold that redemptive historical acts and the divinely revealed meaning of the acts are of equal importance. Biblical revelation is essentially a mental conception, a rational and intelligible communication from the mind and will of God addressed to the mind and will of man. "In whatever mode God speaks," says Henry, "his divine revelation is a mental act . . . . Every mediating alternative not only sacrifices the cognitive significance of divine revelation, but also dissolves revelation itself into a vaporous and insignificant concept."[49]

The biblical faith presupposes an intelligible revelation that has compelling supportive evidence. For the evangelical this implies reasonable sentences and propositional truths in contrast to divine disclosure as basically nonmental. "The biblical witness nowhere depicts God's self-revelation as conceptually imprecise and verbally inexpressible."[50] Henry charges neoorthodoxy with depicting the Christian revelation as paradox and logical contradiction. Karl Barth even implied that revelation and irrationalism are either next of kin or allies. This diluted the importance that should be attached to doctrine or dogma. "Neo-Protestants no longer consider biblical doctrine a *test* of theological truth, but rather a 'testimony' to Truth (the personal Christ)."[51] Barth rejected any attempt to make a rational defense of the Word of God. Henry agrees that no man has an exhaustive knowledge of God even on the basis of revelation, but affirms, on the other hand, the rational character of divine disclosure and the usefulness of human language as a communicator of truth.

With the question of the significance of language coming to dominate recent modern philosophy, Henry and the evangelicals have had to cope with the concerns of religious language. Henry makes the point that the Creator God of the Bible quali-

fies man for communication with himself and others. The *imago dei* guarantees meaning to human language and God-talk. Evangelicals are on the side of any attempt to communicate the truth about God in precise, intelligible statements whose meaning is sure. Long ago Augustine and Calvin insisted that theology requires clear and careful statements. Evangelical language, Henry charges, has sometimes been scandalously loose and obscure, needlessly confusing the hearer or reader about basic religious beliefs. "The doctrines of the Trinity and of the Atonement, for example, are frequently presented in a manner that actually multiplies intellectual problems. . . ."[52] Evangelicals should welcome the recent trend in analytic philosophy (or linguistic analysis) to eliminate vagueness in language and promote clear and definable meaning. Some linguistic analysts are hostile to supernatural theism, but this is no reason to shun the task of clarifying concepts.

The linguistic function of theological statements is to convey some literal truth or information about God and the invisible world. Religious language is subject to the same laws of meaning as all other language. There is no special logic for religious language. Alternative formulations to the literal meaning of theistic statements, stressing instead the analogical, pragmatic, behavioral, pictorial, dialectical, existential, doxological, and political significance of religious language, are not logically persuasive. Language is a whole, lending itself to various fields of interest, including religion. There is no "unique" religious language. Biblical language is logically and verbally related to everyday expressions. "Theology designates a distinctive range of reality, and in view of this has a special vocabulary, as does every science by virtue of its area of concentration and specialization, but theological statements do not on that account require a peculiar meaning-import or truth-significance."[53] Revelational truth obeys the logical rules governing all verbal propositions of whatever field.

Henry asserts that religious language, along with language elsewhere, has a basic cognitive function. Ordinary language

serves as a means for God and man to commune with each other. Language is a gift of God to man to facilitate intelligible communion between man and God and communication of the truth. The immediate consequence of this for Henry is that God gives verbal information, a propositional-verbal divine revelation. The living God of the Bible who speaks conveys precise verbal instructions concerning his present doings as well as his future purpose and past creation. The contrast that neoorthodoxy drew between personal and propositional revelation, between God and truths about God, was a false distinction that undermined any basis for confidence in person-revelation. To be intelligible, to be true or false, revelation must be a communication of sharable truth.

For Henry, a proposition "is a verbal statement that is either true or false; it is a rational declaration capable of being either believed, doubted or denied."[54] In the sense that God communicated himself in terms of cognitive truths, the Bible is a propositional revelation. A contrast between God's self-revelation and propositional truths in the Bible is unnecessary. The Bible, conveying its message in many literary forms such as letters, poetry and parable, prophecy and history, stresses that the truth conveyed by God has conceptual adequacy. There is no basis in the Scripture for the notion that God's revelation is nonpropositional, personal truth. Evangelicals do not insist that all divine disclosures are propositional, but that the biblical revelation is capable of being formulated propositionally. Propositions are the minimal units of meaning and truth.

IV. The Bible As Authoritative Norm

Henry concludes Vol. III of *God, Revelation and Authority* with the assertion that God's revelation is rational communication conveyed in intelligible ideas and meaningful words, that is, in conceptual-verbal form. This leads him in a natural way to a treatment of the significance of Scripture in Vol. IV.

What are some standards that any current book on the authority of Scripture must meet, whether it be evangelical or otherwise? First, it must offer a paradigm of how best to come to terms with the Enlightenment. The Enlightenment changed orthodox theology as nothing did before or after, and orthodoxy has never fully recovered from the shattering upset. Henry is a theological product of the post-Enlightenment orthodox-liberal debate that has warped evangelical thought. That debate raised the problem of authority in a scientific age of a book (the Bible) written in a prescientific age. One of the many ideas that characterized the Enlightenment was the necessity for literary and historical criticism of all documents of the past, including the Bible. Henry's task is not to ignore the Enlightenment (as fundamentalism does) nor to capitulate to it (as liberalism

does). When fundamentalism ignored the Enlightenment it committed itself to obscurantism; namely, anything about the Bible that is addressed by modern learning is denied. Fundamentalism continually castigates biblical criticism, modern geology, the theory of evolution, and scientific anthropology. When liberalism surrendered to the Enlightenment, that is, when it accepted uncritically the development and legitimacy of modern scientific history and the rights of biblical criticism, liberalism surrendered biblical authority. Henry's task is to systematically interact with modern knowledge and agree with the positive gains of the Enlightenment while at the same time preserving the evangelical doctrine of the integrity of the Scripture.

Second, any book on the authority of Scripture must deal realistically with the humanity of the Bible. The biblical scholars of the Enlightenment so highlighted the humanity of Scripture that they embarrassed its divinity. And since then both the humanity and the divinity of Scripture have been difficult to bring into focus: the more humanity has been emphasized, the more divinity has been neglected; and the more divinity has been stressed, the more humanity has been ignored. Fundamentalism put a tight lid on the humanity of Scripture and fell into obscurantism, while the liberals overstressed the humanity and surrendered the Bible as a unique book. Henry's task is to speak to evangelicals who have traditionally hedged the Bible's humanity by surrounding it with divinity. Henry must guard evangelicals from denying the validity of modern learning (obscurantism) by honestly confronting the unabridged humanity of sacred Scripture. Evangelicals must avoid a docetic Bible (fully divine, but not fully human) by taking its languages, cultures and human side in stride. If God is not ashamed of the humanity of the Bible, why should evangelicals be?

Third, in dealing with biblical authority Henry must help evangelicals come to grips with historical criticism where the humanity of Scripture is dealt with most exclusively. Fundamentalism says that if a theologian accepts biblical criticism he

cannot accept the integrity of Scripture. Liberalism capitulated to the Enlightenment, never challenged the rights of biblical criticism, and gave up the ideas of the divine origin, inspiration and traditional modes of interpreting Scripture. Evangelicals, no friends of biblical criticism, have a very guarded attitude toward it. They tend to dismiss any adverse biblical criticism by saying that: critical theories are too subjective (they rapidly come and go); they hold a liberal theology which distorts their interpretation of the facts; or they are betrayed by skeptical philosophical presuppositions. The historical critical method is still a burning issue among evangelicals and Henry must help them to a valid working hypothesis that will interact with it. Henry cannot gloss biblical criticism and still interact with modern knowledge—he must give equal rights to historical science as understood in modern terms and to the theological integrity of the historical element in the Bible.

At 674 pages, Henry's Vol. IV of *God, Revelation and Authority* is half the length of John Calvin's *Institutes of the Christian Religion*. A major undertaking of the highest quality, it has already attracted the interest of evangelicals as the broadest and most learned treatment of the authority of the Bible among them. It is the standard against which young theologs will test their strength, and a challenge to evangelicals to have done with superficial analysis. In addition, it is the best evangelical statement on inerrancy of the Scriptures, and an accurately nuanced approach to final authority that most evangelicals can assent to. It is a closely argued and informative book that will make heavy demands on the average reader.

The Bible As the Authoritative Norm

Henry's eleventh thesis is that the "Bible is the reservoir and conduit of divine truth."[1] For the Christian the Bible is the ongoing source of reliable, objective knowledge concerning God's nature and ways, and should be the Christian's authorita-

tive written record and interpretation of God's revelatory deeds. Only the Bible offers a comprehensive overview of God's will and purpose in the past, present and future.

But contemporary civilization is caught in a revolt against authority. Respect for authority is being challenged on every front, and the Bible has been caught in this general defiance. Both God and his Bible are increasingly edged out of the world. Atheism is the automatic point of departure for a radically secularized culture. Modern man, presuming to reject all finalities, is merely repeating an ancient revolt against spiritual and moral absolutes. "The difference between ancient and modern man is mainly this: Adam stood too close to human beginnings to call his revolt anything but sin, whereas contemporary man rationalizes his revolt in the name of evolution and progress."[2] Both evangelical and nonevangelical Christians are acutely aware of the dilemma concerning biblical authority. In spite of the many attempts to discredit it, the Bible still stands at the heart of the human dispute over absolutes, and multitudes of people still retain a sense of reverence for its message. Henry says: "The more one contemplates recent alienation from the Bible, the more one is inclined to say that its great emphases have never been demonstrably discredited."[3]

All authority is derived from God. In the New Testament we see that God's power and authority are given to Jesus Christ and under him, to his disciples. This power finally comes to rest in Scripture because the Bible is the only knowledge-basis we have for the person and work of Christ. Henry says: "The first claim to be made for Scripture is not its inerrancy nor even its inspiration, but its authority. Standing in the forefront of prophetic-apostolic proclamation is the divine authority of Scripture as the Word of God."[4] Both prophets and apostles claimed to be God's chosen and authorized spokesmen, and behind them stood Christ, the Apostle of God. The prophets and apostles were so confident that they were speaking for God that to deny them was to call God a liar. Christianity is a religion of the "Book," although it may seem incongruous

to speak of God's words in human writings. "The same sense of incongruity overtakes us when on 'the first Palm Sunday' we behold deity astride a donkey."[5]

Henry charges that the twentieth-century church has been confronted by an array of influential theologians who profess loyalty to Scripture but who nonetheless oppose much of what Scripture actually teaches. They appeal to Scripture only in a selective and restricted way and thus evade the authority of Scripture. Henry grants that the Bible does not treat every realm of human inquiry (it is not a textbook on the planets, botany, economics, and so on) because its primary concern is theological and ethical; but on whatever theme it speaks it is not to be relativized.

The failure to honor Scripture as authoritative conceptual-verbal revelation of the nature of God became the pitfall of neoorthodoxy. Even some evangelicals, says Henry, have become timid in their defense of biblical authority. He says, for example, that some "evangelical scholars now apologize for aspects of biblical ethics that are out of tune with the culture of our times, and theorize that apostolic teaching shared the cultural outlook of the past at specific points and must now be superseded by a supposedly superior view more compatible with contemporary insights."[6] Henry agrees that some apostolic admonitions were intended only for a local or particular historical situation, but he says that this provides no basis for clouding the eternal truth of any and all argumentation. Henry is alarmed that some of his fellow evangelicals are saying that the New Testament writers in some respects taught as doctrine what in fact was a reflection of the cultural milieu in which they lived. For example, Henry objects to Paul K. Jewett's 1975 book, *Man As Male and Female.* In it the Fuller Theological Seminary professor writes that the Pauline passages which teach woman's subordination to man are culturally conditioned rabbinic traditions that Jesus had already transcended. Henry says that this approach of Jewett breaches the divine inspiration of Scripture. "Here the affirmation of a wholly trustworthy

Scripture is subverted by a hermeneutic that distinguishes within the teaching what presumably is authoritative and what is not, and thus accommodates twentieth-century cultural preferences."[7] Henry will have nothing to do with this bifurcation of Scripture among evangelicals. He feels that the difference among contemporary theologians turns largely on which facets of the Bible each one elects or rejects.

Henry says that the apostles of Jesus believed Scripture to be authoritative because divinely inspired, and as such, divine truth. For the apostles an attack on the inspiration of Scripture would have been an attack on its authority. Currently many nonevangelical scholars are championing scriptural authority while denying divine inspiration. Henry says: "The current tendency is to redefine biblical authority functionally and therefore not to identify Scripture with any fixed intellectual content. The Bible is said to be authoritative merely in the manner in which it operates existentially in the life of the believing community."[8] The Bible is inspired only when it inspires the believer. This functional approach, says Henry, denies the apostolic view and erodes the authority of the Bible.

Henry, following the lead of B. B. Warfield, holds that the doctrine of inspiration rests logically on the authority of Scripture, and not vice versa. Whatever doctrine Scripture teaches is authoritative. The Bible teaches its own inspiration, and in regard to inspiration teaches biblical inerrancy. This pits the cognitive authority of Scripture against the modern functional authority of Scripture. Henry feels that if the doctrine of inspiration is truncated or dismissed, then biblical authority cannot survive. To say that the writers were inspired, but not the writings, does not help biblical authority. "The insistent modern revolt against rational divine disclosure—particularly God's communication of truths and of other intelligible information—explains why the awakening neo-Protestant interest in revelation has not been paralleled by a recovery of interest in the transcendent divine inspiration of the biblical writings."[9]

What inspired this modern rejection of inspiration as a New

Testament concept? Biblical criticism, says Henry. Most non-evangelical scholars agree that biblical criticism has done away with the Bible as a trustworthy literary deposit that conveys divinely revealed truths. But, observes Henry, "the critical results upon which this repudiation of biblical inspiration and authority is said to rest are much less unanimously shared or logically assured than neo-Protestant theologians assume and imply."[10] Henry says that biblical criticism is still an infant science and scholars remain at serious odds on fundamental issues. "Biblical criticism as a science has not only been marked by sharp conflict but also by evident transition; it therefore holds less prestige among the sciences than does chiropractic among some medics. At any rate, in any other sphere biblical criticism would be considered just an infant science."[11]

The Bible has nothing to fear from a mature criticism. "What accounts for the adolescent fantasies of biblical criticism are not its legitimate pursuits but its paramour relationships with questionable philosophical consorts."[12] Modern biblical criticism has tended to operate on inconclusive philosophical presuppositions. Modern biblical criticism has doggedly maintained a disavowal of the historic Christian commitment to the inspiration and authority of the Bible.

The functional approach to the Bible claims to preserve the authority of the Bible while it rejects divine inspiration as an objective property of the biblical texts and accommodates critical dismemberment of the Bible. Henry says that the functional approach has not retained scriptural authority; it has left theology without absolute truth, and private preference becomes the only basis for doing theology. "To reorient the discussion of inspiration to nontheoretical existential concerns channels and dilutes the objective 'inspiredness' of the texts simply into their 'inspiringness' in the life of the church. This approach dwarfs the former emphasis on inspiredness to merely an arbitrary postulate and exalts inspiringness to decisive significance; the realities of the Christian heritage are thus inverted."[13]

The classical view of inspiration, which Henry advocates, correlates authority with a divinely imparted property of the scriptural texts and not in the common life of the community of faith. The functional view elevates tradition to an equal level with Scripture. Henry concludes: "The current effort to salvage a special role for 'scriptural authority' in a merely functional sense must be recognized for what it is: the newest phase in a continuing anti-scriptural revolt against divine authority. It repudiates the Holy Spirit's inspiration of the scriptural writings, repudiates the contingent divine authority of the apostles in their doctrinal witness to such inspiration, and repudiates the objective truth of the inspired teaching of Scripture."[14]

Henry asks, "Is the Bible literally true?" He replies that the evangelical thinks of the Bible as literally true, if by literal one means that he believes what the Bible purports to say. Figures of speech are regarded as figures of speech, and prose is regarded as prose. To interpret literally is to interpret in terms of normal, usual designations, i.e., the meaning of a word is the basic, customary social designation of that word. The evangelical holds to the grammatical-historical interpretation of the Bible rather than to alternatives that attach to the passage exotic meanings which depend upon reader decisions. The literal interpretation may also be called the historical sense.

Evangelicals recognize that all language is symbolic. Theological truth is true in the same sense that any truth is true, and this is not to ignore the variety of literary forms in the Bible. The Bible conveys truth in poetry and prose, in similes, metaphors, parables, and verbal techniques such as hyperbole. Thus, says Henry, to charge evangelicals with being wooden-headed literalists who cannot distinguish between literary types in the Bible is to resort to ridicule rather than to reason. Evangelicals take figuratively what the biblical writers declare to be figurative. "But if so-called nonliteralists hold that, *because* of their conventional or symbolic nature, words can convey

no literal truth, then their thesis is self-refuting, since if no literal truth can be conveyed because words are symbolic, it is impossible to communicate even *this* literal truth about the nature of truth. Nonsymbolic communication is humanly impossible; without words or signs others are unsure of our meaning. If all we mean by language as being symbolic is that all words are symbolic, then religious language is no more threatened than any other language; if literal truth can be conveyed anywhere, it can be conveyed by religious language as readily as by language about nonreligious reality; if literal truth is precluded because religious language is symbolic, then it is in principle precluded likewise in other realms of dicourse."[15]

Henry holds that biblical or theological language, whatever literary form it assumes, literally tells the truth about God, i.e., concepts and words do convey reliable information about God. Henry makes a careful distinction between "literal interpretation" and "literal truth." He rejects the five current arguments used to support the view that theological language cannot literally tell the truth about God. These arguments are: First, human language is anthropomorphic and hence incapable of providing information about God as he is in himself. Second, all language and knowledge are culturally conditioned and are therefore relative. Third, finite language is too limited to depict the Infinite. Fourth, all language about God is by necessity analogical language. Fifth, religious language is by nature metaphorical or figurative.

Henry says that a prime reason for the current split between literal interpretation and factual representation lies in the rejection of divine inspiration and a distrust of the Bible. "The alternatives to the historic evangelical insistence that Christianity conveys literal truth about God are hardly convincing and lead invariably toward skepticism. There is only one kind of truth. Religious truth is as much truth as any other truth. Instead of being devised for tasks other than to express literal truths about God, human language has from the beginning had this very purpose in view, namely, enabling man to enjoy

and to communicate the unchanging truth about his Maker
and Lord."[16]

The Meaning of Inspiration and Inerrancy

Anyone looking for a contemporary analysis of divine inspiration will look to the evangelicals since they have kept the
issue alive, stressed its importance, and have written most about
the topic in recent times. In circles other than evangelical it
has rated hardly an "honorable mention" in the standard text-
books in Anglo-American systematic theology. But evangelicals
are divided in their account of inspiration because the standard
line "articulated by B. B. Warfield in *The Inspiration and Authority of the Bible* and passed on by writers like J. I Packer in
'Fundamentalism' and the Word of God has not proved wholly
satisfactory to those who would gladly identify with the Evangelical heritage in Christian theology."[17] This evangelical crisis
over the bedrock foundation doctrine of inspiration went public
when Harold Lindsell published his book *Battle for the Bible*
in 1976.

To acquire a passport to the evangelical tradition an adherent
has to confess three things about the Bible: First, the Bible
was "breathed out" by God in such a way as to become the
very Word of God Himself (inspiration). Second, inspiration
applies only to the original copies (the *locus* of inspiration).
Third, the Bible is inerrant (an implication of inspiration). On
the other hand, evangelicals have self-consciously denied four
theories about inspiration: the dictation theory (direct divine
intervention), the intuition theory (naturally endowed religious
genius), the illumination theory (the Holy Spirit heightened
the naturally endowed religious genius of the writers), and
the dynamic theory (the Holy Spirit gave the writer the thoughts
of God, but the writer freely chose his own words and forms
of expression). Evangelicals have advocated what is known as
plenary or verbal inspiration (not only did the Holy Spirit
give to the writer the proper thoughts, but led the writer to

the proper word or words with which to express the thought). The words of the Bible are the very words of God but expressed through the writer's own peculiar style.[18]

Verbal inspiration of inerrant original autographs has not gone unchallenged by a new generation who call themselves evangelicals and who cannot remain satisfied with the views of such thinkers as Warfield and Packer. They are doubtful that inerrancy can be deduced from inspiration. Evangelicals use four arguments for inerrancy: it is required by the teaching of Jesus, by the teaching of the Bible as a whole, by the idea of inspiration, and by the idea of biblical authority. Many of these discontents refuse to brush aside the standard historical critical study of the Bible in academic theology. They don't like to disregard standards of evidence that they rely on in their normal lives. They don't want to abandon the evangelical theology of inspiration, but they don't want to abandon a natural and honest study of the Bible either. They feel uneasy about the term inerrancy since they can't get their hands on the original autographs, and they prefer to use the more ambiguous term "infallible" as a substitute. They hesitate over the deductive, intellectualistic and rationalistic tone of the theory of inerrancy, and they feel that it goes far beyond what the Bible itself teaches on inspiration.

These new evangelicals look at hermeneutics, or the principles one should use to interpret Scripture, in a different way since they have started using the historical critical method. They have been forced to rethink what they had been taught about such interpretive problems as the factuality of the two accounts of creation in Genesis 1 and 2, the historicity of Jonah, the authorship of Isaiah, the puzzle of how Moses could write his own obituary, the place in the canon of the Song of Solomon and Ecclesiastes, the reason for the sharp difference between the synoptic Gospels and the Gospel of John, and the meaning of the book of Revelation.[19]

Further, this new crop of evangelical scholars has faced the "problems" in the Bible without resorting to a false harmoniza-

tion technique. Several problematic areas for them in the Bible include, first, historical difficulties: for example, did Judas kill himself by hanging after throwing his money at the feet of the priest (Matt. 27:3), or by falling on the ground (a field bought with the betrayal money) where his body burst open and his intestines spilled out (Acts 1:18)?

Second, they encounter genealogical difficulties, such as the nonagreement between Matthew 1 and Luke 3, or between Genesis 4 and Genesis 5. Third, they must deal with factual problems, such as the angels at the tomb of Jesus. Matthew says there was one angel at the tomb, Mark says it was a young man sitting down, Luke says two men stood, and John says two angels sat. Fourth, there are numerical problems. For example, 2 Samuel 10:18 records that David slew the men of 700 Syrian chariots while the parallel account in 1 Chronicles gives the number as 7,000.

Fifth, there are inconsistencies. Did the Lord or Satan command King David to take a census of Israel; 2 Samuel 24:1, says the Lord, but 1 Chronicles 21:1 claims Satan. Sixth, there are theological difficulties such as the pessimism and fatalism in Ecclesiastes. And seventh, there are moral problems. The Psalmist (Ps. 137) asks God to slay his enemies and bless those who would smash Babylonian babies against the rocks. These seven representative difficulties the new evangelicals are determined to face straightforwardly.[20] How has Carl Henry responded to these divisions among the more reflective leaders that keep evangelicals at their debating posts?

Henry's twelfth thesis is that the "Holy Spirit superintends the communication of divine revelation, first as the inspirer and then as the illuminator and interpreter of the scripturally given Word of God."[21] He says that this view does not mean the evangelical believes the Bible is a product of mechanical divine dictation or a divine heightening of the psychic powers of the writers. Positively, the evangelical does mean by inspiration that the text of Scripture is divinely inspired as an objective deposit of language, that the humanity of the small company

of chosen writers is not violated, and that the writers were given information beyond their natural resources. Further, God is the ultimate author of Scripture guaranteeing its reliability as a whole and in all its parts. This, says Henry, is the historic doctrine of the Church.

With Henry all evangelicals believe in the inspiration and authority of Scripture. But "inerrancy" is an inference from biblical inspiration which not all evangelicals support and which many refuse to make the dogmatic benchmark of faith. During the last two decades the debate over inerrancy among evangelicals has grown so fierce that outsiders often assume that evangelicals mean by the inspiration and authority of Scripture its inerrancy. At the moment, inerrancy is *the issue* among evangelicals. Inerrancy is an inference from the authority and inspiration of Scripture, but some evangelicals have reversed this order of priority to make inerrancy the watershed for evangelicals. For example, Harold Lindsell and Francis Schaeffer equate inerrancy and a high view of biblical authority, suggesting that the test of evangelical authenticity is the belief in inerrancy. The campaign for inerrancy grows more strident each year and a pall of fear is beginning to hang over the evangelical academic community.

Robert K. Johnston in his 1979 book, *Evangelicals at an Impasse*, distinguishes four positions that are being taken among evangelicals regarding inerrancy.[22] First, "detailed inerrantists" such as Lindsell and Schaeffer hold that a high view of Scripture cannot be defended without recourse to the term inerrancy. This view says that the Bible in its original autographs is inerrant in every detail of chronology, geography, astronomy, measurement, and so on, even when such details are not germane to the intent of the passage. Further, this view implies that to abandon inerrancy is a prelude to discarding other cardinal doctrines of Christian orthodoxy (the "domino theory").

Second, "partial infallibilists" such as Dewey Beegle and Stephen Davis believe that biblical writers may be in error

at points, but such errors do not involve any of the basics of the faith. The gospel is trustworthy and authoritative, and inspired on every essential.

Third, "irenic inerrantists" such as Clark Pinnock and Daniel Fuller hold that the Bible is without error, but the scope of inerrancy must be given a meaning related to standards in biblical times (a biblical "hermeneutic").

Fourth, "complete infallibilists" such as David Hubbard of Fuller Theological Seminary reject the term inerrancy and substitute the term "infallible" in its place. Because of its modern connotations the word inerrancy is misleading since it implies a precision alien to the biblical writers, distracts the church from its main task of preaching salvation, encourages superficial biblical scholarship, imposes an alien category on the Bible, and is too defensive about a Bible that boldly proclaims its own confidence. For this position the option to inerrancy is not "errancy" but total infallibility—trustworthiness versus precision and accuracy.

In this heated debate Henry wants to positively affirm the entire trustworthiness of the Bible. Although unhappy with some of the negative implications of the word "inerrancy," Henry honestly believes it is best not to drop the term today, reckoning this to be less misleading than to deny it. He is not militant on inerrancy and he respects those who have honest reservations about it. He wants to strike a balance between overbelief (which seeks to protect the Bible from its own humanity) and underbelief (which expects too little from the biblical text).

In his book, *Battle for the Bible,* Harold Lindsell dropped a thunderbolt on the evangelical community when he said that only those who affirm detailed inerrancy deserve to wear the badge of "evangelical." Henry reacted strongly to Lindsell, rejecting the purge to remove the evangelical badge from noninerrancy people, denying that the Bible teaches its own inerrancy, and refusing Lindsell's demands to erase the historical-critical method from evangelical seminary curricula. Henry

charges Lindsell with having a reactionary, unscholarly viewpoint about the Bible's authority. "Dr. Lindsell regards the historical-critical method as in itself an enemy of orthodox Christian faith. He seems totally unaware that even Evangelical seminaries of which he approves are committed to historical criticism, while repudiating the arbitrary, destructive presuppositions upon which the liberal use of the method is based. Surely Dr. Lindsell does not want the seminaries to take an uncritical, unhistorical approach to the Bible!"[23] In working out his own approach Henry gives one of the best statements among evangelicals on inerrancy, one that may well lessen the heat in the debate and serve as a model that most evangelicals can assent to.

Negatively, Henry says that inerrancy does not imply "that modern technological precision in reporting statistics and measurements, that conformity to modern historiographic method in reporting genealogies and other historical data, or that conformity to modern scientific method in reporting cosmological matters, can be expected from the biblical writers." Second, inerrancy "does not imply that only nonmetaphorical or nonsymbolic language can convey religious truth." Third, inerrancy "does not imply that verbal exactitude is required in New Testament quotation and use of Old Testament passages." Fourth, inerrancy "does not imply that personal faith in Christ is dispensable since evangelicals have an inerrant book they can trust." Fifth, inerrancy "does not imply that evangelical orthodoxy follows as a necessary consequence of accepting this doctrine."[24] With these five disclaimers, then, Henry tries to correct the error of overbelief. In evangelical circles these "what inerrancy is not" qualifiers are just as significant as positive statements, and they separate Henry from some of his fellow evangelicals such as Lindsell.

Positively, Henry says that inerrancy does imply "that truth attaches not only to the theological and ethical teaching of the Bible, but also to historical and scientific matters insofar as they are part of the express message of the inspired

writings."[25] The Bible is not intended to be a textbook on
scientific and historical matters, but it does give scientifically
and historically relevant information. For example, the "Genesis creation account has implications for God's causal relationship to the cosmos; the Exodus narrative teaches the historical
flight of the Hebrews from Egypt; the Gospel accounts of Jesus'
birth and resurrection describe factual events in the external
world."[26] The Bible is conditioned by its environment, but
this does not make it unscientific. The Bible is expressed in
the idiom of its age, but it has important things to say about
origins, nature, history and the future.

Second, verbal inerrancy "implies that God's truth inheres
in the very words of Scripture, that is, in the propositions or
sentences of the Bible, and not merely in the concepts and
thoughts of the writers."[27] Verbal expression has to be a part
of inspiration because thoughts can be expressed only by certain
pertinent words. The absence of logical contradiction is assured
only by inerrant words. Truth telling is more than pedantic
precision, and inspiration is more than dictation. "If in the
prophetic-apostolic context the category of dictation is at all
appropriate, then the only instance would be Balaam's ass,
where the medium can hardly have contributed significantly
either to the content or to the form of the message."[28] Inerrancy
doesn't require uniformity but it does rule out falsity.

Third, verbal inerrancy "implies that the original writings
or prophetic-apostolic autographs alone are error-free."[29] The
use of secretaries (amanuenses, ghost-writers) does not invalidate this claim because the apostolic writers vouch for the
truth and accuracy of the content. The lack of inerrant originals
is no discomfort since critics cannot produce errant originals
either. "If the originals were errant, then textual criticism would
expect to give us not more truthful readings but only more
ancient ones."[30]

Fourth, verbal inerrancy of the autographs implies that
"evangelicals must not attach finality to contemporary versions
or translations, least of all to mere paraphrases, but must pursue

and honor the best text."[31] The long-cherished King James Version, for example, is based on inferior manuscripts. "What is fundamentally at stake is competence and integrity in the translation of the best available manuscripts."[32] Evangelicals should not be distrustful of good scholarship, because God's truth is communicated in objective propositional form and one is not required to be an evangelical to understand it. Linguistic competence is the most important element in a good translation, assuming that philosophical and theological biases have been excluded.

Infallible Copies?

Henry raises the question, "Are the copies of the Bible infallible?" He says that no informed Christian holds to the inerrancy of the presently existing copies, far less to the inerrancy of the many translations and versions now in print. Claims for inerrancy cannot be extended beyond the original autographs. The question posed by the extant copies concerns their infallibility and not their inerrancy: are they dependable or not? Henry then draws a contrast between infallibility and inerrancy. By inerrancy he means without error; by infallibility he means not prone to err. His conclusion is that the copies may be considered as cognitively dependable carriers of objectively inspired truth.

Henry says that evangelicals attribute inspiration and inerrancy only to the prophetic-apostolic autographs, but never to scribes, amanuenses, copyists, or postapostolic ecclesiastical leaders such as the pope. The church must always submit to the superior authority of Scripture. "Evangelical Christians hold that the Bible as we have it unfailingly communicates God's Word, that it cannot lead men astray in the knowledge of God and his will, and that whatever collides with the express teaching of Scripture is fallacious. In short, evangelicals apply the term infallibility to the extant copies of the inspired prophetic-apostolic writings, rather than to the Roman teaching hierarchy. If the churches were to crumble, but the Bible sur-

vived, men would still find that God personally forgives sins, regenerates the penitent and gives them new life in Christ. But if the Bible were destroyed or hidden, we would soon return to medieval legends or be left to wallow in modern myths."[33]

However good a copy or translation, the evangelical scholar must put at least some slight distance between his best translation and the original autographs. To insist that the copies are without error is unwarranted. Henry quotes with approval F. J. A. Hort's verdict that textual criticism has been successful in restoring copies of the New Testament to within 99.9% accuracy. This is the equivalent of about one-half page of suspect copy in a 500-page New Testament. We have copies of the Bible today in a remarkably pure form and the Bible remains virtually unchanged and its teaching undimmed. "The infallibility of the copies presupposes not only the ongoing special providence of God, and the continuing dependence of copies and translations on the best available texts, but also the inerrancy of the original writings."[34] Conditional perfection is Henry's position.

By infallibility of the copies Henry does not imply four things: that inspiration extends beyond the biblical writers to copyists, translators or interpreters; the inerrancy of the copies; the personal infallibility of the copyists; nor the equal value of all families of texts, versions, and translations. By infallibility of the copies Henry does imply five things: that copies reliably and authoritatively communicate the specially revealed truth and purpose of God to mankind; that the copies unfailingly direct mankind to God's proffer of redemption; that the infallible copies and accurate versions remain the conceptual frame by which the Holy Spirit, Inspirer of the originals, and Illuminator of the transcripts and translations as well, impresses upon human beings their created dignity and duty, their ongoing answerability for moral revolt, and the differing destinies of believers and unbelievers; that copies expound God's will and purpose and truth with clarity; and that the copies preserve the only sufficient divine rule of faith and conduct.[35]

The Holy Spirit and Exegesis

Illumined by the Holy Spirit, special revelation came to and through the apostles and became Bible. The Spirit illumines and interprets the Bible as revelation to us, "and through our witness in turn, revelation proceeds to others who like us must depend for its normative cognitive content upon the inspired writings."[36] Scripture does not say how the Spirit illumines us, but the evangelical exegete is not thereby doomed to hermeneutical nihilism. Henry says that all exegetes are fallible, the evangelical no less so than others, but fallibility doesn't condemn us to skepticism. "Scripture, moreover, not only gives us divine revelation in objective propositional-verbal form, but also sets before us the normative prophetic-apostolic explanation and proclamation of that very revelation."[37]

The biblical text needs to be heard for what it says. The evangelical scholar need not object to literary criticism, form criticism, redaction criticism, or whatever else. The evangelical has no objection to the historical-critical method, but rather the alien presuppositions to which neo-Protestant scholars subject it. When an evangelical runs into a problem passage he should simply acknowledge the problem rather than seeking refuge in an inerrant original text. Henry gives ten guidelines to evangelicals for assessing biblical content. He says "evangelical theology properly affirms that:

1. Historical criticism is not inappropriate to, but bears relevantly on, Christian concerns.

2. Historical criticism is never philosophically or theologically neutral.

3. Historical criticism is unable to deal with questions concerning the supernatural and miraculous.

4. Historical criticism is as relevant to miracles, insofar as they are historical, as to nonmiraculous historical events.

5. Historical criticism cannot demonstrably prove or disprove the factuality of either a biblical or a nonbiblical historical event.

6. To assume the unreliability of biblical historical testi-

mony . . . or in order to believe only what is independently or externally confirmed, unjustifiably discounts the primary sources.

7. Discrimination of biblical events as either historically probable or improbable is not unrelated to the metaphysical assumptions with which a historian approaches the data.

8. A historian's subjective reversal of judgment concerning the probability or improbability of an event's occurrence does not alter the objective factuality or nonfactuality of the event.

9. Although the historian properly stresses historical method, he is not as a person exempt from claims concerning supernatural revelation and miraculous redemptive history, for the historical method is not man's only source of truth.

10. Biblical events acquire their meaning from the divinely inspired Scriptures; since there could be no meaning of events without the events, the inspired record carries its own intrinsic testimony to the factuality of those events."[38]

Henry says that when critical scholars have dealt with problem passages they have made some reckless blunders. First, the errors of the critics far outnumber the alleged errors in the Bible. Second, the errors of the critics grow longer year by year while supposed biblical errors grow shorter. Third, radical discontinuity still plagues the camp of biblical critics. Fourth, radical criticism has moved closer to agnosticism. Henry goes on to say that the failures of skeptical critics do not relieve the evangelical from dealing with critical problems in Scripture. Forcing inerrancy to the forefront does not solve the vexing problem passages in the Bible. Henry has strong words for those evangelicals who avoid serious exegesis by proclaiming inerrancy. "Unbalanced preoccupation with inerrancy can be a costly evangelical diversion," he says. "Some evangelicals concentrate so much on 'the defense of Scripture' that they neglect serious theological exposition. Instead of 'uncaging the lion' to sound its roar in the world, they become lion tamers."[39]

The mark of an evangelical is the proclamation of the crucified and risen Jesus, not inerrancy, says Henry. "The New

Testament supplies no basis for elevating scriptural inerrancy to kerygmatic superprominence."[40] Henry does not like Harold Lindsell's program to declare biblical inerrancy to be the one criterion for distinguishing true from false evangelicals. But what of those evangelicals who are noncommital about inerrancy, yet not committed to errancy? Henry acknowledges that some evangelicals are conscientiously in this camp. "The evangelical who is noncommittal on inerrancy is sometimes motivated by the desire not to commit himself to more than Scripture expressly teaches; he views inerrancy as an inference from the biblical doctrine of inspiration but no more."[41] These noncommitted are not to be called apostate; "the responsibility, instead, is to prod them toward an inerrancy commitment by means of rational considerations."[42] Henry agrees with Lindsell that inerrancy is the evangelical heritage and has been normative for the church since the days of the apostles, and he disagrees with Jack Rogers that biblical inerrancy is an exaggerated imputation by twentieth-century fundamentalists.[43]

Questions to Be Answered

The reader of Vol. IV may feel that Henry overemphasizes the point of revelation as mental communication, but the reader will be impressed that Henry is abreast of the subtleties involved in biblical authority, inspiration and inerrancy. How helpful is Henry's book in the current debate? Liberalism will not be impressed, charging Henry with being a learned but crabby orthodox theologian. Liberalism will accuse Henry with not recognizing that man cannot be delivered from historical relativities even in receiving God's revelation (revelation is indirect and nonobjective), that Henry does not admit that the Bible is essentially a historical document written by fallible men who were wholly human in all they wrote. They will say that Henry does not see that the Bible has no objective authority apart from the Holy Spirit who makes the human words *become* the Word of God. On the other hand, fundamentalism will

reject Henry because he doesn't ignore the Enlightenment, and particularly because he is not militant enough in his attitude toward all higher criticism of the Bible. Again, fundamentalism will reject Henry since he does not make inerrancy his first confession about the Bible.

Turning to the evangelical camp, has Henry provided a viable paradigm to come to terms with the Enlightenment and still retain biblical authority, to take into account the humanity of the Bible and to incorporate the positive benefits of biblical criticism? Three different answers might be given to this question.

First, those evangelicals such as Lindsell and Schaeffer would say that Henry is right in thinking that the older paradigm of evangelical theology still holds, but that he has admitted that there are historical difficulties in the Scripture and thus he cannot affirm the full theological integrity of Scripture.

Second, some neo-evangelicals (Bernard Ramm, for example) will say that Henry clings to the older paradigm of evangelical theology when he should have abandoned it for a better one.[44] These evangelicals are pressing for a better method for interacting with modern knowledge, and they feel that Henry has not developed a method that will allow him to be both evangelical and a man of modern learning. They admit that Henry interacts with modern scholars such as Karl Barth, Morton Kelsey and James Barr, but that he fails to acknowledge in print their positive contribution, that he focuses exclusively on their proposed denials, and that he continues to give them a bad press.

Third, the broad middle group of evangelicals will find a theological guide in Henry even though they may quarrel with him on special points in his presentation. They will credit him with benefitting from the Enlightenment, for retaining the humanity of Scripture, and for accepting a positive biblical criticism. They will appreciate his emphasis that the historical-critical method is a necessary but preliminary method, but only a theological interpretation can get at the meaning of the Bible. They will also like his notion that the truth is in

the witnessing canonical text regardless of critical issues. They will feel that Henry is guilty neither of overbelief nor underbelief.

Henry's treatment of the Bible as authoritative norm has pointed in helpful directions, but many questions relating to the central task of interpreting the Bible remain. For example, what is the best terminology to use—inerrant, infallible, or the truthfulness of the Scripture? Again, what is the best method of dealing with the Scripture—deductive (since God is perfect, the Bible must be perfect) or inductive (since the Bible is also human, it must be investigated and formulated into a structure of truth)? Which affirmation about the Bible should come first, inerrancy (Lindsell) or authority/inspiration (Henry)? How significant is the biblical writer's intention for understanding the text of Scripture? How shall we understand God's accommodation of himself to the Bible writer's limited cultural outlook—God preserved them from teaching error in all matters, in nonrevelatory matters, or in most revelatory matters?

These questions are not easily answered and the wrangling among evangelicals goes on. Henry, the unofficial senior spokesman for the entire tradition, says sadly that the controversy will not go away. By 1980 the scholars had reached a manysided, bitter, no-compromise stalemate among themselves. But by then the battle had moved out from academia and into the denominations just as it had done over fifty years before. In the Lutheran Church—Missouri Synod an inerrancy war had already been waged and the denomination had divided. In 1980 the 14 million member Southern Baptist Convention was in a fierce and continuing political battle over control of the convention leadership positions, a battle centered on loyalty to inerrancy. "The controversy had penetrated rank and file membership, leaving the SBC factionalized and confused over the dangers of yielding too much or else defining 'evangelical' too narrowly."[45] Henry publicly lamented that the controversy was building toward a day of institutional upheaval. Just as the evangelical stance on the Bible as the authoritative norm

was gaining widespread public interest and acceptance, "Henry saw the advance retreating over an issue that need not have produced such a result."[46]

Henry concludes Vol. IV with his three final theses. His thirteenth thesis is that the Holy Spirit, the bestower of eternal life, "enables individuals to appropriate God's truth savingly, and attest its power in their personal experience."[47] The reader may have been surprised when Henry discussed the Holy Spirit as the expositor of divine revelation. Evangelicals have long emphasized the Spirit as inspirer of Scripture, but neglected his role as interpreter. It may surprise the reader again that Henry at this point in Vol. IV sets out his social and political philosophy, but he has reached it out of his discussion of the Spirit and the Scripture. In thesis fourteen he says that the "church approximates God's kingdom in miniature, mirroring to each generation the power and joy of the appropriated realities of divine revelation."[48] His fifteenth thesis is that "God will unveil his glory in a crowning revelation of power and judgment, indicating righteousness and justice and subduing and subordinating evil."[49] In Chapter Six of this book we will return to Henry's social and political thought.

In the first four volumes of *God, Revelation and Authority* Henry has already written a work that is well over twice the length of Paul Tillich's *Systematic Theology*. Like Tillich, Henry is an apologist who tries to drive home a positive point against some injustice done to the faith. One of Henry's primary concerns is the "propositional errorlessness" of Scripture, but his plea for rational consistency does not cause him to lose sight of the mystery of the truth of faith. For him, the decisive role of the Spirit in communicating the intent and purpose of the biblical message may play a subordinate role in his writings, yet I feel that the reader will come away with the conviction that the Holy Spirit looms large in Henry's personal experience. These six volumes are Henry's *magnum opus* and a profound challenge to evangelicals to get on with serious thinking.

V. The Doctrine of God

The doctrine of God brings to a close Henry's monumental six-volume work, *God, Revelation and Authority*. Volume I consisted of preliminary considerations. Volumes II, III, and IV dealt broadly with the subject of revelation and were subtitled *God Who Speaks and Shows*. Volumes V and VI set forth a Christian doctrine of God and are subtitled *God Who Stands and Stays*. These volumes have received high praise from fellow evangelicals. Kenneth S. Kantzer, former editor of *Christianity Today*, says that Henry is the honored and revered dean of evangelical theologians and these six books "provide the most thorough introduction to systematic theology in print." Kantzer says that this work may prove to be *the* outstanding product of twentieth-century evangelical scholarship. Ronald Nash calls Henry's work "the definitive statement of the evangelical theological consensus." Praise for these volumes has come from Roman Catholics and a wide spectrum of Protestants.

Every theological system finds itself under the impossible constraint of having to say everything at once. Henry felt that before he could speak of the nature of God he first had to

show that we can truly know God, and this he did in his first four volumes. In these earlier volumes Henry gave apologetics as well as theology, pausing at each juncture to show where others go wrong, and precisely how and why neoorthodoxy, fundamentalism, existentialism, process thought, naturalism, scholasticism, and such, have departed from the biblical and evangelical truth. In these final two volumes Henry assesses the nature of God as God is revealed in the Bible and in Christ. As in the previous four volumes, Henry tries to digest what the most respected writers and thinkers are saying, show the significance of their insights for the Christian faith, and work out an apologetic for an evangelical position committed to biblical authority. He is particularly keen to speak to fundamentalists who have revolted and swung too far toward liberalism and to the neoorthodox who have not yet swung far enough toward a biblical orthodoxy.

In the first four volumes Henry focused on religious epistemology, that is, on knowledge and revelation as the answer to the question of how we know God. In the last two volumes he emphasizes ontology or metaphysics, that is, the nature of the self-disclosing God. Henry says, "God's existence is the foundational biblical doctrine; from it flow all other Christian principles and precepts."[1] For him the doctrine of God is the most important tenet for comprehending biblical religion; the biblical God remains our only transcendent hope and our only trustworthy support. Revelation is a pointer to the question of God, and a subject of revelation has always been presupposed.

The "God who stands, stoops, and stays" could well have been the subtitle for Henry's Volumes V and VI. The basic Christian axiom for Henry is God's existence, the "I am" who has eternally been *there*. He says, "The living God is the original Christian axiom, both ontologically and noetically, for God discloses himself in revelation as the God who is eternally there."[2] The God who is, Henry contends, is the God who stands, stoops and stays. As the God who stands, God contains in himself the ground of his own existence. As the God who stoops, God

voluntarily forsakes his sovereign exclusivity to both create
and redeem the cosmos. As the God who stays, God governs
in providence and in eschatological consummation his plan
for man and the world. Deliberately deploying these everyday
terms of stands, stoops and stays, Henry structures a framework
to contemplate the doctrine of God.

The God Who Is

Henry begins his doctrine of God with three affirmations.
First, he asserts that God is objectively real. He summarizes
his approach in this sentence: "The Christian says *God is* to
emphasize not simply that more than the world is, but that
other than the world is, and indeed, that only because God
is, the world that need not be, and would not be, is."[3] To
forfeit God's objective existence is to forfeit Christianity. Henry
charges two recent groups, one profaith (neoorthodoxy) and
one antifaith (logical positivism), with sacrificing the objectivity
of God. Neoorthodoxy, in claiming that God is essentially per-
sonal-subjective, turned God into a divine Subject, eclipsed
God as an object of thought, and unwittingly lost God's reality.
Logical positivism, on the other hand, lost the reality of God
"by elevating empirical verifiability as the criterion of all meaningful theological affirmations and, to nobody's surprise, declared that God had failed the test."[4] For logical positivists,
God is a nonsense syllable devoid of all meaning because they
demand a sense-perceptible God. Henry says that both of these
unhelpful approaches are self-destructive.

Second, Henry affirms that God is being, coming, and becoming. As being, the biblical God is the transcendent ground of
the universe, self-sustaining and complete within himself, living
his inner triune life of resplendent self-sufficiency. As coming,
God the eternal Sovereign voluntarily came to create, judge
and redeem the world and man. When God created the world
out of nothing he condescended to be-for-others. As becoming,
God fulfills his plan of salvation by becoming what he was

not, namely, the God-man of Nazareth. Henry says, "The biblical link between the being of God and God's coming and becoming is the promised and expected Messiah."[5] God voluntarily
came in the form of a man to unveil the inmost nature of
the unchanging God.

Third, Henry asserts that God is living, and in living challenges all false gods. Henry writes, "That God lives is at once
the simplest and profoundest statement to be made about him,
for his life embraces the full reality of his sovereign being
and activity."[6] God has life in himself (aseity) or life from
and by himself in independent freedom. He is the only living
God and is so eternally. Since God lives, all pseudo-gods are
doomed as mere mockeries and shams. The Bible leaves no
room for other gods. To serve the living God is to repudiate
all idols—"be they the philosopher's deifying of the elemental
forces of the cosmos (Gal. 4:8 ff.); the political tyrant's imposi-
tion of obligations that God disallows (Acts 4:19, 5:29); the
secularist's idolatry of mammon (Matt 6:24); the glutton's capit-
ulation to appetite (Phil. 3:19); or even the Western tourists'
tolerant curiosity about ancient temple idols (2 Cor. 6:16; 1
Thess. 1:9)."[7]

Having made these three statements about the existence of
God, Henry next turns to a discussion of the essence, nature,
substance or being of God. Theologians have traditionally defined the essence or being of God more precisely by discussing
his attributes (also called perfections or virtues). But theologians
have always faced two problems: how to identify the attributes
and how to best classify them. Henry asserts that the biblical
theology of evangelicals can show that God reveals his attributes, and that this revelation implies a meaningful classifica-
tion system. Henry says: "Evangelical orthodoxy holds that
the attributes of God are to be determined by a logically ordered
exposition of an inscripturated revelation."[8] That is, God in
his biblical revelation is the only intelligible objective source
for statements about God's nature.

This means that scholars have used illegitimate methods

in identifying the divine attributes. Henry quickly names and dismisses five inadequate methods before turning to his own positive statement. (1) The way of negation affirms that any predication of attributes compromises God's perfection. This approach seeks to save God from all earthly attributions, but it ends with a nameless divinity. (2) The way of analogy seeks to rise by analogy from the creaturely world to positive affirmations about God's attributes. Its weakness is that it denies that the terms used of God and man have univocal meaning. (3) The way of causality argues from the world and man as effects to an originating cause or author. Its fault for evangelicals is that it makes man and nature, not God, its starting point. (4) The way of intuition holds that the idea of God's existence is innate in mankind, and that humans can know divine attributes through direct cognitive relationships with God. The weakness of this approach is that it fails to see that sinful fallen man flees from the true God. (5) The way of dialectical and/or existential divine-human encounter affirms God's initiative in revelation through Christ, such revelation being actualized by responsive human trust. Henry says that this approach jeopardizes a rationally consistent doctrine of God. Henry's own confident basis for expounding the divine attributes is the way of scriptural revelation.

How does Henry view the nature of God? Does he believe that there is an underlying divine substance to be distinguished from God's attributes, that attributes inhere in an underlying substance (the position of most conservative Protestants)? And if he does believe substance is the ontological core of all finite entities, does he believe it is nonmental in contrast to mind and spirit, that is, Being is impersonal Thought versus ultimate Reality is personality? Henry has joined the growing revolt against a substance philosophy which conjectures a divine substance distinct from God's own active manifestation in and through his attributes. Henry says, "I reject the realistic view that being is a substratum in which attributes inhere, an underlying substance that supports its qualities or predicates."[9] God's

essence (substance) is not to be separated from God's attributes. God's essence is constituted by his attributes, and God's attributes define his essence more precisely.

God is not a collection of attributes, a compound of parts. Neither is God a substance to which his attributes are additions. God is a living personal center of activity characterized by all his attributes. Henry says, "For this very reason the statement 'God is'—if we know what we are saying—exhausts all that a course in theology can teach concerning him."[10] God's essence and attributes are integral to each other, and each attribute has an absolute divine character. Each attribute is involved in every other attribute, and none is ontologically inferior to another. God's attributes are a divine unity: love, veracity, omnipotence, infinity, personality, reason, goodness, moral perfection, sovereignty, righteousness, holiness and the others, all equally constitute the divine essence as a supernatural personal being.

The Trinity: Eternal and Omniscient

To affirm that God is personal being, as evangelicals routinely do, poses the question of God as triune. How should evangelicals resolve the inherently contradictory notions of God's unity and plurality? As Henry wittily asks, "Are orthodox evangelicals driven to say that anyone who rejects this doctrine may lose his soul whereas anyone who tries to explain it will lose his mind?"[11] Henry repeats historic Christian theology when he affirms that the doctrine of the triune God rests upon sufficient reason, and that alternative views are less than true to fact. He says, "Christian theology affirms neither that three gods are one God nor that three isolated persons are one God. Rather, it affirms three eternal personal distinctions in the one God, in short, 3 X in 1 Y."[12]

The orthodox doctrine has it that three persons—Father, Son and Holy Spirit—exist eternally and coequally within the one divine essence. This is a trinitarian form of monotheism,

a way of emphasizing the complex personal unity of the one living God. "The doctrine of the Trinity organizes the teaching and language of the New Testament in a comprehensively consistent way. To understand the New Testament doctrine of God in any other framework oversimplifies the biblical data, impoverishes the scriptural revelation, and leads to inadequate and heretical views of the one true and living God."[13] There is much light yet to be shed on the Trinity, but, says Henry, the evangelical should speak boldly only where the Bible does so and speak cautiously where the Bible requires caution. Henry says that evangelical scholars have contributed little to current trinitarian literature, and the doctrine is seldom used or preached in evangelical churches. Henry pleads with evangelicals to return to the doctrine of the Trinity both in its ontological and practical implications. God is the ultimate Spirit, immaterial and invisible, self-conscious and self-determining, and evangelicals need to see how this applies to every aspect of their Christian pilgrimage.

Is God (Father, Son and Holy Spirit) infinite and eternal, or limited and time bound? Orthodoxy has traditionally claimed that God is the infinite Creator of a finite universe, timelessly eternal yet interacting with history in an all-knowing way. Henry admits that neither the Old Testament nor the New Testament use the precise term "infinity" for God, yet infinity must be predicated as one of the attributes of the self-revealing God. The universe is limited but God is not. Henry says, "On the surface the doctrine of divine incarnation might seem to relativize the conception of divine infinity. Yet the doctrine affirms that the infinite Logos stepped into history in one Jesus of Nazareth who bears both divine and human natures. The infinite is no less infinite because of its distinctive infinite-finite disclosure."[14]

A corollary of God's infinity is his eternality. God's attributes such as wisdom, righteousness, omnipotence and omniscience characterize the divine nature before he created the universe. God has no time span; he has neither temporal limits nor

temporal location. There are three current views about God's eternity: (1) God is timeless; (2) God has limited temporal duration; and (3) God lives in an "eternal now" in which there are no distinctions of past and future. Henry opts for divine timelessness, over which there is a heated debate in evangelical circles with some theologians wanting to abandon the "God everlasting" tradition.

What light does the Bible throw on the question of God's eternity? Henry says that we must admit that the Bible contains no express declarations about God's timeless eternity or about time's pervading the nature of God. But, he says, "As long as we do not violate the express biblical teaching where the inspired writers touch on the themes of time and eternity, we may draw doctrinal inferences from what they affirm about other divine perfections, and thus bring to light and formulate what is inherent in the scriptural data."[15] Henry feels that a proper inference leads to God's timelessness, a necessary truth implicit in the very idea of God. Negatively, however, divine timelessness does not immobilize God and preclude divine creation, preservation, activity in history, or incarnation in Christ. Henry says, "Evangelical orthodoxy affirms that God has vital and stable personal relationships with the entire space-time universe; it repudiates the idea that time is an illusion, and declares time, rather, a divine creation correlative with God's fashioning, ordering and sustaining of the universe."[16] Time is real, but temporal events do not temporalize God.

If God is eternal, then his knowledge is eternal and perfect (omniscient). God's understanding is very great: he knows himself, his creation, and the thoughts and motives of all created minds. God's knowledge is both eternal (from eternity) and complete. "His knowledge is unerringly correct; it involves no mistaken assumptions or false beliefs."[17] God's knowledge has no temporal limitations since he is eternal. To deny God's eternity is to deny his omniscience. God's cognition is not a temporal activity, yet God's eternity does not preclude him from mental relationships with his creatures. Henry summarizes

his view in this sentence: "The biblical view, it seems to me, implies that God is not in time; that there is no succession of ideas in the divine mind; that time is a divine creation concomitant with the origin of the universe; that God internally knows all things, including all space-time contingencies; that this knowledge includes knowledge of the temporal succession prevalent in the created universe."[18] God knows the past, the present and the future as the future. God knows what man will voluntarily choose.

If God is eternal, it follows then that he does not change. The triune, eternal, omniscient God is also immutable; he can neither increase nor decrease; he is not subject to development or decline. The Bible stresses especially God's moral constancy or ethical stability. Henry says, "The biblical view is that the living God, alone worthy of worship, is timelessly eternal and that immutability characterizes all his perfections. He does not change either for better or for worse for he possesses all perfections from eternity."[19] Process philosophy says that God grows with the universe and with the times, but if this were so, Henry notes, then God could never fully know himself. Without immutability, all other attributes of God lose their efficacy. Henry will allow no inner ontological or epistemological change forced by external limits on God's power or presence.

God is the absolute king of all that is. He is omnipotent. God's absolute power is revealed in his divine creation *ex nihilo* and preservation of the cosmos. The Bible nowhere uses the term "omnipotence," but from the outset the Bible focuses on God as the sovereign creator of man and the world. God can do what he wills to do and he always wills to do the good; God's might and right are always together. Are there some things that God in his power cannot do? Henry says that there are limits to God's possibility and impossibility. Henry notes, "Having willed moral and mathematical distinctions in the creation of the universe, God will not affirm vice to be virtue or two times two to be three; he is faithful to himself and to the relative unity and continuity he wills for

his creation."[20] God's free will is constant and orderly. God wills the law of contradiction because the nature of God is logical. God thinks logically, so the impossible is not a possibility with God since God himself is the ground of all possibility. Contradiction would be nonsense in the world God created. The problem of evil (one of the most troublesome aspects of twentieth-century theology) has questioned God's omnipotence. Henry says, "The global presence of natural and moral evil lifted the discussion of divine omnipotence to a special context."[21] (Henry deals with this problem at length in Volume VI.) God's power is most clearly demonstrated in the Lordship of Jesus Christ. As Henry says, "The modern church's failure to let Jesus Christ function fully in its midst as Lord is the worst scandal of the twentieth-century ecclesiology."[22]

An immediate corollary of God's perfect, logical thinking for Henry is that God's sovereignty upholds truth. The reader would have anticipated that Henry should claim that the laws of logic are grounded in God, that intelligence *per se* is an element (an attribute) in God's personality. The divine Logos gives the world its meaning. Henry writes, "God's truth distinguishes him as true in himself, veracious in all his words and deeds, author of all truth in the creaturely world, and foreign to all falsehood and pretense."[23] God is transcendent Reason, his mind consisting of rational propositions. When we have valid knowledge our thoughts mirror the thoughts of God. Reason and meaning have a supernatural foundation, says Henry, and "Christian theology insists that God maintains the logical rationality of his creation and rules the universe as an intelligible order."[24] Henry bemoans the fact that recent scholars have expounded God's intellectual attributes less fully than God's moral and volitional attributes. Neoorthodoxy, Henry says, even championed irrationalism in the name of piety.

Process Theology: A Major Opponent

The God of the Bible is the transcendent, omnipotent, personal creator *ex nihilo* of the space-time universe, and so Chris-

tian orthodoxy has always confessed. But the growing modern tendency is to blur the supernatural into the natural, to assimilate God to nature and sideline the supernatural. Naturalism, or antisupernaturalism, is the modern megaview, and the deadly foe of biblical theism. Henry believes the trend toward atheism and the eclipse of biblical theism in the twentieth century is caused by several developments. He says, "Among these were metaphysical counterclaims by absolute idealists, personalists and panpsychists; insistence on empirical verification by logical positivists and linguistic philosophers; concessive modernist views that denied the literal significance of scriptural representations of God's being; phenomenological emphasis on the creative contribution of the individual knower; and neoorthodox denial of the objective metaphysical importance of special revelation."[25]

Outside of biblical theism, says Henry, there are four major theories that have tried to relate God to the world. (1) God as efficient cause shapes the cosmic process from preexistent matter and forms. (2) God is the source of the cosmic process which arises as an inner self-manifestation or emanation from the divine Being. (3) God is the ever-changing final stage of the ongoing cosmic process. (4) God is the final cause of the cosmic process.[26] None of these four, says Henry, are biblical. But the fourth ("God is the final cause") is the position of current process philosophy/theology which in some respects rejects the Judeo-Christian heritage but in others professes to champion it. As in classical Christian theism, process thought tries to sustain interest in supernaturalism.

All theologians state their position in relation to an opponent; Paul was against Judaism, Thomas Aquinas was against Augustine, and Luther was against Roman Catholicism. Carl Henry, in stating his doctrine of revelation, worked mostly against neoorthodoxy. In setting forth his doctrine of God (particularly God as creator) Henry's opponent is process thought. For the reader it may be helpful at this point to give a quick survey of process thought to get a feel for Henry's major opponent.

Process theology has its roots in the thought of Alfred North

Whitehead (1861–1947), particularly as stated in his masterpiece *Process and Reality*, 1929. There he conceived of God
as having both an eternal (or primordial) and temporal (consequent) nature. This conception has been appropriated for theology by Charles Hartshorne, John Cobb, Jr., Daniel Day Williams
(1910–1973), Bernard Loomer, Schubert Ogden, Norman Pit-
tenger, and many others—names that appear repeatedly in
Henry's volumes on the doctrine of God. Its basic assertion
is that reality consists of organic societies of value-seeking
events ordered and urged forward into creative advance by a
God who is an all-inclusive Persuasive Purpose.

Whitehead, a Britisher, taught mathematics at Cambridge
University for more than thirty years and then was a teacher-
administrator at the University of London for a decade. In
his mid-sixties he went to teach at Harvard University where
he was to have a monumental impact on the American scene.
In some half-dozen books he set forth a remarkably comprehensive view of the world under the general heading of "a world
in process." His most fundamental idea is that the evolution
of all reality must be taken seriously. Reality is not static
being, but dynamic process. Roughly sketched, Whitehead's
position was that the universe is an organismic whole within
which lesser organismic wholes are related to one another by
a system of feeling or "prehension" at various levels of consciousness. Through the persuasive lure of an initiating and
guiding principle (God) such organisms (component occasions
or entities) move toward their fulfillment of potentiality in a
widening sharing in good. The universe is a society of "energy-
events" (not a collection of "things") moving from potentiality
to actuality ("becoming") by selecting certain courses of action
and rejecting others. God supplies the direction of the energy
events and lures them toward fulfillment. All entities are influenced by, and themselves affect, all other entities. Entities respond better to persuasion and love than to coercive power
or brute force. God is in process with the universe, enjoying
it and suffering with it, directing it and being enriched by it.

This Whiteheadian position, adopted and modified by Charles Hartshorne, the American philosopher, has become the vehicle for the theological enterprise of an increasing number of younger Christian thinkers. Hartshorne has been directly useful to the process group in that he brought to the fore and developed the concept of God that was latent in the thought of Whitehead. Process theology has found in the Whitehead-Hartshorne view of reality a natural theology by means of which belief in God can be recommended to the secular skeptic, and has developed concepts by means of which the Christian God can be described. The process work on the doctrine of God has basically been done in the past three decades and at present the focus is on Christology and hermeneutics.

Classical Western theology has generally believed that there is an unchanging realm of truth and reality, as Henry has stated. Process thought opposes this view for two reasons: first, it is internally inconsistent (God cannot be both free and necessary), and second, it rules out some characteristics of the Christian God that are essential to his being (if the Son suffers, the Father cannot impersonally stand aside). The classical doctrine was right, process thinkers say, in affirming God's stability but wrong in not affirming God's dynamism. By contrast, the process doctrine of God says that God is totally involved in the cosmic process and in time, moving along with his creation, and totally omniscient only of the past and the present. God is not to be identified with the universe (pantheism), but is involved in it and suffers with his creatures (panentheism). Everything that happens in the cosmos, for good or ill, also happens to God, the world's fellow traveler. What emerges is the concept of a God whose reality is both stable and dynamic, both immutable and infinitely relative. Everything is a series of momentary events (versus substances) related to every other momentary event (to be is to be related) all the way up the scale from a subatomic particle to the most complex self-conscious person. By experiencing and remembering all of reality, God gives cohesion and unity to the momentary events. By

remembering the past and seeing the possibility for the future, God provides an ever enriched fund of "material" that the process may draw from to enhance tomorrow's ever greater good in the container of time.

In the process view of God lies both its chief virtue and its chief danger. Process theologians insist against the classical view that God is not an immutable substance, but they have had a problem in saying just how God can be said to act. God's function is to experience and remember all that is past, an essentially passive role as cosmic memory. Process thinkers like to use words such as "influence" and "lure" to describe the way in which God acts upon the creation, but they are quite vague when it comes to isolating an act of God in history. They seem to say that a particular act initiated by God is unnecessary because of the inevitable progress inherent in the cosmic process. What Christian theology wants to say about God's initiative in creation, incarnation, and eschatology may play a secondary role in process thought. What the Bible wants to say may require a more "activist" God than the process account is willing to allow. Apparently process hermeneutics has concluded that the "act of God" terminology involves a mythology that is incredible to the secular mind.[27]

Henry's judgment is that the process view of God is not the God of the Bible. He says, "Process theology lacks not only the authority of Scripture, but also the commendation of rational consistency and coherence and the full support of experience."[28] Henry offers the fond hope that there are signs of a slackening interest in process theology.

God the Creator

Henry begins his discussion of creation where some of the Reformers began—with God's foreordination of the entire course of world and human events. And he no more hesitates than did some of the Reformers in saying that God predestines some to salvation and some to nonsalvation. Henry says, "God

shows his love in electing some undeserving human beings to salvation and his justice in redemptively passing over others who are equally undeserving."[29] Henry says that the Bible points up God's freedom at the heart of the election doctrine. Henry says that three objections have been raised to God's election: (1) God's foreordination is inconsistent with human freedom. (2) Foreordination makes God the author of sin. (3) It undermines all human motive for exertion. Henry replies that election gives man freedom, that God cannot do evil, and Scripture correlates divine election with personal spiritual decision and faith in the Savior. Divine providence excludes resigning oneself to one's "fate," since moral responsibility is a biblical teaching. Election should be a message of joy, and not of horror and dismay. God elects only some, but he does it in loving freedom since he is good to all. "But while God's sovereignty is absolute it is not tyrannical; he does not use his power unjustly and he coerces no one into personal salvation apart from individual decision for Christ."[30]

In turning to the doctrine of God the sovereign creator, Henry says that it is the bedrock foundation for every major doctrine of the church. In Volume VI he devotes 143 pages to the doctrine, pointing to its significance in his own system. How does Henry approach Genesis 1 and 2? Very carefully indeed. He wants the biblical account to be as factual or literal as possible, yet he doesn't want to fall into the trap of turning Genesis 1 and 2 into a textbook in science. He says, "If proper principles of hermeneutics are observed, there is no reason why a distinction between literal and figurative sense cannot be made within the creation account."[31] He wants the creation account to be straightforward prose in contrast to myth or symbol, but he knows that he cannot have it that simply. To turn to Genesis 1 only for science (e.g., geological ages) is to miss the theology, but to say that Genesis 1 is only a salvation drama (e.g., interpersonal relationships) is to miss its value to modern science. Henry says, "It is true, of course, that the creation account was not written with a scientific intention;

it is nonempirical in the sense that it does not offer laboratory observation and verification as the ground of its affirmations. Yet in another sense it is both profoundly scientific and broadly empirical. . . . It is empirical in the sense that it employs a linguistic content readily intelligible to persons in all ages and places."[32]

Henry quotes with approval his fellow evangelical, Bernard Ramm, that the Bible aims to narrate *who* created and *why*, rather than *how*. Yet Henry wants to retain some measure of the *how*; for example, God creates by divine fiat, in an orderly time-sequence, both once-for-all and by repetitive patterns of action, by distinguishing types and by making man ruler over creation. There are apparent clashpoints between Genesis 1 and modern science, but Henry doesn't want the biblical exegete to surrender to scientific determinism. He says, "What Genesis says about the *how* may not be extensive or comprehensive, but it is not on that account either negligible or irrelevant. What it says may bear significantly on empirical realities and hold scientific implications as well that either accord with or dispute scientific theories of man and the world."[33]

For Henry, the chief *how* of God's creation is that God created *ex nihilo* (out of nothing), consciously and rationally. This means that the universe is neither an ultimate necessity nor an inevitable divine emanation. *Ex nihilo* also eliminates the other two options about origins: that the universe has always existed, or that it is self-caused. *Ex nihilo* is uneasy with the three competing theories of origins in contemporary astronomy: the "big bang," the steady-state theory, and the oscillating model. Henry is unwilling to commit himself to any contemporary theory of cosmology. He says, "In short, the big bang requires a Big Banger, and the Big Banger more and more reminds us of the omnipotent, intelligent and purposive Creator portrayed in the Genesis account."[34] But his main objection to the "big bang" theory, even though he finds areas of compatibility with Genesis 1, is that the "big bang" implies that creation

is still continuing while the Bible teaches that God created the world at a definite point in time.

Henry constantly struggles with the *how* of Genesis and the way it intersects with modern science. He feels the two do intersect, and that Genesis is history, rather than legend or saga, with bearing on scientific method and conclusions. He is determined that a scientific naturalism not be allowed to determine the way Genesis 1 is understood, and he is particularly hostile at the way atheistic evolution has replaced theism. He says, "In Christendom the modern conflict over origins has in recent generations centered around biblical creationism as against naturalistic evolution; the former rests on the conviction that Genesis is an authoritative account that discloses the creative activity of the self-revealing God while the latter stems from the empirically oriented philosophy of naturalistic scientism."[35] Theology has tried to correlate evolution and theism in four different ways: (1) deistic evolution, in which God started the process and then abandoned it; (2) pantheistic evolution, in which nature and man are part of the divine life; (3) theistic evolution, in which God created the process but miracles are minimized in deference to continuity and process; and (4) "scientific creationism," which contends that theistic evolution is scientifically unjustified and that the earth is no older than 10,000 to 15,000 years. Henry is not happy with any of the four approaches, but he does agree with most evangelical scholars who have continued to insist that the formation of Adam by God was *de novo* and involved no dependence upon prior animal life.

Charles Darwin's earlier evolutionary speculation lay in his assertion that all complex species arise slowly by chance variation and natural selection from simpler forms. Today Darwin's theory is in disrepute and there is a breakdown in the scientific community of the evolutionary consensus. Henry is gleeful over the demise of the modern synthesis and says, "It is therefore deplorably inaccurate from the standpoint of science itself to

champion evolutionary theory as an incontrovertibly established dogma that one questions only on religious grounds."[36] He rejoices that a major perspectival shift is taking place in evolutionary science away from an advanced commitment to naturalistic evolution, since this shift opens the door once again to theistic creationism. Only a halting return to special creation is being made, but Henry finds the signs hopeful. He is determined to show that Genesis 1 in its *how* statements repudiates the idea that man came from animal ancestry. He says, "The view of Genesis is that God created distinct kinds of life propagated by natural generation, a propagation that preserves a normal condition or fundamental likeness within which variations occur."[37] Both Genesis 1 and the mathematical odds are against the chance origination of man, the world, or the universe. Naturalistic science has turned evolution into a religious faith, a false god. Henry says, "Biblical theists lay no claim to special information about processes governing the solar system. They do insist, however, that a theistic view of origins will guard science from hasty and false assumptions of naturalistic development."[38] For Henry special creation is compatible with the scientific data and with Genesis 1.

More central to the creation-evolution debate than the origin of man is the nature of man. For evangelicals the crucial factor about man is his being created by his Maker in the image of God. In evolutionary theory morphological similarity to other mammals is the crucial factor. Evolution focuses on man before the Genesis Adam, while theology focuses on man's possibilities after Adam. Henry says, "The theological problem is whether the Genesis account lends itself to evolutionary interpretation; the scientific problem, whether scientific research confirms evolutionary theory."[39] There are four views about man's origin and nature that fix the perimeters in the current debate: (1) naturalistic evolution, in which man is the product of unthinking nonpurposive forces; (2) theistic evolution, in which God directs the natural processes that shaped man; (3) progressive creation, in which God acts at special stages to create all species and

finally man in his image; and (4) fiat creation, in which God creates *de novo* all life forms at a recent date in the past. Henry is sympathetic to progressive creation because it lends itself to the scientific representation of the antiquity of the earth and man, and he shows a partial sympathy to fiat creation because it reflects the immediate impression given by the Genesis account.

Henry's conclusion is that he can live with and appreciate a modified theory of evolution as long as no animal species is regarded as the progenitor of man. Second, he can live with an ancient earth idea, since the Genesis account does not fix the precise antiquity of either the earth or of man. He says, "The Bible does not require belief in six literal 24-hour creation days on the basis of Genesis 1–2, nor does it require belief in successive ages corresponding to modern geological periods."[40] Third, he is squarely against modern humanism and naturalism. Fourth, evangelicals need to reaffirm that Adam or man "is a creation supernaturally made in the image of God, an historical being divinely fashioned from the dust of the earth and rationally, morally, spiritually, genetically and culturally different from any prior species of life."[41]

God Is Good

Goodness is an intrinsic attribute of the biblical God. He articulates that good for his creation. Everything he creates is good, and whatever corresponds to his will is good. When God's good will is violated the good loses its winsomeness, truth its goodness, and beauty its wholesomeness. For Henry the good God's revealed commands are the core structure of biblical ethics. To oppose divine command ethics is to flaunt the goodness of God since the law is a provision of God's goodness. When man tries to define goodness on his own terms he inevitably accommodates himself to a soft view of evil.

But if God is both omnipotent and good, how does evil enter in? Henry insists that evil is very real, but he does not

consider its presence in the universe inconsistent with God's omnipotent benevolence. Since God commands only the good, evil arises when those commands are disobeyed. Both good and evil are defined by the sovereign Creator's will and purpose. Henry believes in the agency of a malevolent fallen spirit from the angelic world called Satan. Western thought has eroded faith in any invisible spiritual world, but Henry holds firmly to the idea that Satan is an apostate angel introduced in Scripture as far back as Genesis 3. He says that it is theologically plausible to affirm a real evil, real death, real hell, and a real Satan. He states, "To speak of moral concepts—e.g., sin and evil—only in terms of an impersonal principle is unjustifiable symbolism; from the standpoint of Scripture, moreover, it is an intolerable fiction."[42] Evil arose when Satan voluntarily rebelled in God's perfect creation. After that, man fell and cosmic disorder and suffering are now the lot of the universe.

God's goodness is most perfectly expressed in Christ's substitutionary redemption for penitent sinners. God brackets the problem of evil and suffering through Christ who suffered injustice at its height and death at its depth. By his resurrection Christ was victorious over Satan, and God anticipates the final triumph of good and the conquest of evil.

Further, God's goodness does not accommodate him to a soft view of evil before that final triumph over Satan. The good God further brackets evil in the present through the efforts of his people, the church. The world now is scarred by sin and victimized by injustice, but "the regenerate church is nonetheless a healing body that cancels sin's condemning and enslaving power, moderates its consequences by prayer and the Spirit, and relates and relegates its legacy of believers' suffering to a promised future glory."[43] Again, the good God in his providential purpose brackets Satan by subordinating all the pain and suffering of regenerate believers to a higher good that involves a new heaven and a new earth wholly free from suffering. For Henry, God's free activity is what defines his character and God's activity is unfailingly good. Evil, the "bone in the

throat" to a doctrine of a good God, is answered by Henry with a personal Satan. And the answer to Satan, for Henry, is the suffering of Christ as God-man.

An immediate corollary of God's goodness is God's fatherhood. God's paternity must be known by revelation just as all the other attributes are known. Social injustice, sickness, death and destructive natural evils like earthquakes and floods are anything but fatherly, so God's paternity cannot be arbitrarily predecided by human ideas of fatherhood. Henry says, "If legitimate points of comparison exist between human and divine fatherhood, these can be ascertained only by divine revelation and not on the basis of human expectation."[44] The Old Testament looked upon God's fatherhood as a living divine unrest over Israel's neglect of her special privileges and duties as God's chosen people. The Judaism of the interbiblical period tied God's fatherhood to the individual redemptively, but the New Testament connects God's paternity primarily to Jesus Christ. The full revelation of divine fatherhood occurs in the Son, an exclusive yet exemplary sonship. Christ's sonship leads immediately to the sonship of individual believers through redemptive restoration. God in Christ divinely adopts the regenerate sinner. Jesus then authorized his disciples to use the intimate term *abba* ("daddy" or "papa"). "This deliberate use of *abba*, which corresponded to baby-talk, signaled a directness and intimacy that Jewry must surely have considered overfamiliar . . . . because of its exaggerated view of God's transcendence."[45]

Jesus brought new depth and dynamic to the revelation of God as Father, and it almost routinely became a New Testament designation. Divine fatherhood means creation, providential interest in just and unjust alike, forgiveness for the undeserving, special care for his adopted disciples, and discipline on his sons for their good. For Henry, fatherhood does not summarize all of God's perfections, since God's mercy and forgiveness do not automatically flow from his paternity. Only as God's self-giving *agape* (love) is additionally implied can salvation be associated with the term Father.

God's incomparable love (*agape*) is a revelation of a fundamental and eternal divine attribute and reflects God's whole
being in specific actions and relationships. *Agape* is not an
exhaustive definition of God, but it is the shaping principle
of his creative and redemptive work. The *agape* of God, a
disarming love for the undeserving, is the very lifeline of the
Bible. Jesus was *agape*-incarnate and "presupposes the exclusive voluntary initiative of the sovereign divine being whom
no external power can manipulate."[46] Christ's atoning death
was the peak of God's love and God's love for us is always
expounded by reference to the cross. To ignore the death of
Christ is to ignore God's *agape*, and to ignore *agape* is to
neglect the one thing that would fully satisfy the justice of a
sovereign God.

God is good and in his goodness he is just. But how can
both *agape* and righteousness relate in the same God? Henry
says, "The warp of the biblical doctrine of justification is love,
its woof is righteousness or justice."[47] For Henry, God's *agape*
and righteousness are coextensive and equally ultimate. No
relationship can compromise the ethical priorities that exist
in God, and *agape* does not intercept God's final punishment
of evil; in fact, God vindicates his essential goodness by eschatological retribution. Henry will have nothing to do with the
subordination of righteousness to love, which he says is a modernist and neoorthodox accommodation. There is no universal
salvation, hell cannot be emptied of its terrors, and God's last
judgment is not benevolent toward the impenitent. Henry says,
"During his earthly ministry Christ, *Agape* incarnate, repeatedly coupled references to declarations of his lordship with
warnings that Hades awaits the impenitent."[48] According to
Henry, when the neoorthodox did away with divine judgment
in favor of salvation for all, they also evaporated the faculty
of divine love. Henry sees no conflict between divine love and
divine righteousness because both are reconciled in the blood
atonement of Christ. Reconciliation in Christ removes God's
wrath, and Henry quotes the Bible and the Reformers to support

this traditional evangelical interpretation. He says, "That Christ's death removes God's enmity against man—that a new relation exists of God toward the sinner no less than of the sinner toward God—is at the heart of the doctrine of salvation."[49]

Since God is holy, he is especially separated from humanity in its sin and wickedness. The wrath of God is not simply the reverse side of his love, nor can wrath be subordinated to love. But wrath is related to love in that God offers himself in Christ to achieve a just and merciful forgiveness of sinners. Justice is a divine attribute, and justice invites judgment since justice grants each person his due. Because God's punishments are just, justice does not have the character of grace. But justice and mercy come together in God to voluntarily save the sinner. *Agape* and justice are not to be confused. Henry says, "However much Scripture speaks about God's holy love and mercy, and of God's provision of his Son as the penitent sinner's righteous substitute, Scripture focuses first and foremost upon God's transcendent righteousness that rewards moral creatures according to their works and requires reparation for sin."[50] To subordinate divine righteousness to forgiving grace is to lose God as lawgiver and preclude any final act of divine condemnation. Justice has its roots in heaven, and it will ultimately defeat unrighteousness on earth.

God's Providence

Henry spoke of the God who stands (who eternally exists) and who stoops (who created, and who redeemed his fallen creation). Next he speaks of the God who stays (who preserves, renews and consummates his creation). Henry says, "The Bible depicts God as the providential sustainer of the universe by his omnipotent omnipresence and also the divine governor of all things. The living God everywhere upholds and maintains the created universe; he does so, moreover, for the sovereign purpose and goal for which he initially created it."[51] The uni-

verse is dependent on its Creator and is not metaphysically ultimate.

Just as creation *ex nihilo* was a distinct act, so preservation is a continuing series of acts that rules out continuous (perpetual) creation and ongoing evolutionary creation. Preservation means that God is more for the world than against it, that he intends to redeem the world and not destroy it. God preserves the world to move it toward moral and spiritual ends in anticipation of a climactic consummation. Henry says, "God has always been concerned with ends. In his divine program redemption is not simply an unplanned supplement suddenly added to the plan of creation; rather it is creation's renewal and restoration."[52] Since God rules the universe for a goal, it is a cosmos rather than a mere chaos, chance, or vague benevolence.

The biblical view of providence is that God works out his purpose in the details and minutiae of life; nothing falls outside God's concern. God is interested in every individual, and even seemingly chance events should be considered providential. God's greatness is seen in specific actions whereby he sustains nature in a certain order, in the pattern he preserves in history, and in his miraculous redemptive acts. God can alter our very history and destiny, achieve good for all who love him, lead us to praise him even in the midst of adversity, free us from all delusive nature-myths and historical ideologies, lead us to challenge all mechanistic idolatries and improvident fates, and free us for the pursuit of natural science and the true meaning of history. Providence is the most contested of biblical doctrines in a secular culture, but only sin and wickedness cause us to doubt God's shaping of our ends.

Scripture neither minimizes adversity nor dwarfs the fact of evil. Man's disorderliness and degeneracy do not befall us for an immediate good. To say that God has a purpose in history merely compounds the problem of evil. Henry says "the fact that a child dies of leukemia; a bride-to-be is raped; a gifted collegian dies in a car accident; a company executive

succumbs to a heart attack the morning of a well-deserved
retirement and a godly woman suffers from ravaging cancer
represent providences that tend to drive believers and unbelievers alike 'up the wall.' "[53] Evil and injustice are awesome live
factors, yet God's special providence works selectively, for the
good of all who trust him. Only on the basis of revelation
can the Christian affirm that God's providence will be undictated
in a life beyond this life, that evil will be defeated in an end-
time reckoning, that fruitful obedience will finally be rewarded,
and that cosmic beneficence will be made manifest. Jesus said
and demonstrated that no human concern is too insignificant
for God's attention; that puts the debate over providence in
proper focus and should relieve the feeling of gloom and despair
hanging over contemporary life. The Christian knows that miracles and prayer are integral elements in the achievement of
God's purpose. The unbeliever forfeits the peace and confidence
"which stem from knowing that events are shaped not by
chance, not by mechanical necessity, not by blind fate, not
by Satan, but by the sovereign Creator and Preserver of all."[54]

But a modern secular culture refuses to posit a providential
coherence in history, and even people of faith sometimes stumble at the notion of providence. For example, Henry says that
Auschwitz (Hitler's destruction of six million Jews) is a harsh
verdict on Christians and for many a suspension of providence.
"No post-biblical event has so shattered Jewish faith in divine
providence as the Auschwitz holocaust."[55] Many secularists,
Jews and Christians would rather abandon God than accept
the idea that God would use Auschwitz to implement his purpose. Henry says that with rare exception (he names Karl Rah-
ner and Wolfhart Pannenberg) Christian theologians have not
discussed the significance of the holocaust for the doctrine of
providence. Henry makes several observations, the first of
which is that while Christians failed to respond properly to
the plight of the Jews under Hitler, "to infer from this failure
the invalidity of Christian teaching would be as erroneous as
to infer the invalidity of prophetic teaching from the fact of

the Hebrew exile to Babylon."[56] Second, Henry observes that
Christians can find no glimmer of triumphalism in the holocaust
since the New Testament warns of a coming persecution of
Christians. Third, the destruction of the Jews was not willed
by a Christian sanhedrin but by the mad and inhuman Hitler.
Fourth, totalitarianism spares neither the Jew nor the Christian:
Hitler destroyed six million non-Jews in concentration camps;
Stalin may have killed fifteen million persons and Mao, thirty
million. Fifth, the holocaust was a horror, yet it was not hell,
the ultimate horror, the whole of horror. And sixth, the holocaust led the Jews to take up the neglected possibility of a
national homeland.

But the final answer to all the probabilities and evils of
history is that the future belongs to God. The God who stays
will prevail, determine and assure the finalities of history and
nature. "God's mighty purpose is sweeping the entire universe
toward the final climax of his master plan. In every succeeding
age he has been bringing to himself dedicated followers from
every race and nation; now he is moving all creation toward
the eschaton."[57] Christ, at the center of the eschaton (the end),
will return to the earth in great power and glory to judge
mankind and bring the final kingdom of God. "Within that
framework will occur the resurrection of the dead, the full
conforming of believers to Christ's moral and spiritual image
and their unending blissful service in the presence of God,
as well as the doom of Satan and of those eternally separated
from God to unending divine punishment."[58] This present sinful
world will be displaced by a future world restored by God to
its creation-purpose. The wicked will have neither joy nor rest,
but the redeemed will fully bear the image of God. To say
that God *stays* is the final reminder that God knows us through
and through. In eternity the wicked will not be on speaking
terms with God, whereas the redeemed saints will join the
God of heaven in a chorus of holy laughter and joy in a community in which righteousness reigns voluntarily and evil has
no place.

God's Kingdom

Until that time when God unveils his glory in a crowning revelation of power and judgment, vindicating righteousness and justice and subduing and subordinating evil, the Christian must live in a sinful world. More than most evangelicals, Henry is concerned with the redemption of the moral life. In 1957 he published his 615-page book, *Christian Personal Ethics,* in which he diagnosed the loss of human worth in modern life and the hope of its recovery in the zone of Christian redemption. He has never considered ethics the dull hobby of duller academicians, but the incisive and universal requisite for survival with the life and death of civilization hanging in the balance.

Henry's own educational pilgrimage had not prepared him to teach ethics in the classroom. His college and seminary experience had not adequately grounded him in biblical ethics or the ethics of revelation, and in his doctoral studies his professors had a semi-concealed, albeit gentlemanly, distaste for an ethic of special revelation. Henry confesses that his earliest days of formal lecturing reflected his rather inadequate articulation of Hebrew-Christian morality. As he continued to teach two convictions began to emerge in his thinking: "the impotence and sterility of speculative ethics derive largely from its self-enforced segregation from the ethics of revelation; Christian ethics becomes impoverished when unrelated to the problems of secular morality to which the man of the world seeks an answer."[59] His 1957 book on ethics is an enlargement on these two convictions, especially in the sphere of personal ethics.

Henry's controlling assumption in *Christian Personal Ethics* is that in the Bible God has revealed his will for man's moral conduct. True to his apologetic disposition he spent the first 120 pages of the book showing that speculative philosophy (naturalism, idealism and existentialism) has not been able to recover modern man from his sense of moral loss. Secular ethics, he says, is conceived not in God's revelation but in sin. Secular ethics usually misrepresents man as capable of

reasoning his way out of his moral dilemmas. Revelational ethics, on the other hand, identifies the good with God and God's will. *Agape* becomes the divine imperative in personal relations. *Agape* as the will of God is particularized in the Sermon on the Mount, and the larger New Testament reinforces the ethics of creation, of Sinai (ten commandments) and of the Sermon. Christ's death (atonement) is the presupposition of Christian morality. Jesus is the ideal of all ethical behavior. The Christian life is one of liberty in grace, and the Holy Spirit promotes and sustains higher levels of morality. The believer's life is not one of moral perfection but of growth in purity, the education of conscience, and the cultivation of gratitude. Henry's book has become a standard text on Christian ethics in evangelical schools and has been praised as "the best treatment of personal ethics from the evangelical point of view."

Private and public justice is an integral part of Henry's theology, close to his evangelical heartbeat and the subject of much of his reflection and writing. When he was editor of *Christianity Today* many of his articles addressed the thorny relationship between *agape* and social justice. Much of his advice may have been more politically conservative than liberal, but he never hesitated to throw himself into the moral struggle. In 1973 he edited the massive volume, *Baker's Dictionary of Christian Ethics.* In numerous books he has prodded American evangelicals to renew their influence in the public realm. Just as he has paced evangelical theology, so he has paced evangelical ethical thought. For decades he has pleaded with, exhorted, scolded, preached at and challenged evangelicals to see the social implications of the gospel. His 1947 book, *The Uneasy Conscience of Modern Fundamentalism*, was a key document in Evangelicalism's emerging social conscience. Sadly, he says, "Evangelicals seem to divide increasingly over the relation between social concern and evangelism and over what program Christian social ethics implies."[60] Henry helped guide some young evangelicals in 1973 to issue the Chicago Declaration,

a vigorous indictment of injustices in the American scene and a call to all evangelicals to take up their social duties. In his six volumes of *God, Revelation and Authority* there are passages that virtually soar in their eloquent appeal for evangelicals to be responsible to God's world outside the local congregation of believers. In the elder statesman there is still the young newspaper reporter eager to know what is "going on" in the world, quick to assess the latest world crisis and then apply the gospel revelation with serpent wisdom and dove harmlessness. Henry has written with a sense of heartbreak that the "evangelical failure to elaborate a schematic social ethic is a blemish on the record of that religious community to which more than any other, America owes its distinctive heritage."[61]

For Henry, God is the proper subject of Christian theology, and from that main axis flow all discussions of social ethics no less than soteriology and eschatology. In God's attributes, righteousness and love are equally ultimate. He says, "In the sphere of social ethics it is reflected in the biblical emphasis that the role of government in the world is to preserve justice, with an eye on human rights and duties as sanctioned and stipulated and supported by the will of God. The Church's role in the world, on the other hand, is essentially redemptive and benevolent, alert to man's spiritual needs."[62] For Henry this means that love must modify political and social justice while preserving human rights. To get to this new society of equal justice we must go back to the man of love, Jesus of Nazareth. In his life Jesus manifested the kingdom of God and in his resurrection he pictured the ideal person that God approves in eternity. Jesus is the ideal man and the content of the new society is found in the regenerate church's reflection of the kingdom of God.[63] The kingdom of God includes an inner conformity of the human heart to the law of God. "The Bible relates its data concerning divine manhood to Jesus Christ as the ideal man; in the incarnation God has already published in human nature the content of a divinely approved moral compliance."[64] Jesus established a whole new world that defied

the existing society of alien powers, and the church was called to challenge the powers for their illusory claims to ultimacy and for their accommodation to and support of injustice.

The alien powers were first created for God's service, but they now work rebelliously to elevate themselves to absolute value, to enslave mankind and separate the believer from God's love. The church is not to forcibly demote the alien powers, but to support their rightful claims while challenging their wrongful ways and calling them back to God's service. Christ has liberated the church from the powers, and the church is to live its daily existence in a corporate life of truth, righteousness and mercy. The evangelical churches, fragmented and with their witness to the world lamentably reduced, must begin to bear a corporate social witness as divinely designated "salt" and "light" in the world. The evangelical churches have tragically neglected their fullest sense of mission while imposing legislation on the unregenerate world (concerning alcohol, abortion, race, housing and so on) that church members themselves refuse or fail to practice. Henry says, "The church must reject trying to politicize an unregenerate world into the kingdom of God; it must also reject interpreting evangelical conversion devoid of active social concern as fulfilling Christian responsibility."[65] God works through the church to change the world, not by the church forcing new structures on society but by being a new society in its own ranks. The church, witnessing to the world by voluntary subjection to the Lord as the coming King, has a joyful good word to speak in the sphere of politics: "that God is the true King; that God's faithful and gracious action toward man puts his seal on the dignity of the individual; that the coming kingdom is not merely a future possibility but is already in some sense actual; that even in the political arena God's main concern is not ideology, isms or ideals, but rather persons and their relationships to God and to one another."[66] Each Christian becomes an important moral agent reflecting the character of God, that is, blending righteousness and love in equal ultimacy.

Henry says, "The Jesus Way is indeed not the way of Zealot revolutionary violence aimed to overthrow the oppressive powers; nor is it the way of Herodian acceptance of wicked secular powers for the sake of private favor; nor the way of Pharisaic cooperation with alien authority to preserve sectarian religious interests; nor the way of Essene retreat from socio-political realities to hopefully expect the coming future Teacher."[67] Nor is it the way of radical political pacifism, since the evangelical may have to engage in a "just war" to bring about social justice. In regard to war, the church stands on the side of peace. In regard to property, the church stands on the side of survival needs. In regard to justice, the church has a mandate to challenge social injustice. In regard to isms, the church refuses to baptize either Marxist socialism or secular capitalism as Christian. In regard to the oppressed, the church has a message that Christ the Liberator has already doomed sin and injustice and no one is forced to accept the crush of evil powers as final. In regard to the staggering breadth and depth of human need, talk is no more a substitute for action than faith is a substitute for works. In regard to evangelicals, Henry feels that it is a time of resurgence of evangelical conviction regarding social involvement. Evangelicals are recognizing that nothing has done more in history to stimulate a passion for justice than the Bible, that social compassion is a part of the evangelical message, that feeding the hungry is a duty to Christ, and that evangelicals must criticize their own social or cultural traditions. "Evangelical commitment to the new birth involves also commitment to the new society—to preservation of human justice and order, and to fuller humanization of man's fallen life through divine renewal and reorientation."[68] Evangelism and the pursuit of justice should be equally served.

Justice in the context of the kingdom of God is the evangelical ideal, but giving political expression to this ideal is not easy. The crucial problem is how to move from normative principles to specific proposals. The God who *stays* expects his disciples to make concrete commitments. Since the church is the approxi-

mation of the kingdom of God in history, it is to manifest
the ideals of the new covenant in its own life. But, says Henry,
the church has no mandate to work out a particular ideology
as the preferred social utopia. The church is not charged by
God to transmit a specific political ideology, but to preach
the Christ whose message pleads for and demonstrates new
community. Henry says, "The Christian community is first and
foremost a purging movement, a part of the world washed by
the Savior's blood and touched by the Spirit's flame. If this
expectation pricks an uneasy conscience, then both judgment
and charity must begin in the house of the Lord. To offer
any other solution reflects neither judgment nor agape, and
can guarantee only a redistribution of the world's burgeoning
problems."[69]

Evangelicals have traditionally debated four different strategies for implementing social justice.[70] (1) The "conservative"
position declares that evangelism—winning individuals to
Christ—is primary, though believers should be benevolent and
compassionate citizens and accept the structure of American
society. (2) The "moderate" position holds that believers should
support the American political system, that evangelism is the
priority mission of the church, but that implementing social
justice is a parallel calling. All governments are imperfect and
individual salvation remains America's only ultimate hope. Social action grows out of evangelism. (3) The "reformist" stance
says that evangelism and social action are equal partners, that
individual conversion through preaching and political restructuring for greater social justice through social action are joint
priorities. (4) The "radical" perspective, molded in the Anabaptist tradition and suspicious of all political power and governmental institutions, is committed to rigorous discipleship,
corporate lifestyle, and societal critique. This approach seeks
to build up the life of the church as an alternate lifestyle to
the American way of life, and associates itself with the powerless
and dispossessed.

Carl Henry recognizes that neither the "conservative" nor

the "radical" approach have thus far been effective in changing society. Henry is more at home with the "moderates" and "reformists" but finally falls into neither camp. He is willing to offer structural critiques of the American political system, but unwilling to dictate specific political and social policy. He prefers to elucidate socially related biblical principles and leave the structuring of specific programs to governmental agencies. He continues to emphasize the need for spiritual renewal, ministry through humanitarian care, biblically principled citizenship, a theory of limited government, societal restructuring, individual effort, and justice as a guide for love in implementing social policy. His final assumption is that the God who *stays* is intimately involved in the effort to rescue society from its woes, and the Christian also has the obligation to stay and serve as a redeeming agent of Christ.

VI. Carl Henry and His Critics

Carl Henry writes Christian theology, a discipline which is called the "science of God" and the "most beautiful of all the sciences." Theology is an attempt to think seriously about the central convictions of the faith, to set out what Christians believe about their religion, and to interpret Christianity as a Christian sees it. Theology deals with the eight fundamental doctrines of revelation, God, creation, man, Christ, salvation, church and last things (eschatology). Each doctrine is intimately connected with the other seven doctrines, and the arrangement given to them by the theologian is only a matter of expediency. Henry has not given equal time to each doctrine since he is not trying to write an evenly balanced textbook in systematics. Rather, he has focused on revelation and God, and the other six doctrines blend into his treatment of these two doctrines. He has deliberately chosen this format because he feels that revelation and God are the crucial doctrines at this stage of the twentieth century, and this two-foci style suits his apologetic thrust.

Emil Brunner once remarked that the task of the theologian

is to stand in the doorway of the church kitchen tasting the food to see that the congregational fellowship is not poisoned. Henry agrees with this and holds that "this, and no other, is the doctrinal food that the church should be eating." This firmly held conviction implies several things: first, theology is something to be believed, not merely studied in detachment. Further, the theologian's task should be a happy one since he is devoted to apprehending, understanding and speaking of God. Henry is a "Christ intoxicated" believer, and he is happy about it. His commitment to God is open and obvious. At the same time his writings are sprinkled with a healthy humor that reminds himself, his fellow evangelicals, and his opponents of their common humanity. Evangelicals seem to have a built-in weakness for some aspects of totalitarianism and need a touch of humor to counteract fanaticism.

Second, there is a norm in belief, and for Henry that norm is the evangelical one. But what is the norm for one theologian may not be normative for another. Hence there have been numerous theological systems (Apologetic, Patristic, Greek Orthodox, Scholastic, Lutheran, Reformed, and so on), traditions, creeds, confessions and organizations (historical, systematic, practical). The theologian should be modest about his efforts (as Henry is) because he is constantly exposed to the judgment of God and that of his colleagues.

Third, theologians may affirm the centrality of the eight basic doctrines and still legitimately differ. Fellow evangelicals Donald G. Bloesch, Dale Moody, Helmut Thielicke and G. C. Berkouwer have recently published systematic theologies that differ radically from Henry's opinions.[1]

Fourth, the range of theology is infinitely wide, since anything in the cosmos is a matter of theological interest if it touches one of the eight doctrinal convictions. Consequently, Henry is the perpetual learner, exploring and mastering as many aspects of knowledge (past and present) as time and energy will permit.

Fifth, the thought of the past must be studied in order to see the true colors of the present.

Sixth, theology receives, it does not create. The theologian is dependent upon the prior experience and consequent convictional testimony of the church. Theology is always in motion between the eternal truth of its foundation and the contemporary setting as it interprets the context of the faith.

Seventh, theology is justified in its existence by summarizing and explaining the faith, by instructing old and new Christians, and by combating false doctrine. Measured by these seven standards, Henry is a "true theologian."

To the eight basic doctrines theology attempts to bring biblical teachings, Christian thinking yesterday and today, and modern understanding. Theology is an attempt to unpack the biblical witness of the past and apply it to the present in the light of tradition. Biblical, traditional and contemporary are blended in a dynamic way that produces wisdom, not precisely defined scientific knowledge. How does Henry fare with his critics (friendly and unfriendly) on this level? Henry is at his very best in philosophy of religion and contemporary theology, and this is to be expected because of his interest in the apologetic task. Only one who has mastered current philosophy and theology has the grounds on which to accept or repudiate them. Henry leaves his readers with the feeling that he has read everything in print in these two areas, evaluated it, and separated the superficial from the authentic. He far surpasses most other American evangelicals in contemporary philosophy and theology. In the history of doctrine up to the modern period he is moderately successful. But his critics have charged him with being less than successful in dealing with historical and critical issues relating to the biblical text and with having an unsteady hand in the area of biblical exegesis. Bernard Ramm says that "Henry sets out his views of revelation, inspiration and authority against all options," but his monumental effort "stumbles because he glosses biblical criticism."[2] That is, Henry still has not come to terms with the Enlightenment.

Yet the expression "unevenness in quality of scholarship" is a traditional one used by the biblical specialist for the theologian who is ordinarily a generalist. Henry is a specialist in contemporary thought, an apologist by instinct and inclination, a generalist by training, and not a professional or technical biblical scholar.

Henry has set himself to understand and critique the modern mind. How successful has he been in this effort according to his critics? America has now reached that inevitable period in its history when its technologically induced economic growth has shaped its way of thinking. America's cultural commitments are now structured by an elite class of workers—a New Class— who create and manipulate symbols in the knowledge industries. Modernity, or highly rational modes of thought, humanism, secularism, left-liberal politics, rejection of traditional authority, a concern for the "best interest of mankind" publicly, and moral tolerance privately, provide the structure of the New-Class ideology.

Secularists make up 9 percent of the American population and solidly support the public agenda of the New Class. Liberal (nonevangelical) Protestants, who make up 35 percent of the general American population, largely sympathize with the ideology of the New Class. More than one of every five Americans (22 percent) eighteen years of age and older claims to be an evangelical, and evangelicals are placing the blame for America's ills on the New Class.[3] Evangelicals tacitly know that they are being replaced as the dominant political, social, and cultural force in American society by this cohort of knowledge elites. The New Class is deinstitutionalizing evangelical religious authority, and the rise of evangelical apologetic activity, such as Henry's, can be seen as one response to this clash of ideologies.

Henry is at the heart of this apologetic effort to reassert traditional evangelical theology and counteract the modernity that is inimical to traditional religious beliefs. We have seen in Chapter V that Henry reaffirms the evangelical doctrine of

God and applies it to the specific problems raised by modernity. Henry's God is one of reasonableness, order, and balance—a timeless, absolute, immutable, supernatural Being. The evangelical tendency is to highlight God's transcendence, which implies that God reveals himself objectively by breaking into history via special acts, rational words, and an authoritative book, all given in a sacred past. The primary image of God is that of a Judge-Father who both represses and protects. Such a theology would necessarily be traditional, orthodox, stable and nurturing.

Henry's critics have charged him with being overly concerned with reason, with being obsessed about propositional revelation and advocating a God who reveals himself only in Euclidean terms. But it may be Henry's penchant for reason that will appeal most to a technological culture since the college and professionally trained people of the New Class in America have a "marked tendency toward rationalistic modes of thought and discourse unmatched by any social grouping its size in history."[4] The New Class carries on its critical discourse solely on the basis of rationally deduced arguments, and Henry has said in a hundred different ways that God reveals himself in intelligently formed statements. Christianity, like any logically formed system, has its basic "axioms" on which all other claims depend. The God of the Bible is not a deaf mute, and biblical ideas are not just human guesses, but truths that God has provided. Innumerable times Henry has said, "I believe that divine revelation is rational, that the inspired biblical canon is a consistent and coherent whole, that genuine faith seeks understanding, that the Holy Spirit uses truth as a means of persuasion, that logical consistency is a test of truth, and that saving trust in Christ necessarily involves certain revealed propositions about him."[5] Henry's stance has a natural affinity for modernity's highly rational mode of thought and discourse, a modern rationalism that insists that religious beliefs and moral convictions stand up to the test of logic and reason. Modernity itself is predictably creating circumstances that evoke a bold reassertion of reasonable Evangelicalism.

Modernity in America is so powerful that it is not surprising that in the popular imagination of evangelicals some concessions to it have been made. The evangelical model for God has begun to embody some of the dimensions of modernity. That is, God is being domesticated. In traditional evangelical theology God's wrath, terror and justice (transcendence) have loomed over his kindness and mercy (immanence). But among contemporary evangelicals God's transcendence is largely reinterpreted as a benign, bureaucratic tolerance.[6] In popular imagination *agape* has been refined to mean more a lifestyle of civility than self-effacing and sacrificial giving. Henry has set himself in opposition to this accommodation to a tolerant, familiar and subjectivistic God and is determined that evangelicals must return to the majesty that formerly pervaded their imagery of God. Faith must not collapse into sentimentality.

Henry's critics will say that as Henry attempts to reassert a God as the Judge of nations and of peoples he is creating a lack in his own theology, an imbalance that makes him sound like the neoorthodox of thirty years ago. His critics will say that he fails to see in different traditions strengths which will complement his own weakness. They will want to know why Henry does not also picture God as ecstasy, a personal power ever moving and becoming, a dynamic energy risking freedom, novelty, and tolerance. They will question why he cannot accept from the process theologians, for example, the challenge to dance, to play and to invite the freedom that revolutions inevitably invite. They will say that process theology, although it has not fully articulated a complete system of Christian thought, has many fine and corrective things to say and offers some helps and challenges. They will accuse Henry of being more afraid of embracing error than of losing truth.

Not all evangelicals are happy with Henry's bent toward rationalism and his argument that the truth of revelation can be known prior to becoming a Christian, otherwise people would not be guilty for its rejection. For example, Donald G. Bloesch objects to Henry's giving reason a creative role prior to faith, and indicts Henry along with several other evangelicals for

holding that revelation can be comprehended by reason alone. He says: "In John Warwick Montgomery's scheme Christianity can be objectively validated by the historical method alone. Norman Geisler, in his *Philosophy of Religion*, seeks to state the case for belief in God without ever once appealing to divine revelation. For him as for Hegel, the rationally inescapable is real, and, so it seems, rational verification is the presupposition of faith as well as its necessary preparation. Francis Schaeffer contends that one does not believe until one examines the evidence and is satisfied intellectually that the claims of faith are true."[7] Bloesch and many other evangelicals prefer to say that only God can illumine the mind of the unbeliever to recognize and understand revelation, that revelation is not at the disposal of reason. The non-Christian can understand the historical side of revelation by examining the Bible's literary and historical context but he cannot understand its divine intent. Only a God-given faith can see the divine meaning in biblical history and propositions. Bloesch says, "The method of Gordon Clark and Carl Henry is deductive, deriving conclusions from given rational principles,"[8] and Bloesch objects to this because he feels that revelation remains mysterious even to the believer, and Jesus Christ is more than rational. Theology's goal is not to think *the* right thoughts, but in our thought to approximate the transcendent truth. Our theology will forever fall short of the mind of God. Bloesch says, "We *intend* the truth in our theological statements, but we do not *possess* the truth, since reason is always the servant and never the master or determiner of revelation."[9]

Again, some evangelicals are uneasy with Henry's emphasis on reason because they feel that reason can be a two-edged sword cutting the one who wields it. They know that when the church has placed too high a premium on reason to defend the faith, reason has in turn been used to undermine the faith. The Enlightenment discredited all the traditional Christian evidences and apologetics by turning the rationalism originally used by Christianity against it. Reason admits the validity only

of that which can be perceived or conceived, so reason can give only approximate not final certainty. The positiveness of rational knowledge is illusory. Even a Christian must have his reason sanctified by God's grace since the sinner cannot be divorced from his logic. Henry, his critics say, does not make enough of the idea that the unbeliever's mind is depraved and the believer's mind is enlightened by grace, that our knowledge of God is a pure gift and not a rational or philosophical achievement. Grace accomplishes what apologetics cannot, but once the intellect is saved it comes alive and is given the right point from which to think. Revelation, not reason, must be the final authority; if revelation is first tested for truth, then truth is greater than revelation. Henry continually responds to these criticisms by saying that revelation is a disclosure of higher truth that stands in continuity with rational truth.

Uneasy lies the head that projects the future of theology, because there is always the unexpected genius such as Karl Barth who cannot be predicted but who might change the whole course of theology like an earthquake. Certain evangelical theologies are in the budding stage and all seem to be concerned with our technologically oriented or secular culture. These theologies seek to be faithful to the doctrinal structure of the biblical and Christian tradition while at the same time being contemporary. Liberal theology's weak spot was the failure to maintain a clear continuity with tradition, and the weakness of evangelical theology has been the failure to be contemporary. This "critical conservatism" is trying to make highly original statements about wholly unoriginal doctrines in an age of great sophisticated technology. It is a reaffirmation of orthodoxy in the context of modernity, a holding to substance without reduction but with respect for the appropriate claims of human reason. Dale Moody says, "Biblical theology, modern science, various types of biblical criticism (textual, source, form, redaction), historical theology, and the history of doctrine—all these have a significant part to play in the development of a systematic

theology."[10] For an evangelical theology to succeed it will have
to be very close to "technical reason" (as Tillich called the
mentality of scientists and technologists) and unafraid to submit
itself to a thorough rational investigation. The creative thinking
of the Free University of Amsterdam (e.g., G. C. Berkouwer)
already serves as an evangelical model that can survive the
future. The Free University thinkers write an updated theology,
alert to modernity, and interact with contemporary thought
where they think it is relevant. In America, Carl Henry is an
advocate of the same kind of clear headedness in theology.
Heresy may be clearly stated, but untrue; right belief may be
true, but not clearly stated. Reason is the key to separating
the true from the false.

Henry preaches to his fellow evangelicals that if they are
to be the church of tomorrow some byways must be avoided.
Evangelicals have much promise but many dangers; they are
a cohesive growing movement but they could become "a wilder-
ness sect." Henry's evangelicals may think he is wrong, but
they don't think he is mad: when he persists in prophetically
telling them where they are off-base they generally pay attention. He has been one of popular Evangelicalism's staunchest
internal critics, often describing evangelicals as "majoring on
minors," underplaying crucial doctrines, and failing to recover
evangelical distinctives. He has made them aware of heresies
on both right and left: experimentalism—a search for extraordinary signs and a yearning for transforming experiences; obscurantism—the denial of the validity of modern learning and
technology; worldliness—using the gospel to gain the goods
of life; hyperorthodoxy—the tendency to interpret God's Word
only through the lens of one's own cultural and theological
setting; false rationalism—in which the logical conclusions of
dogma are equated with dogma itself; individualism—where
the concern is with one's own soul to the neglect of prophetic
insights regarding social sin, naively trusting providence to
remedy public injustice; legalistic perfection—where abstinence
is equated with righteousness and only the unqualified good

can be supported; and aggressive orthodoxy—dispensationalism, hyperfundamentalism and perfectionism. Wherever theology is taken seriously, controversy abounds. Evangelicals are a particularly "scrappy" people, and Henry has always been in the middle of the war. Evangelicals have not always heeded Henry, but they are grateful for the criticisms that he has fired at them.

Evangelicals define and experience life in a certain way. No one can say for sure if the broader evangelical traditions—Baptist, Holiness-Pentecostal, Reformed-Confessional, Anabaptist—will come unglued by the beginning of the next century. If evangelicals retain and gain strength and purity they will owe an incalculable debt of gratitude to Carl Henry. His influence in theology, personal and social ethics, evangelism and socio-political involvement is unparalleled among evangelicals, and his writings give promise of continuing contributions to American thought and life.

Notes

CHAPTER I

1. Richard Quebedeaux, *The Worldly Evangelicals* (New York: Harper and Row, 1978), p. 7.
2. "The House Divided: An Interview with Carl Henry," *Eternity* (October 1976): 36.
3. James Davison Hunter, *American Evangelicalism: Conservative Religion and the Quandary of Modernity* (New Brunswick, N.J.: Rutgers University Press, 1983), pp. 7–9.
4. "Born Again!" *Newsweek* (October 25, 1976): 76.
5. James Leo. Garrett, Jr., E. Glenn Hinson, James E. Tull, *Are Southern Baptists "Evangelicals"?* (Macon, Ga.: Mercer University Press, 1983).
6. Hunter, *American Evangelicalism*, p. 47.
7. Jeremy Rifkin with Ted Howard, *The Emerging Order* (New York: G. P. Putnam's Sons, 1979), p. xi.
8. Carl F. H. Henry, "Confessions of an Editor," *Christianity Today* (March 29, 1968): 627.
9. Carl F. H. Henry, "Twenty Years a Baptist," *Foundations*, I (January 1958): 46.
10. Henry, "Confessions," p. 627.
11. Henry, "Twenty Years," p. 46.
12. Henry, "Confessions," p. 627.

13. Ibid.   14. Ibid.   15. Ibid.

16. Henry, "Twenty Years," p. 46.   17. Ibid.

18. Ibid., pp. 46–47.   19. Ibid., p. 47.   20. Ibid.

21. Ibid.   22. Ibid.   23. Ibid.   24. Ibid.

25. Ibid., p. 48.   26. Ibid., p. 49.   27. Ibid., pp. 52–53.

28. Ibid., p. 54.

29. For brief histories of the evangelicals, see Richard Quebedeaux, *The Young Evangelicals* (New York: Harper and Row, 1974); Martin E. Marty, *A Nation of Behavers* (Chicago: The University of Chicago Press, 1976); David F. Wells and John D. Woodbridge, eds., *The Evangelicals* (Nashville: Abingdon Press, 1975); Peter L. Berger and Richard John Neuhaus, eds., *Against the World for the World* (New York: Seabury Press, 1976); Kenneth S. Kantzer, ed., *Evangelical Roots* (New York: Thomas Nelson, Inc., 1978). For a brief, but fine treatment of the theological roots of Evangelicalism, see Bernard L. Ramm, *The Evangelical Heritage* (Waco, Tex.: Word Books, 1973). For both history and theological themes see John D. Woodbridge, Mark A. Noll, and Nathan O. Hatch, *The Gospel In America: Themes In The Story of America's Evangelicals* (Grand Rapids: Zondervan Publishing House, 1979), p. 86. James Davison Hunter, *American Evangelicalism* (New Brunswick, N.J.: Rutgers University Press, 1983).

30. See Ramm, *The Evangelical Heritage*, pp. 23–39.

31. Ibid., pp. 55–56.

32. Ibid., p. 70.

33. Carl F. H. Henry, *Evangelicals in Search of Identity* (Waco, Tex.: Word Books, 1976), pp. 30–31.

34. Martin E. Marty, *A Nation of Behavers* (Chicago: University of Chicago Press, 1976), p. 83.

35. Carl F. H. Henry, "The Perils of Independency," *Christianity Today* (November 12, 1956): 20–23.

36. Carl F. H. Henry, "The Vigor of the New Evangelicalism," *Christian Life* (January, 1948): 32.

37. Ibid.

38. Carl F. H. Henry, *The Uneasy Conscience of Modern Fundamentalism* (Grand Rapids: Wm. B. Eerdmans Publishing Company, 1947), p. 18.

39. Ibid., p. 20.   40. Ibid., p. 32.   41. Ibid., p. 76.

42. Ibid., p. 76.

43. Carl F. H. Henry, "The Vigor of the New Evangelicalism," *Christian Life* (March, 1948): 35–8;85 (April, 1948): 32–5: 65–9.

44. Ramm, *The Evangelical Heritage*, p. 114.

45. Donald G. Bloesch, *The Evangelical Renaissance* (Grand Rapids: Wm. B. Eerdmans Publishing Company, 1973), pp. 37–41.

46. Bloesch, pp. 80–100.

47. Quebedeaux, *The Young Evangelicals*, p. 28.

48. Henry, *Evangelicals in Search of Identity*, p. 94.

49. Quebedeaux, *The Young Evangelicals*, p. 41.

50. Carl F. H. Henry, "Winds of Promise," *Christianity Today* (June 5, 1970): 829–30.

51. Henry, *Evangelicals in Search of Identity*, pp. 19, 22, 24.

52. Ibid., p. 46.

53. Quebedeaux, *The Worldly Evangelicals*, p. 164.

54. Quebedeaux, *The Young Evangelicals*, p. 74.

55. See Richard Quebedeaux, *The New Charismatics: The Origin, Development, and Significance of New-Pentecostalism* (Garden City, N.Y.: Doubleday, 1976).

56. Henry, *Evangelicals in Search of Identity*, p. 72.

57. John D. Woodbridge, Mark A. Noll, and Nathan O. Hatch, *The Gospel In America: Themes In the Story of America's Evangelicals* (Grand Rapids: Zondervan Publishing House, 1979), p. 86.

58. Ibid., p. 12.

CHAPTER II

1. Carl F. H. Henry, *Remaking the Modern Mind* (Grand Rapids: Wm. B. Eerdmans Publishing Company, 1946), p. 7.

2. For a sample of early evangelical apologetics, see Edward John Carnell, *An Introduction to Christian Apologetics* (Grand Rapids: Wm. B. Eerdmans Publishing Company, 1948); Gordon Clark, *A Christian View of Men and Things* (Grand Rapids: Wm. B. Eerdmans Publishing Company, 1952); Bernard Ramm, *Varieties of Christian Apologetics* (Grand Rapids: Baker Book House, 1961).

3. Besides his 1946 work, *Remaking the Modern Mind*, see his *Notes on the Doctrine of God* (Boston: W. A. Wilde, 1948); *The Protestant Dilemma* (Grand Rapids: Wm. B. Eerdmans Publishing Company, 1948); *Giving a Reason for Our Hope* (Boston: W. A. Wilde, 1949); *Fifty Years of Protestant Theology* (Boston: W. A. Wilde, 1950); and *The Drift of Western Thought* (Grand Rapids: Wm. B. Eerdmans Publishing Company, 1951).

4. See Ramm, *Varieties of Christian Apologetics*, pp. 15–17.

5. Henry, *Remaking the Modern Mind*, p. 231.

6. Ibid., p. 213.

7. Carl F. H. Henry, "Science and Religion," *Contemporary Evangelical Thought*, ed. Carl F. H. Henry (New York: Holt, Rinehart and Winston, 1962), p. 262.

8. See Frederick Ferré, *Language, Logic and God* (New York: Harper and Row, 1961), pp. 162–163.

9. Carl F. H. Henry, *God, Revelation and Authority*, I (Waco, Tex.: Word Books, 1976), p. 10.

10. Henry, *Remaking the Modern Mind*, pp. 232, 171.

11. Ibid., p. 227.

12. Henry, *God, Revelation and Authority*, I, p. 215.

13. Ibid., p. 217.   14. Ibid., p. 216.   15. Ibid., p. 224.

16. Ibid., p. 227.   17. Ibid., p. 229.   18. Ibid., p. 235.

19. Ibid., p. 240.   20. Ibid., p. 243.   21. Ibid., p. 14.

22. Ibid.   23. Ibid., p. 85.   24. Ibid., p. 90.

25. Ramm, *Varieties of Christian Apologetics*, p. 149.

26. Ibid., p. 150.

27. Henry, *God, Revelation and Authority*, I, p. 273.

28. Ibid., p. 279.

29. Only Plato and Kant have been selected from Henry's lengthy treatment: he gives attention to many others in pp. 273–394 of Vol. I of *God, Revelation and Authority*.

30. Ibid., p. 286.   31. Ibid., p. 387.   32. Ibid., p. 384.

33. Ibid., p. 388.   34. Ibid., p. 279.   35. Ibid., p. 387.

36. Ibid., p. 38.   37. Ibid., pp. 135–36.

38. Here Henry depends for his analysis on Langdon Gilkey, *Naming the Whirlwind: The Renewal of God-Language* (Indianapolis: Bobbs-Merrill Co., 1969).

39. Henry, *God, Revelation and Authority*, I, p. 138.

40. Ibid., p. 23.   41. Ibid., p. 140.   42. Ibid., p. 142.

43. Ibid., p. 151.   44. Ibid., p. 43.   45. Ibid., p. 96.

46. Ibid., p. 97.   47. Ibid., p. 98.   48. Ibid., p. 110.

49. Ibid., p. 111.   50. Ibid., p. 113.   51. Ibid., pp. 120–21.

52. Ibid., p. 123.   53. Ibid., p. 126.   54. Ibid., p. 248.

55. Ibid., p. 250.   56. Ibid., p. 262.   57. Ibid., p. 265.

CHAPTER III

1. Carl F. H. Henry, *God, Revelation and Authority*, II (Waco, Tex.: Word Books, 1976), p. 8.

2. Ibid., pp. 20–21.   3. Ibid., p. 23.   4. Ibid., p. 24.

5. Ibid., p. 30.   6. Ibid., p. 43.   7. Ibid., p. 44.

8. Ibid., p. 47.   9. Ibid., p. 52.   10. Ibid., p. 69.

11. Ibid., p. 77.   12. Ibid., p. 80.   13. Ibid., p. 98.

14. Ibid., p. 126.   15. Ibid., p. 136.   16. Ibid., p. 151.
17. Ibid., p. 157.   18. Ibid., p. 167.   19. Ibid., p. 172.
20. Ibid., p. 173.   21. Ibid., p. 178.   22. Ibid., p. 186.
23. Ibid., p. 201.   24. Ibid., pp. 220–21.   25. Ibid., p. 225.
26. Ibid., p. 246.   27. Ibid., p. 247.   28. Ibid., p. 314.
29. Ibid., p. 320.   30. Ibid.   31. Ibid., p. 321.
32. Ibid., p. 330.   33. Ibid., pp. 309–10.
34. Carl F. H. Henry, *God, Revelation and Authority*, Vol. III (Waco, Tex.: Word Books, 1979), p. 9.
35. Ibid., p. 19.   36. Ibid., p. 47.   37. Ibid., p. 97.
38. Ibid., p. 102.   39. Ibid., pp. 121–2.   40. Ibid., p. 160.
41. Ibid., p. 162.   42. Ibid., p. 164.   43. Ibid., p. 171.
44. Ibid., p. 192.   45. Ibid., p. 229.   46. Ibid., p. 248.
47. Ibid., p. 251.   48. Ibid., p. 252.   49. Ibid., p. 271.
50. Ibid., p. 302.   51. Ibid., p. 279.   52. Ibid., pp. 354–55.
53. Ibid., p. 382.   54. Ibid., p. 456.

CHAPTER IV

1. Carl F. H. Henry, *God, Revelation and Authority*, IV (Waco, Tex.: Word Books, 1979), p. 7.
2. Ibid., p. 13.   3. Ibid., p. 22.   4. Ibid., p. 27.
5. Ibid., pp. 39–40.   6. Ibid., p. 55.   7. Ibid., p. 64.
8. Ibid., p. 68.   9. Ibid., p. 74.   10. Ibid., p. 77.
11. Ibid., p. 77.   12. Ibid., p. 81.   13. Ibid., p. 92.
14. Ibid., p. 97.   15. Ibid., pp. 105–6.   16. Ibid., p. 128.
17. William J. Abraham, *The Divine Inspiration of Holy Scripture* (Oxford, England: Oxford University Press, 1981), p. 1.
18. Ibid., pp. 2–4.
19. Erling Jorstad, *Evangelicals in the White House: The Cultural Maturation of Born Again Christianity 1960–1981* (New York: The Edwin Mellen Press, 1981), pp. 48–49.
20. Michael J. Christensen, *C. S. Lewis on Scripture* (Waco, Tex.: Word Books, 1979), pp. 16–19.
21. Henry, *God, Revelation and Authority*, IV, p. 129.
22. Robert K. Johnston, *Evangelicals at an Impasse* (Atlanta: John Knox Press, 1979), pp. 15–47.
23. Carl F. H. Henry "The War of the Word," *The New Review of Books and Religion*, September, 1976, p. 7. See also Carl F. H. Henry in "The Battle for the Bible: An Interview with Dr. Carl F. H. Henry," *Scribe*, Spring 1976, p. 4.

24. Henry, *God, Revelation and Authority,* IV, pp. 201–204.

25. Ibid., p. 205.　　26. Ibid., p. 205.　　27. Ibid., p. 205.

28. Ibid., pp. 206–7.　　29. Ibid., p. 207.　　30. Ibid., p. 209.

31. Ibid., pp. 209–210.　　32. Ibid., p. 210.　　33. Ibid., p. 229.

34. Ibid., p. 241.　　35. Ibid., pp. 243–55.　　36. Ibid., p. 276.

37. Ibid., p. 351.　　38. Ibid., p. 403.　　39. Ibid., p. 365.

40. Ibid., p. 365.　　41. Ibid., p. 367.　　42. Ibid., p. 367.

43. The "heritage" question is being fiercely debated among evangelicals. For the claim that the heritage affirms the infallibility of Scripture in matters of faith and conduct but allows it to be incorrect on matters of historical and scientific detail, see Jack R. Rogers and Donald K. McKim, *The Authority and Interpretation of the Bible: An Historical Approach* (San Francisco: Harper & Row, 1979), xxiv—p. 448. For a claim that Rogers and McKim have produced shoddy scholarship see John D. Woodbridge, *Biblical Authority: A Critique of the Rogers/McKim Proposal* (Grand Rapids: Zondervan Publishing House, 1982), pp. 7–237.

44. Bernard Ramm, *After Fundamentalism: The Future of Evangelical Theology* (San Francisco: Harper & Row, 1983), pp. 26–27. Ramm makes a case that Karl Barth's theology will best serve evangelicals as a model for doing theology.

45. Jorstad, *Evangelicals in the White House: The Cultural Maturation of Born Again Christianity 1960–1981,* p. 58.

46. Ibid., p. 58.

47. Henry, *God, Revelation and Authority,* IV, p. 494.

48. Ibid., p. 542.　　49. Ibid., p. 593.

CHAPTER V

1. Carl F. H. Henry, *God, Revelation and Authority,* V (Waco, Tex.: Word Books, 1982), p. 9.

2. Ibid., p. 10.　　3. Ibid., p. 40.　　4. Ibid., p. 21.

5. Ibid., p. 58.　　6. Ibid., p. 66.　　7. Ibid., p. 79.

8. Ibid., p. 100.　　9. Ibid., p. 119.　　10. Ibid., p. 131.

11. Ibid., p. 165.　　12. Ibid., p. 165.　　13. Ibid., p. 208.

14. Ibid., p. 233.　　15. Ibid., p. 249.　　16. Ibid., p. 260.

17. Ibid., p. 269.　　18. Ibid., p. 276.　　19. Ibid., p. 289.

20. Ibid., p. 319.　　21. Ibid., p. 312.　　22. Ibid., p. 330.

23. Ibid., p. 334.　　24. Ibid., p. 355.

25. Carl F. H. Henry, *God, Revelation and Authority,* VI (Waco, Tex.: Word Books, 1983), p. 52.

26. Ibid., p. 26.

27. See Bob E. Patterson, "Theology," *The Theological Educator*, Vol. IX, Number 2, Spring 1979, pp. 65–92.

28. Henry, *God, Revelation and Authority*, VI, p. 74.

29. Ibid., p. 107.   30. Ibid., p. 107.   31. Ibid., p. 116.

32. Ibid., p. 114.   33. Ibid., p. 115.   34. Ibid., p. 130.

35. Ibid., p. 138.   36. Ibid., p. 159.   37. Ibid., p. 174.

38. Ibid., p. 181.   39. Ibid., p. 200.   40. Ibid., p. 226.

41. Ibid., p. 227.   42. Ibid., p. 239.   43. Ibid., p. 304.

44. Ibid., p. 306.   45. Ibid., p. 311.   46. Ibid., p. 349.

47. Ibid., p. 356.   48. Ibid., p. 351.   49. Ibid., p. 358.

50. Ibid., p. 413.   51. Ibid., p. 455.   52. Ibid., pp. 457–58.

53. Ibid., pp. 460–61.   54. Ibid., p. 482.   55. Ibid., p. 485.

56. Ibid., pp. 486–87.   57. Ibid., p. 492.   58. Ibid., p. 504.

59. Carl F. H. Henry, *Christian Personal Ethics* (Grand Rapids: Wm. B. Eerdmans Publishing Co., 1957), p. 16.

60. Carl F. H. Henry, *Evangelicals in Search of Identity* (Waco, Tex.: Word Books, Publisher, 1976), p. 57.

61. Carl F. H. Henry, *A Plea for Evangelical Demonstration* (Grand Rapids: Baker Book House, 1971), p. 25.

62. Carl F. H. Henry, *Aspects of Christian Social Ethics* (Grand Rapids: Wm. B. Eerdmans Publishing Company, 1964), p. 47.

63. Henry, *God, Revelation and Authority*, Vol. IV, p. 522.

64. Ibid., p. 524.   65. Ibid., p. 530.   66. Ibid., pp. 530–31.

67. Ibid., p. 534.   68. Ibid., p. 591.   69. Ibid., p. 577.

70. See Johnston, *Evangelicals at an Impasse*, pp. 77–112.

CHAPTER VI

1. See Donald G. Bloesch, *Essentials of Evangelical Theology*, Vols. I, II (New York: Harper & Row, 1978–1979); Dale Moody, *The Word of Truth* (Grand Rapids: William B. Eerdmans Publishing Company, 1981); Helmut Thielicke, *The Evangelical Faith*, Vols. I, II, III (Grand Rapids: Wm. B. Eerdmans Publishing Company, 1974, 1977, 1981); and G. C. Berkouwer, *Studies In Dogmatics* (Grand Rapids: Wm. B. Eerdmans Publishing Company), a multivolume series still being published.

2. Ramm, *After Fundamentalism*, pp. 26–27.

3. Hunter, *American Evangelicalism*, p. 111.

4. Ibid., p. 108.

5. "The Concerns and Considerations of Carl F. H. Henry," *Christianity Today*, March 13, 1981, p. 21.

6. Hunter, *American Evangelicalism*, p. 122.

7. Donald G. Bloesch, *Essentials of Evangelical Theology*, II (San Francisco: Harper & Row, 1979), p. 267.

8. Ibid., p. 268.

9. Ibid.

10. Dale Moody, *The Word of Truth: A Summary of Christian Doctrine Based on Biblical Revelation:* (Grand Rapids: Wm. B. Eerdmans Publishing Company, 1981), p. xi.

Books by Carl F. H. Henry

PUBLICATIONS BY WORD BOOKS:

The God Who Shows Himself (1966)
Evangelicals at the Brink of Crisis (1967)
Evangelicals in Search of Identity (1976)
God, Revelation and Authority, Vol. I, *God Who Speaks and Shows: Preliminary Considerations* (1976)
God, Revelation and Authority, Vol. II, *God Who Speaks and Shows: Fifteen Theses, part one* (1976)
God, Revelation and Authority, Vol. III, *God Who Speaks and Shows: Fifteen Theses, part two* (1979)
God, Revelation and Authority, Vol. IV, *God Who Speaks and Shows: Fifteen Theses, part three* (1979)
God, Revelation and Authority, Vol. V, *God Who Stands and Stays: part one* (1982)
God, Revelation and Authority, Vol. VI, *God Who Stands and Stays: part two* (1983)

BY OTHER PUBLISHERS

A Doorway to Heaven (1941)
Successful Church Publicity (1943)

The Uneasy Conscience of Modern Fundamentalism (1947)
Remaking the Modern Mind (1947)
Giving a Reason for Our Hope (1950)
The Protestant Dilemma (1948)
Notes on the Doctrine of God (1948)
Fifty Years of Protestant Theology (1950)
The Drift of Western Thought (1951)
Personal Idealism and Strong's Theology (1951)
Glimpses of a Sacred Land (1953)
Christian Personal Ethics (1957)
Evangelical Responsibility in Contemporary Theology (1957)
Aspects of Christian Social Ethics (1964)
Frontiers in Modern Theology (1966)
Faith at the Frontiers (1969)
A Plea for Evangelical Demonstration (1971)
New Strides of Faith (1972)

SYMPOSIUMS

Contemporary Evangelical Thought (1957)
Revelation and the Bible (1959)
consulting ed., *Dictionary of Theology* (1960)
The Biblical Expositor, 3 vols. (1960)
Basic Christian Doctrines (1962)
Christian Faith and Modern Theology (1964)
Jesus of Nazareth: Saviour and Lord (1966)
ed. with W. Stanley Mooneyham, *One Race, One Gospel, One Task*, 2 vols. (1967)
Fundamentals of the Faith (1969)
Baker's Dictionary of Christian Ethics (1973)
Horizons of Science (1978)

DATE DUE

DEMCO

CAN'T GET ENOUGH OF ROBIN JONES GUNN?

Christy Miller Collection, Volume 1 (Books 1-3)
Christy Miller Collection, Volume 2 (Books 4-6)
Christy Miller Collection, Volume 3 (Books 7-9)
Christy Miller Collection, Volume 4 (Books 10-12)

Sierra Jensen Collection, Volume 1 (Books 1-3)
Sierra Jensen Collection, Volume 2 (Books 4-6)
Sierra Jensen Collection, Volume 3 (Books 7-9)
Sierra Jensen Collection, Volume 4 (Books 10-12)